# Arkansas Criminal Law
## *A Guide for Enforcement*

Adam J. McKee, Ph.D.
University of Arkansas – Monticello

*To the Sheepdogs*

# Contents

**PART THREE**

**CHAPTER 19: EVIDENCE LAW** .................................................................. **159**

**CHAPTER 20: THE FOURTH AMENDMENT** ............................................. **171**

# Preface

This book is an attempt to fill a void in the professional literature on law for Arkansas Law Enforcement. It is intended to be a user friendly introduction and reference to the aspects of Arkansas law that are critical to law enforcement. In addition to serving law enforcement, I have endeavored to make it general enough to be useful in the college classroom. The brevity and "black letter law" format necessitate that any college professor considering it will no doubt need to supplement the material presented here with applicable court cases and explanatory lectures.

My decision to write this book was driven by the simple fact that someone needed to do it. Many large states have publications that achieve the objectives I have set for myself with this book. If there is a comparable text on Arkansas law, I have been unable to find it. That is not to say that Arkansas has no quality legal publications—far from it! Our law schools and legal scholars have produced an outstanding body of quality legal literature. The problem is that this material is aimed at lawyers, not law enforcement officers. The Attorney General's office has produced some outstanding publications aimed at police officers, but these are generally of a very narrow focus and difficult for the inexperienced officer or student to bring together in a systematic way. My goal with this book was to provide a systematic treatment of a very broad spectrum of law in a way that is accessible to law enforcement officers and the interested Arkansas citizen.

The book is divided into three major sections. The first section is an introduction to the general principles of the criminal law. It provides an understanding of the critical ideas and vocabulary that make understanding specific criminal offenses possible. The second section deals with the substantive criminal law. This section details the specific elements of selected criminal offenses and attempts to simplify the technical jargon found in the text of the Arkansas Criminal Code. The third section deals with criminal evidence and procedure. These are the rules and regulations that every officer needs to know in order the protect the civil liberties guaranteed to the citizens of Arkansas, ensure that evidence is admissible in court, and protect themselves and their departments from civil liability.

## Omitted Code Sections

This text omits many provisions of the criminal code. Those omitted sections are those that are not generally applicable to law enforcement, such as perjury and contempt. Also omitted are complex areas of criminal law that are generally investigated by special agencies, such as the Attorney General's office; and those sections that are of such obscurity that they are not likely to be needed on a frequent basis, such as the prohibition against using natural gas to produce carbon black.

## Caveats

This text is for educational and reference purposes only. ***It does not constitute law or legal advice.*** Always consult the *Code* or your legal counsel on matters that might incur liability if handled improperly. While an effort has been made to verify the accuracy of the information within this text, keep in mind that when information herein conflicts with primary sources of law, *those primary sources are correct and must be followed.*

## Abbreviations and Acronyms

To limit the size of this text, several commonly used terms are shortened to acronyms. Consult the following table for interpretation.

| Abbreviations and Acronyms | |
| --- | --- |
| **Abbreviation** | **Stands For** |
| A.C.A. | Arkansas Code Annotated |
| AR | Arkansas |
| ARSC | Arkansas Supreme Court |
| Code | (Generically) the *Arkansas Criminal Code* |
| LE | Law Enforcement |
| LEO | Law Enforcement Officer(s) |
| PC | Probable Cause |
| US | United States |
| USSC | United States Supreme Court |
| DOC | Department of Corrections |
| DCC | Department of Community Corrections |

## Acknowledgements

I would like to thank Kristin Finch and Janet Allison-Wilson for their helpful comments on a very rough first draft of this book. The final product is much more readable due to their efforts.

I would also like to thank the Arkansas criminal justice professionals who contributed their experiences, ideas, and opinions. Many of these were members of the Criminal Justice Institute's *CopShare* Listserv; accordingly, I am grateful to CJI staff for all of their efforts to improve criminal justice in Arkansas. Many individuals contributed to this work, even if they didn't know it at the time—much of the practical material herein was gathered through conversations with veteran officers long before I decided to write it all down. Those who contributed their time are gratefully acknowledged below, in no particular order.

*Ken Slocum, Jefferson County SO*
*Ryan Baker, Sherwood PD*
*Rodney Pickens, UAM DPS*
*John Kidwell, UAM DPS*
*Ken Vanderzwalm, UAM DPS*
*Debbie Haralson, DCC*

*Jami Cook, ASP*
*John Morgan, CJI*
*Robert Thomason, UAM DPS*
*Mike May, UAM DPS*
*Jeff Peebles, UAM DPS*
*Kelly King, DCC*

Please feel free to contact me with any comments, criticisms, and suggestions. I am quick to acknowledge that this is an imperfect work and that future editions have much room for improvement.

Adam J. McKee, Ph.D.
Associate Professor of Criminal Justice

E-mail: mckee@uamont.edu

School of Social and Behavioral Sciences
University of Arkansas at Monticello
P.O. Box 3619
Monticello, AR  71656

# PART ONE

# BASIC CONCEPTS

# Chapter 1: Nature of Criminal Law

## (1.1) Nature of the Criminal Law in General

The social and economic stability of any society depends on people treating each other in acceptable and predictable ways. In our modern society, a critical element in the social control of each individual is our system of laws. Because our form of society is democratic and places a high value on equality, we adhere to the **rule of law**. This concept centers on the idea that a safe and orderly society depends on governance by established principles and publicized codes that are applied to everyone uniformly and fairly. Under the rule of law, no one is above the law. Those who make the law and those who enforce the law must abide by it.

The term **law** is very general. It can be defined as a rule of conduct, given down by authority, which prohibits or commands certain behaviors. The law can be broken down into several types. The most common way to do this is to consider what types of behaviors the law seeks to control. **Civil law** is the body of law that regulates relationships between private individuals. Civil law deals with such things as contracts and torts. A **tort** is a wrongful act that often results in money **damages** being paid to the aggrieved party. This is different (at least theoretically) from the criminal law.

**Criminal law** (a.k.a. *penal law*) concerns itself with regulating acts that harm society as a whole. Take murder for example. Obviously, there is a victim that has been harmed, which constitutes a private wrong—something for the civil law to deal with. But, the legal logic is that because that person was killed, we all have suffered. We all are deprived of the victim as a member of our society, and we all feel a little less safe because of it.

Many legal writers have found it convenient to divide the criminal law into two branches: substantive and procedural. The **substantive criminal law** deals directly with specifying exactly what acts are prohibited and what punishments are associated with committing those prohibited acts. **Procedural law** is the part of the criminal law that specifies the methods that are used to enforce the substantive criminal law. That is, it dictates how government agents (LE, court officers, corrections officers, etc.) can treat people.

The criminal law is a complex subject, but it is not so difficult that those with average intelligence cannot learn it with some effort. The largest barrier to understanding the law is the use of legal jargon and the large degree of precision that must be used when defining those legal terms and phrases.

## (1.2) Anatomy of a Crime

### a. Criminal Liability

The Arkansas Code[1] (the major source of AR criminal law) stipulates that no person may be convicted of an offense unless the following are proved beyond a reasonable doubt:
(1) Each **element** of the offense, (2) jurisdiction, (3) venue[2], and (4) the commission of the offense within the time period specified in the statute of limitations[3].

---

[1] § 5-1-111

Thus, the prosecution (the state) must prove all of the elements of a crime beyond a reasonable doubt to secure a conviction. In its most basic form, a crime consists of three general **elements**:

1. **Actus Reus** refers to the criminal act. Note that when the law commands something to be done, an *omission* can count as an act.

2. **Mens Rea** refers to the criminal intent. This is the mental element of the crime.

3. **Concurrence** refers to the idea that the criminal act and the criminal intent are joined in the sense that the criminal intent sets the criminal act in motion.

Some crimes are more complex because they require that some criminal **harm** occur. Murder is such a crime: it requires that the criminal act result in the death of a person.

These types of crimes have two additional elements:

1. **Causation** refers to the idea that the criminal conduct must produce the harm as defined by the statute.

2. The **resulting harm** must actually occur.

### (1.3)  Grading Offenses

Arkansas recognizes several different grades of both felonies and misdemeanors. Generally, a **felony** is a serious crime that is punishable by more than a year in prison. A **misdemeanor** is a less serious offense that is punishable by less than a year. Sentences for misdemeanors are usually served in county jails.

Specifically, Arkansas law[4] recognizes an offense as a felony under two circumstances. An offense is a felony if it is designated as such by the criminal code, or if it is designated as such by another statute that is not part of the criminal code. Arkansas uses a letter system to grade felony offenses, based on seriousness. Class Y felonies are the most serious, followed by Class A felonies, Class B felonies, Class C felonies and Class D felonies. Anything graded below the least serious grade of felony (Class D) is classified as a misdemeanor.

As with felonies, misdemeanors are graded using a letter system. An offense is legally defined as a felony if it is explicitly made so by the criminal code or other statute, or if a sentence of imprisonment is authorized upon conviction and the offense has not been designated as a felony. Misdemeanors range from the most serious being a Class A misdemeanor to the least serious being a Class C misdemeanor[5]. Rare offenses can be considered as "unclassified" misdemeanors.

The least serious offenses are considered **violations**. An offense is a violation (as opposed to a felony or misdemeanor) "if the statute defining the offense provides that no sentence other than a fine, or fine or forfeiture, or civil penalty is authorized upon conviction."[6] A culpable mental state is not required if "the offense is a violation, unless a culpable mental state is expressly included in the definition of the offense."[7] Because violations do not require proof of a mental element, they are known as **strict liability** offenses.

---

[2] The state is not required to prove jurisdiction or venue unless evidence is admitted that affirmatively shows that the court lacks jurisdiction or venue
[3] § 5-1-109
[4] § 5-1-106
[5] § 5-1-107
[6] § 5-1-108 (b)
[7] § 5-2-204 (c) (1)

## (1.4) Punishment

Sentencing in Arkansas is entirely a matter of statute[8]. Most crimes are classified by the legislature when the law is enacted. The range of penalties is dictated by §5-4-401. There are also enhanced penalties for habitual offenders[9].

| Offense Classifications and Sentences | | |
|---|---|---|
| **Grade of Offense** | **Minimum Sentence** | **Maximum Sentence** |
| Class Y felony | not less than ten (10) years | not more than 40 years<br>*or*<br>life |
| Class A felony | not less than 6 years | not more than 30 years |
| Class B felony | not less than 5 years | not more than 20 years |
| Class C felony | not less than 3 years | not more than 10 years |
| Class D felony | *none specified* | not more than 6 years |
| unclassified felony | *as specified by statute* | *as specified by statute* |
| Class A misdemeanor | *none specified* | not more than 1 year |
| Class B misdemeanor | *none specified* | not more than 90 days |
| Class C misdemeanor | *none specified* | not more than 30 days |
| unclassified misdemeanor | *as specified by statute* | *as specified by statute* |

## (1.5) Criminal Law in a Federal System

Our system of laws is complex because we have several different levels of government. When laws from different levels of government conflict, the higher level of government wins. That is, if an Arkansas law is in conflict with a federal law, then the federal law is the one that is valid law.

Constitutions are superior to statutory law on both the federal and state level. The federal constitution supersedes state constitutions.

## (1.6) Sources of Criminal Law

The primary sources of criminal law include:

- U.S. Constitution
- Arkansas Constitution
- Common Law
- U.S. Criminal Code
- Arkansas Criminal Code
- Municipal / County Ordinances
- Judicial Decisions Interpreting Codes and Constitutions

These various sources of the law can be described by how they are made.

A *constitution* (under our system of government) is the supreme law. All other laws must meet constitutional standards to be valid. Constitutions generally require much more effort to change than do other laws.

A *statutory law* is one passed by a legislative body, such as the Congress of the United States or the Arkansas General Assembly.

---

[8] *State v. Freeman*, 312 Ark. 34, 846 S.W.2d 660 (1993)
[9] See § 5-4-501.

*Case law* (sometimes referred to as *common law*) refers to laws made by judges and promulgated in written decisions. The requirement that *Miranda* warnings must be read before custodial interrogations can occur is an example of case law.

The most important source of criminal law for Arkansas is the **Arkansas Criminal Code**, which is Title 5 of the *Arkansas Code*.

Our system of government allows for judicial review—judges get to determine whether or not a particular statute is constitutional. If a particular law is contrary to the constitution, it is void.

The process of judicial review also applies to particular actions performed by the government. Of interest to us is the idea that the constitutionality of a particular police practice can be evaluated by the courts. If such a practice is found to be unconstitutional, the courts will punish law enforcement for the violation. For example, this is the purpose of the **exclusionary rule**.

As we previously discussed, it is common for the criminal law to be divided into two major divisions: First, there is the *substantive criminal law*. The substantive criminal law is the part of the law that specifies what acts are crimes and what punishments go with those crimes. These are almost entirely statutes today in Arkansas.

The other division of the criminal law is called *procedural law*. Procedural law dictates how the criminal justice system treats people. Most procedural law consists of the Federal and the Arkansas constitution and court cases that interpret these constitutions. This means that to find the criminal law, we will generally look to the criminal code. To find procedural law, we will generally look to court cases.

Most of the cases we are concerned with come either from the Arkansas Supreme Court or the United States Supreme Court. As these are the highest courts, once they make a decision, only they can change it.

Most cases come to these courts by way of appeal. An *appeal* is when one party to a case in not satisfied with the result and seeks to have the decision of the lower court reviewed by a higher court. This is why supreme courts are referred to as *appellate courts*. The party bringing the appeal to the higher court is called the *appellant*, and the parties appealed against is called the *appellee*.

Not all procedural law is case law, however. Arkansas has a codified set of rules called the *Arkansas Rules of Criminal Procedure*. These are essentially an effort to bring together many legal doctrines decided by the courts over many years together in one place.

### (1.7) Finding the Law

The *Arkansas Criminal Code Annotated with Commentaries* is published by LexisNexis in a frequently updated edition. This in essence takes the criminal law section of the larger *Arkansas Code* and adds commentary to aid in understanding and interpreting the statutes. The constitution and code[10] are also available online.

USSC case law can be found in *United States Reports*, the official publication of the court. The bound volumes are available in most federal depository libraries. These cases are also online in many places[11].

### (1.8) Jurisdiction and Venue

In all criminal cases, the prosecution must be able to prove both *jurisdiction* and *venue*. *Venue* means that cases must be tried in the county where the crime occurred (unless there is a successful change of venue motion).

---

[10] http://arlaw.iejs.com
[11] see http://www.findlaw.com

*Jurisdiction* (in reference to courts) means that a particular court has the legal right to decide the case at hand. This is usually dealing with the level of the court and the subject matter that it may hear. For example, a municipal court does not have jurisdiction to hear a murder case.

*Jurisdiction* (in reference to LE) generally means the geographic and political areas where an officer has authority.

Arkansas law provides for the reach of the criminal code outside the political boundaries of the state under certain circumstances (See §5-1-104).

---

**§ 5-1-104. Territorial Applicability**

(a) A person may be convicted under the laws of this state of an offense committed by his own or another's conduct for which he is legally accountable if:

(1) Either the conduct or a result that is an element of the offense occurs within this state; or

(2) Conduct occurring outside this state constitutes an attempt to commit an offense within this state; or

(3) Conduct occurring outside this state constitutes a conspiracy to commit an offense within this state and an overt act in furtherance of such conspiracy occurs within this state; or

(4) Conduct occurring within this state establishes complicity in the commission of, or an attempt, solicitation, or conspiracy to commit, an offense in another jurisdiction that is also an offense under the law of this state; or

(5) The offense consists of the omission to perform a legal duty imposed by the law of this state based on domicile, residence, or a relationship to a person, thing, or transaction in the state; or

(6) The offense is defined by a statute of this state that expressly prohibits conduct outside the state, when the conduct bears a reasonable relation to a legitimate interest of this state and the person knows or should know that his conduct is likely to affect that interest.

(b) When the offense is homicide, either the death of the victim or the physical contact causing death constitutes a "result" within the meaning of subsection (a)(1) of this section.

---

### *(1.9) Strength of Evidence*

The criminal law recognizes that different levels or degrees of proof are necessary for different functions of the criminal justice system. Obviously, we would never get criminals into court if we had to have proof "beyond a reasonable doubt" before we can begin an investigation. The most important factor that the courts consider when determining how much surety is required before a certain criminal justice task can be undertaken is the degree to which the suspect's constitutional rights are hampered. This makes good sense. A "hunch" is good enough to ask someone for identification—the suspect suffers very little inconvenience from compliance. On the other hand, our basic sense of justice would be offended if a person could be imprisoned for 20 years on a hunch.

The courts have had a very difficult time trying to establish various standards for what is "enough" proof for LE to take certain actions. Even though we have words and phrases to guide us, the precise meaning of those words is uncomfortably vague. Criminal justice professionals are left trying to apply these hazy concepts to real life situations. Unfortunately, judges don't always agree with decisions made by officers in the field.

We will delve into the requirements of probable cause in more dept in later chapters. What follows is a brief summary of a continuum of evidence strength that will hopefully shed light on the meaning of the various statutes we will cover.

### a. Mere Hunch

This term means that you cannot articulate any specific facts which led you to form the opinion that criminal activity is taking place. This degree of evidence requires that you conduct further investigation with voluntary cooperation in dealing with citizens. That is, it will not support investigative detentions or searches that are more intrusive.

### b. Reasonable Suspicion

Reasonable suspicion requires less certainty than probable cause but more than a mere hunch. You must base your suspicion on facts that you articulate and not on mere intuition. This is the standard for investigative detentions.

### c. Probable Cause

Probable cause has no fixed definition. In essence, it means that there is adequate objective information to form a belief that it is more likely than not that a crime has occurred (or is occurring) and that the suspect is involved.

### d. Preponderance of the Evidence

This is the evidentiary standard in most civil cases and is also the standard for several "tests" under criminal procedure. It requires that the facts are more probably one way than the other. Think of this as weighing the evidence from both sides on a balance—the side that makes the balance tip wins. This standard takes into account the relative strength of the evidence, not merely the amount of evidence. One side may show a preponderance of the evidence with only one strongly compelling piece of evidence.

### e. Beyond a Reasonable Doubt

This is the highest standard of evidence known to law (no legal contest requires absolute proof) and is the standard needed for the prosecution to win in a criminal trial. If the defense can interject any doubt about the prosecution's case, and if that doubt is reasonable, the defense will win.

# Chapter 2: Constitutional Limits on Criminal Law

## (2.1) Constitutional Law in General

The broad topic of constitutional law deals with the interpretation and implementation of the *United States Constitution* and the constitutions of states. The U.S. Constitution is the legal foundation of the United States, as the Arkansas constitution is to Arkansas. The U.S. Constitution deals with many important relationships in our country, including relationships among the states, the states and the federal government, the three branches of the federal government, and the rights of the individual in relation to both federal and state government. The constitution specifies that the government be divided into three branches such that no single branch of government can become too powerful. Traditionally, those branches are the Executive, the Legislature, and the Judiciary. The legislature makes the law, the judiciary interprets the law, and the executive enforces the law. Thus, as a law enforcement officer, you are an agent of the executive branch.

As the interpreter of the Constitution, the Supreme Court of the United States has provided the foundation of modern constitutional law through its many decisions. As a consequence, study of Constitutional Law focuses heavily on Supreme Court cases.

For Arkansas law enforcement officers, the constitution of the State of Arkansas is critically important. As the federal constitution is interpreted by the U.S. Supreme Court, the Arkansas constitution is interpreted by the Supreme Court of Arkansas.

The fact that the United States is a federal system can cause some confusion. As a police officer, you have two constitutions and two supreme courts telling you the law and providing guidance as to how to enforce that law. What if they say different things?

The basic rule is that the United States Constitution is the supreme law of the land. ***The U.S. Constitution, as interpreted by the U.S. Supreme Court, trumps every other source of law.*** That is, the legislature and courts of Arkansas cannot restrict the liberty of any person in violation of the U.S. Constitution. And, since police officers are agents of the state, you must be sure to do exactly what the Constitution tells you to do to the best of your ability. Failure to do so can result in a lawsuit naming you, your agency, and your municipal government (this is discussed in detail in the chapter on *Remedies*).

The Supreme Court has the power to decide whether a law is constitutional or not. This power reaches beyond the Congress of the United States. The Supreme Court can assess the validity of state and local laws as well. In addition to being able to assess the constitutionality of written laws, they can also determine if certain acts by government agents (for example, police officers) are constitutional. The Arkansas Supreme Court does not have the power to interpret federal law, only the laws of the state of Arkansas. The Arkansas Supreme Court can interpret the constitution of Arkansas to provide a higher degree of protection to citizens, but it cannot interpret state law such that it offers less protection that the minimum standards of the U.S. Constitution allow.

Professor Joel Samaha describes seven major constitutional limits on the criminal law in his book *Criminal Law*[12]. His list is as follows:

1. The rule of law
2. The prohibition of ex post facto laws
3. The right to "due process of law"
4. The right to "equal protection of the laws"
5. The right to free speech, association, press, and religion
6. The right to privacy
7. The right against "cruel and unusual punishment"

We will add "double jeopardy" as an eighth element.

### (2.2)  The Rule of Law

The rule of law refers the democratic idea that the government can punish people only if there is a specific law that defines a crime and spells out the punishment for committing the crime.  This is also called the *principle of legality*[13].

### (2.3)  Ex Post Facto Laws

A law enacted to punish behavior after the behavior occurs is known as an *ex post facto* law.  Such laws are prohibited by Article 1, Section 9, of the United States Constitution.  Article 2, Section 17, of the Arkansas constitution prohibits such laws as well.  The idea is that it is unfair to punish people for acts that they had no way of knowing were prohibited.

### (2.4)  Void-for-Vagueness Doctrine

This doctrine requires that lawmakers use clear and precise language so that people of reasonable intelligence do not have to guess at the meaning of a law.  The courts have determined that vague laws are a violation of due process, and such laws must be struck down.  Many ordinances dealing with vagrancy, loitering, loud music, and so forth have been struck down by the courts under this doctrine.

This is very similar to the *Void-for-Overbreadth Doctrine* which makes a statute unconstitutional if the way in which it is written has an unnecessarily broad sweep and invades protected freedoms.

### (2.5) Equal Protection

Equal protection refers to the principle that all persons must be treated alike, not only in statutory law but also in law enforcement.  The government cannot make laws that treat one group of people differently from other groups without a rational reason.

### (2.6) Free Speech

The first amendment protects the rights of American's to write, speak, and communicate thoughts and ideas without government interference.  There are, however, five categories of speech that the First Amendment does not protect[14]:

1. *Obscenity* refers to material whose primary appeal is to nudity, sex, or excretion.
2. *Profanity* refers to irreverence toward sacred things, such as the name of God.
3. *Libel and Slander* refer to the defamation of another person.

---

[12] Samaha, J. (2005). *Criminal Law* (8th Ed.).  Belmont, CA: Wadsworth., p. 26-27.
[13] Samaha, J. (2005). *Criminal Law* (8th Ed.).  Belmont, CA: Wadsworth., p. 27.
[14] Samaha, J. (2005). *Criminal Law* (8th Ed.).  Belmont, CA: Wadsworth., p. 35.

4.  *Fighting words* refers to words that are likely to provoke the average person to retaliate.
5.  *Clear and present danger* refers to expression that creates a danger to the public, such as shouting "fire" in a crowded theater.

### (2.7) Right to Privacy

The phrase *right to privacy* never appears in the Constitution of the United States. The USSC, however, has established that it is a fundamental constitutional right by interpreting several amendments[15]. This right to privacy is extremely important to the law of search and seizure.

### (2.8) Cruel and Unusual Punishment

This is an 8th Amendment protection where the words "cruel" and "unusual" have never adequately been defined. The courts have followed an approach that makes a distinction between "ancient" and "modern" forms of punishment. Ancient methods are generally unconstitutional while most modern methods are upheld. Recent controversy has arisen concerning the extended sentences created by habitual offender laws. Most of these questions center on the *doctrine of proportionality*. For example, in *Soelm v. Helm*[16] the USSC ruled that a series of relatively minor non-violent crimes could not be used to sentence a person to life in prison.

### (2.9) Double Jeopardy

The prohibition against *double jeopardy* means that the same sovereign entity (state or federal government) cannot prosecute the same individual twice for the same crime. This means that both state governments and the federal government *can* try the same person for the same act. As a practical matter, this rarely happens unless there are differences to be found in the elements of the crime or the first jurisdiction to prosecute is not successful.

Under AR law, a person can generally be prosecuted where the same conduct constitutes more than one offense. There are five basic circumstances where this is *not* the case:

1.  Where one offense is an included offense of the other
2.  One offense consists only of a conspiracy, solicitation, or attempt to commit the other
3.  Inconsistent findings of fact are required to establish the commission of the offenses
4.  The offenses differ only in that one is defined to prohibit a designated kind of conduct generally and the other to prohibit a specific instance of that conduct
5.  The conduct constitutes an offense defined as a continuing course of conduct and the defendant's course of conduct was uninterrupted, unless the law provides that specific periods of such conduct constitute separate offenses

The first of these prohibitions to prosecution above is often referred to as a **lesser included offense**. Most jurisdictions bar the state form convicting a person for two offenses where the elements of one offense are part of a greater offense. For example, in jurisdictions where breaking and entering are elements of burglary, a person cannot be convicted of both the burglary *and* the breaking and entering.

Note that capital murder[17], first degree murder[18], and continuing criminal enterprise[19] can all be charged along with their attendant felonies.

---

[15] See *Griswold v. Connecticut*, 381 U.S. 479 (1965)
[16] *Solem v. Helm*, 463 U.S. 277 (1983)
[17] § 5-10-101
[18] § 5-10-102
[19] § 5-64-405

# Chapter 3: Action in Criminal Law

## (3.1) Criminal Act in General

The *actus reus* (criminal act) is on of the elements of criminal liability that must be proven beyond a reasonable doubt in a criminal trial. Generally, the act must be voluntary. Thus, acts that are not voluntary, such as a reflex or convulsion, do not count. Contrary to the everyday use of the word, an omission (failing to do something) can satisfy the *actus reus* requirements for crimes.

---

**§ 5-2-201. Definitions generally**

As used in this code, unless the context otherwise requires:

(1) "Act" means a bodily movement, and includes speech and the conscious possession or control of property;

(2) "Omission" means a failure to perform an act, the performance of which is required by law;

(3) "Conduct" means an act or omission and its accompanying mental state;

(4) The verb "act" means either to perform an act or to omit to perform an act.

---

## (3.2) Voluntary Act Requirement

There is a general legal requirement that a criminal act must be voluntary. This means that under the law a criminal act generally must consist of some movement of the body and free will. For example, if your doctor is checking your reflexes and the reflex action causes you to kick him in the face, then the act is not a battery since you did not intend to kick him.

The courts have ruled that the voluntariness requirement does not protect you from criminal liability if what you do is dangerous under the circumstances. For example, people who know that they are subject to epileptic attacks at any time and operate a vehicle with that knowledge are criminally liable if they kill someone while having a seizure.

## (3.3) Status as an Act

In this context, **status** refers to who we are. Some conditions, such as race, ethnicity, and sex are always with us. Others are developed over time, such as diseases and addictions. Generally, the criminal law cannot punish people for who they are, only what they do. The basic idea is that our legal system is based on the principle that people have free will; if that will is not involved, then we do not like to punish people.

Thus we cannot make it illegal to be a drug addict[20]. We can make it illegal to manufacture, distribute, or possess drugs—these are all acts, not statuses. Similarly, we can still prohibit public drunkenness—a behavior voluntarily engaged in[21]. On the other hand, we could not constitutionally make it illegal to be an alcoholic.

### (3.4) Failure to Act

Most crimes are the result of some action that causes a resulting harm. However, it can also be criminal to do nothing. The most common *criminal omission* is the failure to report something when the law obliges you to do so such as a traffic accident, child abuse, or your earnings to the IRS. Many jurisdictions make it a crime to fail to intervene in order to prevent certain harms.

In *Jones v. United States* (1962)[22], the court indicated that there are at least four situations in which the failure to act may constitute breach of legal duty. One can be held criminally liable:

1. Where a statute imposes a duty to care for another;
2. Where one stands in a certain status relationship to another;
3. Where one has assumed a contractual duty to care for another; and
4. Where one has voluntarily assumed the care of another and so secluded the helpless person as to prevent others from rendering aid.

### (3.5) Possession

Most criminal codes make the conscious *possession* of certain things a criminal act even though we understand it to be a passive state in everyday language. Under Arkansas law, this is part of the statutory definition of an *Act*[23].

The law generally recognizes two types of possession: *Actual possession* and *constructive possession*.

**Actual possession** means that suspects have the prohibited items on them.

**Constructive possession** means that the suspects have control of the prohibited items, but they are not on them, such as when items are in a vehicle or home.

To prove constructive possession, the State must establish beyond a reasonable doubt that the defendant exercised care, control, and management over the contraband and that the defendant knew the matter possessed was contraband[24]. The Arkansas courts have indicated that constructive possession can be implied when the contraband is in the joint control of the accused and another person. However, joint occupancy of a vehicle, standing alone, is not sufficient to establish possession. You must prove some additional factor that demonstrates the suspect's knowledge and control of the contraband, such as:

1. Whether the contraband was in plain view
2. Whether the contraband was found on the accused person or with his personal effects
3. Whether it was found on the same side of the car seat as the accused was sitting or in near proximity to it
4. Whether the accused is the owner of the vehicle or exercises dominion or control over it
5. Whether the accused acted suspiciously before or during the arrest[25].

---

[20] *Robinson v. California*, 370 U.S. 660 (1962)

[21] *Powell v. Texas*, 392 U.S. 514 (1968)

[22] *Jones v. United States*, 308 F. 2d 307 (1962)

[23] § 5-2-201

[24] *Walker v. State*, 77 Ark. App. 122, 72 S.W.3d 517 (2002)

[25] *Porter v. State*, Ark. App. LEXIS 320, (2003)

Arkansas statutory definitions take both ideas into account by defining a criminal act to include "conscious possession or control of property."

Note the word "conscious" in the above description. This word means that you need to have knowledge of what you possess for the possession to be criminal. *Mere possession* is the term used to indicate that a possession is not "conscious"—the person does not know what they possess.

# Chapter 4: The Guilty Mind

## (4.1) Criminal Intent in General

Most serious crimes require a criminal act (Chapter 3) and criminal intent. The intent element is fundamental to our legal system because we generally only want to punish those who are worthy of blame.

In law, blameworthiness is often referred to as **culpability**. When we purposefully commit a criminal act, then we can be held accountable for it. We are even willing to punish people who may not have meant to do something, but should have known better. However, if an act was purely accidental or unavoidable, then we generally will not punish the actor.

Arkansas law recognizes 4 culpable mental states, as define in §5-2-202.

---

### § 5-2-202. Culpable mental states -- Definitions

As used in this code, unless the context otherwise requires, there are four (4) kinds of culpable mental states, which are defined as follows:

(1) "Purposely." A person acts purposely with respect to his conduct or a result thereof when it is his conscious object to engage in conduct of that nature or to cause such a result;

(2) "Knowingly." A person acts knowingly with respect to his conduct or the attendant circumstances when he is aware that his conduct is of that nature or that such circumstances exist. A person acts knowingly with respect to a result of his conduct when he is aware that it is practically certain that his conduct will cause such a result;

(3) "Recklessly." A person acts recklessly with respect to attendant circumstances or a result of his conduct when he consciously disregards a substantial and unjustifiable risk that the circumstances exist or the result will occur. The risk must be of a nature and degree that disregard thereof constitutes a gross deviation from the standard of care that a reasonable person would observe in the actor's situation;

(4) "Negligently." A person acts negligently with respect to attendant circumstances or a result of his conduct when he should be aware of a substantial and unjustifiable risk that the circumstances exist or the result will occur. The risk must be of such a nature and degree that the actor's failure to perceive it, considering the nature and purpose of his conduct and the circumstances known to him, involves a gross deviation from the standard of care that a reasonable person would observe in the actor's situation.

---

## (4.2) Determining Mens Rea

Criminal intent is almost never proven in court by direct evidence. This is primarily because testimonial evidence, such as a confession, is the only direct evidence of a suspect's mental state. The mental element of crimes is usually proved by **circumstantial evidence**. Fortunately, the old expression "actions speak louder than words" holds some truth. That is, by observing what a suspect *does*, it is possible to infer what they *intend*[26].

---

[26] *Chadwell v. State*, 37 Ark. App. 9, 822 S.W.2d 402 (1992)

For example, in *Easter v. State*[27], the court said that the "jury could reasonably have inferred defendant purposely killed his victim, based on the type of weapon used, the manner of its use, and the location of the wounds."

In fact, under Arkansas law there is a presumption that "a person intends the natural and probable consequences of his acts[28]."

### *(4.3) Kinds of Mens Rea*

#### a. Four Levels of Criminal Intent

There are several ways to divide up levels of criminal intent. The most common way is based on the degree of blameworthiness. Arkansas law provides for four levels:

1.  **Purpose** is a level of culpability which has an obvious meaning. The perpetrator did it on purpose—he meant to cause the result of the criminal act.

2.  **Knowledge** means that the perpetrator didn't want to produce the criminal harm, but knew that it would happen.

3.  **Recklessness** means that the perpetrator didn't mean to cause the harm, but knew the odds of it happening were very high and did it anyway.

4.  **Negligence** means that the perpetrator didn't mean to cause the harm and didn't know the odds of it happening, but should have known the odds were high.

Reckless and negligent conduct are very similar in nature. The important difference between the two is that with reckless conduct, there is a conscious disregard for a perceived risk—the person knew the risk was there. With negligence, it is assumed that there is no awareness of the risk[29].

If a statute defining an offense prescribes a culpable mental state and does not clearly indicate that the culpable mental state applies to less than all of the elements of the offense, the prescribed culpable mental state applies to each element of the offense[30]. When a statute defining an offense provides that acting negligently suffices to establish an element of that offense, the element also is established if a person acts purposely, knowingly, or recklessly. Similarly, when acting recklessly suffices to establish an element, the element also is established if a person acts purposely or knowingly, and when acting knowingly suffices to establish an element, the element also is established if a person acts purposely.

Knowledge that conduct constitutes an offense or knowledge of the existence, meaning, or application of the statute defining an offense is not an element of an offense unless the statute clearly so provides[31].

#### b. Types of Intent

The section above divides intent into levels based in the degree of culpability. There are also terms that divide intent up based on what exactly was intended.

1.  **General intent** simply means the intent to commit the criminal act; it does not speak to an intention to achieve a specific outcome or result.

---

[27] *Easter v. State*, 306 Ark. 615 (1991)
[28] *Tarentino v. State*, 302 Ark. 55, 786 S.W.2d 584 (1990); *Furr v. State*, 308 Ark. 41, 822 S.W.2d 380 (1992)
[29] *Smith v. State*, 3 Ark. App. 224, (1981)
[30] § 5-2-203
[31] § 5-2-203

2.  **Specific intent** applies to crimes that require a specific resulting harm, such as in homicide.  The specific intent for homicide is the intent to cause the death of a person.

3.  **Transferred intent** applies to situations where the intent was to harm one person and the result was harm to another.  This is often called *bad aim intent*—often a perpetrator trying to shoot one person shoots another instead.

4.  **Constructive intent** applies to situations where the harm done is greater than expected.

### *(4.4) Strict Liability*

The necessity of criminal intent is a cornerstone of our legal system.  Sometimes, however, lawmakers deem it appropriate to remove this mental element from various crimes and punish people for merely committing the prohibited act.  Acts that do not require a mental element to be criminal are called **strict liability** offenses.

The most common strict liability offenses are *violations*, such as citations for speeding and littering.

As specified in §5-2-204, the legislature may dispense with the mental element by specifically stating so in the statute.

---

**§ 5-2-204.  Elements of culpability -- Exceptions to culpable mental state requirement**

(a) A person does not commit an offense unless his liability is based on conduct that includes a voluntary act or the omission to perform an act which he is physically capable of performing.

(b) A person does not commit an offense unless he acts with a culpable mental state with respect to each element of the offense that requires a culpable mental state.

(c) However, a culpable mental state is not required if:

(1) The offense is a violation, unless a culpable mental state is expressly included in the definition of the offense; or

(2) An offense defined by a statute not a part of this code clearly indicates a legislative intent to dispense with any culpable mental state requirement for the offense or for any element thereof.

---

# Chapter 5: Concurrence and Causation

## (5.1) Concurrence

The idea of **concurrence** (a.k.a. *contemporaneity* and *simultaneity*) is rarely considered in criminal cases. This is not because the idea is unimportant, but because its presence is usually obvious. Concurrence means that the guilty act (*actus reus*) must be triggered by the guilty mind (*mens rea*). Brody, Acker, and Logan[32] provide and excellent example of a situation when concurrence comes into play:

> A enters a mountain cabin during a blizzard without the owner's permission to take refuge from the storm. After entering, he sees valuables and decides to take them with him when the weather calms. He is not guilty of burglary if that offense is defined as "breaking and entering a dwelling with the intention to commit a felony therein." This is so because at the time of his entry into the cabin A had no intention of committing felonious larceny or another felony; he sought only to escape the blizzard. His intention to steal, formed after his entry, did not concur with his breaking and entering the cabin.

While there is no section of the AR code dealing directly with concurrence, we can infer it from the text of §5-2-204(b): "A person does not commit and offense unless he acts with a *culpable mental state with respect to each element of the offense* that requires a culpable mental state." That is, action must be coupled with intent. "… there must be a union or joint operation of act and intention or criminal negligence."[33]

## (5.2) Causation

It is a general rule of the criminal law that an individual is not guilty of a crime unless his or her conduct causes the harm that the law seeks to prevent.

The idea of cause in law is complicated because the term is often broken down into two distinct ideas: **cause-in-fact** and **proximate cause**.

**Cause-in-fact** (also called "but-for" causation) must always be shown. That is, it must be concluded that "but-for" the defendant's conduct, the prohibited harm would not have occurred.

The **proximate cause** language is not present in the Arkansas code, but the idea is maintained in the final clause of §5-2-205. The key idea behind proximate cause is distance between the act and the harm; if the distance is too great, we will not hold the defendant culpable.

---

[32] Brody, D.C., Acker, J. R., & Logan, W. A. (2001). *Criminal Law*. Gaithersburg, Maryland: Aspen. (p. 213)
[33] *Yoes v State*, 9 Ark. 42 (1848)

The "but-for" language has been used by the Arkansas courts in several cases. For example, in *Anderson v. State*[34], the court stated that "… testimony that death would not have occurred but for the trauma and that the alcohol consumption alone was not the cause of death satisfies the statutory requirement."

Under the ARSC interpretation of the statute, where conduct hastens or contributes to a person's death, it is a [legal] cause of the death[35].

---

### § 5-2-205. Causation

Causation may be found where the result would not have occurred **but for** [emphasis added] the conduct of the defendant operating either alone or concurrently with another cause unless the concurrent cause was clearly sufficient to produce the result and the conduct of the defendant clearly insufficient.

---

### (5.3) Harm

In crimes where causation is a factor, it is obvious that something must be caused. **Harm**, then, refers to the specific result prohibited by the statute. In murder, for example, the result is the death of a living human being.

---

[34] *Anderson v. State*, 312 Ark. 606; 852 S.W.2d 309 (1993)

[35] *Tackett v. State*, 298 Ark. 20; 766 S.W.2d 410 (1989). In this case a doctor testified that the victim's comatose condition was caused by the automobile accident which made her more susceptible to infection and that pneumonia was the immediate cause of her death and that the car accident was the proximate cause of her death. Also, there was testimony by other witnesses that the appellant had caused the accident. Under these circumstances, the court held that the evidence was sufficient to prove the cause of the victim's death was the automobile accident.

# PART TWO

# SUBSTANTIVE OFFENSES

# Chapter 6: Parties to Crime

*A person may commit an offense either by his own conduct or that of another person.*

—A.C.A. § 5-2-401

## (6.1) Complicity in General

When an actor is liable for someone else's action or conduct, it is called **complicity**. Generally, a person can be held criminally liable under AR law for the conduct of another person under three circumstances:

1. A specific statute makes the first person liable for the actions of the second
2. The person is an accomplice of another
3. The person causes a person with a defense available to commit the crime[36]

Under the old common law rules, there were four distinct parties to crime:

1. **Principals in the first degree**: These were persons who actually committed the crime.
2. **Principals in the second degree**: These were persons present when the crime is committed, such as lookouts.
3. **Accessories before the fact**: These were people who were not present when the crime was committed, but who helped before the crime was committed (e.g., providing weapons).
4. **Accessories after the fact**: These were people who helped after the crime was committed, such as harboring a fugitive.

Most states have reduced the number of distinct categories. Arkansas has chosen to eliminate nearly all of these distinctions under a single "Accomplices" statute. The exception is the fourth element (accessories after the fact), which has been classified along the lines of a crime against the administration of justice. This category of persons can be described as criminal protectors.

## (6.2) Accomplices

Under Arkansas law[37], a person is considered an *accomplice* if, with the purpose of promoting or facilitating a crime, he or she does any of the following:

1. Solicits, advises, encourages, or coerces the other person to commit the crime
2. Aids, agrees to aid, or attempts to aid the other person in planning or committing the crime
3. Having a legal duty to prevent the commission of the offense, fails to make a proper effort to do so

---

[36] §5-2-402
[37] §5-2-403

For crimes that require a specific result, the above three acts apply to promoting or facilitating the *result*.

*The statute governing accomplice liability requires a culpable mental state sufficient for the commission of the offense*[38]. That is, the accomplice must have the criminal intent that the crime be committed. A defendant who helps others to commit a crime is not an accomplice to the crime when he or she has no knowledge that the activities constitute a crime[39].

There is no difference in the liability of an accomplice and the person who actually commits the criminal act[40]. When two or more persons help each other commit a crime, each is legally an accomplice and liable for the conduct of all[41].

There is *no* statutory requirement that an accomplice be present at the scene of the crime[42]. Mere presence and knowledge that a crime is being committed is not enough to establish a person as an accomplice, regardless of whether the person informs LE[43].

Working together to commit a crime may be shown by circumstantial evidence, without any *direct* proof of a prior agreement. A defendant can be found guilty of the offense not only by his or her own actions, but also by that of accomplices[44].

To prove liability as an accomplice, you only need to show that the defendant encouraged or aided in the commission of the crime[45].

### (6.3) Accomplice Defenses

---

**§ 5-2-404.  Defenses**

(a) Unless otherwise provided by the statute defining the offense, a person is not an accomplice in an offense if:

(1) He is a victim of the offense; or

(2) The offense is defined so that his conduct is inevitably incident to its commission.

(b) It is an affirmative defense to a prosecution for an offense respecting which the liability of the defendant is based on the conduct of another person that the defendant terminates his complicity prior to the commission of the offense and:

(1) Wholly deprives his complicity of effectiveness in the commission of the offense; or

(2) Gives timely warning to appropriate law enforcement authorities; or

(3) Otherwise makes a proper effort to prevent commission of the offense.

---

### (6.4) Accessories
The common law idea (and the former Arkansas Code) of accessories to crimes has been abolished in the Arkansas Code.

---

[38] §5-2-403
[39] *Martinez v. State*, 269 Ark. 231, 601 S.W.2d 576 (1980)
[40] *Riggins v. State*, 317 Ark. 636, 882 S.W.2d 664 (1994)
[41] *Parker v. State*, 265 Ark. 315, 578 S.W.2d 206 (1979)
[42] *Roleson v. State*, 277 Ark. 148, 640 S.W.2d 113 (1982)
[43] *Scherrer v. State*, 294 Ark. 227, 742 S.W.2d 877 (1988), *Pilcher v. State*, 303 Ark. 335, 796 S.W.2d 845 (1990)
[44] *King v. State*, 271 Ark. 417, 609 S.W.2d 32 (1980)
[45] *Cooper v. State*, 324 Ark. 135, 919 S.W.2d 205 (1996)

Under the present code, what was an accessory before the fact is now an *accomplice.*

Perpetrators who were considered *accessories* after the fact under former law are now guilty of a separate crime under §5-54-105, "hindering the apprehension and prosecution[46]."

---

**§ 5-54-105. Hindering apprehension or prosecution**

(a) A person commits an offense under this section if, with purpose to hinder the apprehension, prosecution, conviction, or punishment of another for an offense, he:

(1) Harbors or conceals the person; or

(2) Provides or aids in providing the person with a weapon, money, transportation, disguise, or other means of avoiding apprehension, discovery, or effecting escape; or

(3) Prevents or obstructs anyone from performing an act which might aid in the discovery, apprehension, or identification of the person by means of force, intimidation, or the threat of such, or by means of deception; or

(4) Conceals, alters, destroys, or otherwise suppresses the discovery of any fact, information, or other thing related to the crime which might aid in the discovery, apprehension, or identification of the person; or

(5) Warns the person of impending discovery, apprehension, or identification; or

(6) Volunteers false information to a law enforcement officer; or

(7) Purposefully lies or attempts to purposefully provide erroneous information, documents or other instrumentalities which he knows to be false to a certified law enforcement officer that would distract from the true course of the investigation or inhibit the logical or orderly progress of the investigation.

(b) Hindering apprehension or prosecution is a Class B felony if the conduct of the person assisted in violation of this section constitutes a Class Y or Class A felony, provided that if the defendant shows by preponderance of the evidence that he stands to the person assisted in the relation of parent, child, brother, sister, corresponding steprelationships of the preceding, husband, or wife, hindering is a Class D felony.

(c) Hindering apprehension or prosecution is a felony classified one (1) degree below the felony constituted by the conduct of the person assisted in violation of this section if such conduct is a Class B or C felony.

(d) (d) Hindering apprehension or prosecution is a Class A misdemeanor if the conduct of the person assisted in violation of this section is a Class D felony or unclassified felony unless the person in violation of this section was assisting an escapee from correctional custody sentenced after being found guilty of a felony. If so, the violation of this section is a Class D felony. Otherwise it is a misdemeanor classed one (1) degree below the misdemeanor constituted by the conduct of the person assisted in violation of this section.

---

[46] *Fight v. State*, 314 Ark. 438, 863 S.W.2d 800 (1993)

# Chapter 7: Uncompleted Crimes

### (7.1) Uncompleted Crimes in General

Crimes that have not yet been completed but still incur some form of criminal liability are called **inchoate offenses** (pronounced "in-co-hate"). The term *inchoate* means *underdeveloped*. The defining quality of inchoate offenses is that they seek to prevent additional harms that have not come to pass. That is, the state seeks to prevent the commission of crimes. Arkansas law recognizes the inchoate offenses of (1) criminal attempt, (2) criminal solicitation, and (3) criminal conspiracy.

Inchoate crimes are rather unique in criminal law because they do not require that some social harm be done. Generally, the mental element is the intent to commit the substantive offense. The criminal act, however, is different. With these types of offenses, the act needs to be merely some step in furtherance of the crime.

Rather than have an attempt statute to match every crime (such as a statute that deals with attempted murder specifically), Arkansas has a general attempt statute that can be applied to most substantive offenses elsewhere specified in the Criminal Code.

### (7.2) Criminal Attempt (§5-3-201)

Attempt is the most frequently charged of the inchoate offenses. The essence of attempt is making an effort to accomplish a particular criminal purpose. Another way to look at it is that "an attempt, by nature, is a failure to accomplish what one intended to do."[47]

The *criminal act* element of attempt can be satisfied in two ways:

1. If the person purposely engages in conduct that would constitute an offense if the attendant circumstances were as he believed them to be; or
2. If the person engages in conduct that constitutes a substantial step toward the commission of an offense (whether or not the attendant circumstances are as he believed them to be)

When considering crimes that require a specific result (such as the death of a person in murder), the person commits the offense of criminal attempt if he or she purposely engages in conduct that constitutes a substantial step in a course of conduct intended or known to cause the result. Conduct cannot be considered a "substantial step" unless it is strongly corroborative of the person's criminal purpose.

### (7.3) Complicity [Attempted] (§5-3-202)

The basic purpose of this provision is to criminalize conduct designed to aid the commission of an offense not actually committed.

---

[47] *State v. Kimbrough*, 924 S.W.2d 888 (Tenn. 1996).

Complicity is the crime of attempting to aid in the commission of an offence not actually committed.

A person *attempts* to commit an offense if, with the purpose of aiding another person in the commission of the specific offense, he engages in conduct that would establish his complicity under §5-2-402 if the offense were committed by the other person [see the previous section on **Accomplices** for a detailed discussion of §5-2-402].

It is not a defense to a prosecution that the other person did not commit or attempt to commit an offense.

It is also not a defense that it was impossible for the actor to assist the other person in the commission of the offense, provided the actor could have done so if the attendant circumstances had been as he believed them to be.

It can be taken from the language of the statute that complicity is a form of attempt and is classified as such. Criminal attempts are classified as one grade below an actual commission of the crime. If the offense attempted is capital murder, a Class Y felony, or treason, the attempt will be classified as a Class A felony. Class B felony attempts are classified as Class C offenses, and so forth. Attempted Class C misdemeanors are *violations*.

### (7.4) Criminal Solicitation (§ 5-3-301)

A person solicits the commission of an offense if, with the purpose of promoting or facilitating the commission of a specific offense, he commands, urges, or requests another person to engage in specific conduct which would amount to any of the following:
1.  Constitute that offense
2.  Constitute an attempt to commit that offense
3.  Cause the result specified by the definition of the offense
4.  Establish the other person's complicity in the commission or attempted commission of that offense

Solicitation is classified in the same manner as attempt, with the exception that solicitation of a class C misdemeanor is an *unclassified misdemeanor* rather than a violation (see **7.3** above).

It is an affirmative defense to prosecution for solicitation that the defendant prevented the commission of the offense solicited under circumstances manifesting a voluntary and complete renunciation of the criminal purpose.

Solicitation is complete when the request to engage in criminal activity is made, and it does not matter if the person solicited agrees or if the offense is carried out. This is very different from the law of attempt: for an attempt, some substantial step must be taken toward the commission of the crime. Solicitation does not require that any overt act be made.

### (7.5) Conspiracy (§5-3-401)

Under common law, conspiracy consisted of an agreement by two or more persons to accomplish a criminal act or to use unlawful means to accomplish a noncriminal purpose. The essence of the offense was the *unlawful agreement between the parties*—no overt act was required.

The logic of criminalizing conspiracy is that the actions of people working together increase the chances of successfully completing the crime. In addition, people working together can successfully complete crimes of greater complexity (and possible social harm) than any of the individuals acting alone[48].

Under AR law, a person *conspires* to commit an offense if with the purpose of promoting or facilitating the commission of any criminal offense:

---

[48] *Callanan v. United States*, 364 U.S. 587 (1961)

He agrees with another person(s) that one or more of them will engage in conduct that constitutes a criminal offense, or that he will aid in the planning or commission of that criminal offense;
*and*
He or another person[49] with whom he conspired does any overt act in pursuance of the conspiracy.

If a person knows (or could reasonably expect) that one with whom he conspires has himself conspired or will conspire with another to commit the same offense, he shall be deemed to have conspired with the other, whether or not he knows the other's identity[50].

If a person conspires to commit a number of criminal offenses, he commits only one conspiracy if the multiple offenses are the object of the same agreement or continuous conspiratorial relationship.

Conspiracy is classified in the same manner as an attempt, with the exception that no provision is made for Class C misdemeanors[51].

It is an *affirmative defense* to a prosecution for conspiracy to commit an offense that the defendant does *any* of the following:

- Thwarted the success of the conspiracy under circumstances manifesting a complete and voluntary renunciation of his criminal purpose
- Terminated his participation in the conspiracy and either gave timely warning to LE
- otherwise made a substantial effort to prevent the commission of the offense under circumstances manifesting a voluntary and complete renunciation of his criminal purpose

---

[49] This language suggests that Arkansas subscribes to the *Pinkerton* Rule, *Pinkerton v. United States*, 328 U.S. 640 (1946). In *Pinkerton* the USSC determined that it was constitutionally acceptable to hold members of a conspiracy liable for all offenses committed in furtherance of the conspiracy.
[50] §5-3-402
[51] §5-3-404

# Chapter 8: Defenses

## (8.1) Defenses in General

In a criminal prosecution, the state must prove that the defendant is guilty of the crime charged beyond a reasonable doubt. In practice, this means that the government must prove each element of the crime charged at the legally appropriate level. Most of the time, if the prosecutor successfully does this, the result is a conviction. It is possible, however, for the state to prove each element of the crime and the defendant still be acquitted. This can happen when the defendant successfully proves a **defense**.

Arkansas criminal law permits a number of affirmative defenses that can greatly reduce or eliminate altogether a defendant's criminal liability. Criminal defenses can be divided into two major branches: Affirmative defenses and non-affirmative defenses.

**Non-affirmative** defenses attack the elements of the crime that the prosecution is trying to prove. For example, a defendant may raise an **alibi** defense where he states that he was not present when the crime occurred and thus could not have committed it. The big idea is that non-affirmative defenses attack the prosecutor's proof. If a non-affirmative defense can cause the jury to have a reasonable doubt, then the defense has worked and the defendant will be acquitted.

When an **affirmative** defense is used, the defendant essentially admits guilt but offers an excuse or justification for his or her criminal actions. In most jurisdictions, the defendant must submit enough evidence to the trail judge to show that an affirmative defense possibly exists before the jury can hear the evidence for the defense. The requirement that this initial evidence must be submitted to the judge is called the **burden of production**.

Once the defendant meets this burden of production, the burden then shifts to the prosecution. The burden placed on the prosecution is much higher than that of the defendant. While the defendant does not have to produce a large amount of evidence, the prosecutor must counter the defense with evidence beyond a reasonable doubt that no legal defense exists.

Affirmative defenses can generally be divided into two categories: **excuse defenses** and **justification defenses**.

**Excuse** defenses involve situations where the defendant admits to committing the crime, but claims that he or she is not blameworthy because of some extenuating circumstances, such as *insanity* or *duress*.

**Justification** defenses involve situations where the defendant admits to committing the crime and that the action was appropriate under the circumstances surrounding the act. Normally it is criminal to cause the death of another living human being. If, however, the death comes about as the lawful execution of a death warrant, then the executioner is not held criminally liable because he or she is bound to cause the death by *public duty*. Similarly, if a police officer kills a person that is trying to stab him with a knife, then the killing is considered self-defense and so the officer is not criminally liable.

## (8.2)Justifications

According to §5-2-602, "in a prosecution for an offense, *justification* … is a defense." This means that the prosecution has to prove the defense wrong beyond a reasonable doubt once evidence tending to support the defense has been demonstrated.

### a. Execution of Public Duty (§5-2-603)

This rule protects public servants from being prosecuted when their official duties, sanctioned or commanded by law, would otherwise be offenses. The most common example of this is when a person executes another in the name of the state, pursuant to a lawful death warrant. There is no murder because law commanded the death and the executioner acted with legal authority.

This rule also protects persons acting at the direction of public servants who are compelled by law to perform acts that would otherwise be criminal. This section covers private persons who are acting at the direction of and in cooperation with law enforcement, such as informants who purchase narcotics under LE supervision.

### b. Choice of Evils (§5-2-604)

The choice of evils justification is based on the idea that sometimes it is necessary to perform an "evil" act to prevent an even greater one. Destroying property to prevent the spread of a dangerous fire is a common example.

The statute requires two circumstances be present to use the choices of evil justification:

1.     The conduct was necessary as an emergency measure to avoid an imminent public or private injury.
2.     The desirability and urgency of avoiding the injury outweigh, according to ordinary standards of reasonableness, the injury sought to be prevented.

If the actor is reckless or negligent in bringing about the circumstances requiring the "choice between evils" or in appraising the necessity of the conduct, then the justification may not be used.

### c. Use of Physical Force Generally (§5-2-605)

Under this section, the use of physical force on another person is justified under 5 basic conditions:[52]

1. A person legally entrusted with the care of a minor or incompetent person may use reasonable and appropriate physical force when and to the extent necessary to maintain discipline or promote the child's or incompetent person's welfare.
2. Correctional staff that are authorized to do so may use physical force such as is reasonably necessary to maintain order and discipline.
3. A person responsible for maintaining order on a common carrier[53] (or another person acting under his or her direction) may use nondeadly physical force to the extent reasonably necessary to maintain order.
4. A person may use nondeadly force to the extent reasonably necessary to prevent persons from committing suicide or inflicting serious physical injury to themselves.
5. Physicians may use physical force in the performance of their medical practice so long as proper consent is obtained.

---

[52] This section does not cover all justifiable use of force circumstances. See §6-18-501 for teachers disciplining students, and see §27-66-602 for treatment of county convicts.
[53] According to §5-2-601(1), "Common Carrier" means any vehicle used to transport for hire any member of the public.

**d. Defense of Persons (§5-2-606 & §5-2-607)**

A person may use *nondeadly force* to defend himself or another person from unlawful physical force.  Both the need to defend yourself or another and the amount of force used in the defense must be reasonable.

A person is *not* justified in the use of force under three conditions:

1. If the person provokes the use of unlawful physical force by the attacker with the purpose to cause physical injury or death
2. If the person is the initial aggressor
3. If the physical force is the product of a combat by agreement not authorized by law

A person may use *deadly force* if he reasonably believes:

- That the other person is committing or is about to commit a felony involving force or violence
- That the person is using or is about to use unlawful deadly physical force
- That the person is imminently endangering his or her life or imminently about to victimize the person as described in §9-15-103(a) [see Textbox].

A person *may not* use deadly force in self-defense if he knows that he can avoid the necessity of using that force with complete safety, by:

1. Retreating, except that the person is in his or her dwelling and was not the initial aggressor or the person is a law enforcement officer or someone under the direction of a law enforcement officer
2. By surrendering property to a person claiming a lawful right to the property

---

**§ 9-15-103. Definitions**

(a) "Domestic abuse" means:

(1) Physical harm, bodily injury, assault, or the infliction of fear of imminent physical harm, bodily injury, or assault between family or household members; or

(2) Any sexual conduct between family or household members, whether minors or adults, which constitutes a crime under the laws of this state.

(b) "Family or household members" means spouses, former spouses, parents and children, persons related by blood within the fourth degree of consanguinity, any children residing in the household, persons who presently or in the past have resided or cohabited together, and persons who have or have had a child in common.

---

The reasonableness standard for the use of force as a justification is one of objective reasonableness: what would a "reasonably prudent person" have believed under the circumstances?[54]

**e. Defense of Premises (§5-2-608)**

A person in lawful possession or control of premises or a vehicle is justified in using *nondeadly* force on another person if he or she reasonably believes it necessary to prevent a criminal trespass.

A person may only use *deadly force* when it is reasonably necessary to prevent an arson or a burglary by the trespasser, or circumstances are such as described in §5-2-607 [See 8.2(d) above].

The same degree of force authorized to prevent a trespass may be used to eject the person once they have entered.

---

[54] *Plumley v. State*, 116 Ark. 17, 171 S.W. 925 (1914)

### f. Defense of Property (§5-2-609)

A person is justified in using nondeadly force upon another person when and to the extent that he or she reasonably believes necessary to prevent or stop the commission or attempted commission of theft or criminal mischief or flight.

**Caveat**: *Deadly force may never be used in the defense of property*.  However, it must be remembered that both robbery and burglary are not merely crimes against property and may be met with deadly force.

### g. LEO Use of Force §(5-2-610)

A LEO is justified in using *nondeadly* physical force, or threatening to use deadly force, on a person when he reasonably believes that it is necessary:

1. To effect an arrest or to prevent the escape of an arrested person unless the officer knows that the arrest is unlawful
2. To defend himself or herself from what he or she reasonably believes to be the use or imminent use of force while effecting or attempting to effect an arrest or while preventing or attempting to prevent escape

A LEO is justified in using *deadly physical force* on a person when he reasonably believes that it is necessary:

1. To effect an arrest or to prevent the escape from custody of an arrested person whom he reasonably believes has committed or attempted to commit a felony
2. To defend his or herself from the imminent use of deadly force

When it comes to self-defense, the only difference between a LEO and a private citizen is that a LEO is under no obligation to retreat.

**Caveat:** despite the obvious interpretation of §5-2-610(b)(1), it is *unlawful* for an officer to use *deadly force* to arrest or prevent the escape of an unarmed, nondangerous felony suspect[55].

### h. Use of Force by Private Persons Aiding LEOs (§5-2-611)

A person is justified in using nondeadly physical force when and to the extent he reasonably believes it necessary:

1. To effect the arrest of one reasonably believed to be committing or to have committed a felony
2. To prevent the escape of one reasonably believed to have committed a felony

A person who has been directed by a LEO to assist in effecting an arrest or in preventing an escape is justified in using *nondeadly* force when and to the extent that the person reasonably believes it necessary to carry out the LEOs direction.

**Caveat**: A private person may only use deadly force under the rules governing self-defense—*this statute provides no special provisions for the use of deadly force.*

### i. Force in Resisting Arrest (§5-2-612)

A person *may not* use physical force to resist arrest, whether the arrest is lawful or unlawful, by a person who is known is reasonably appears to be a LEO or someone acting under the direction of an LEO[56].

---

[55] *Tennessee v. Garner*, 471 U.S. 1 (1985)
[56] This provision may seem odd today, but it must be remembered that the common law allowed for the resistance of an *unlawful* arrest with physical force.  Here the legislature is making it known that the common law rule no longer has force.

### j. Force to Prevent Escape (§5-2-613)

Correctional officers (Both DOC and municipal/county employees) may use deadly force to prevent escape from custody, so long as it is *not known* (or reasonably should have known) to the officer that the person attempting escape has only been convicted of a misdemeanor.

### k. Reckless or Negligent Force (§5-2-614)

If a person is reckless or negligent either in making the decision to use force or excessive in the degree of force used, then the justification available in the various use of force provisions above is not available.

The justification is also not available to those who, when otherwise justified in the use of force, recklessly or negligently harms a third party.

### (8.3) Excuses

### a. Former Prosecution

**See 2.9**

### b. Ignorance or Mistake (§5-2-206)

Ignorance or mistake is of two types. **Mistake of fact** means that circumstances were not as you thought. **Mistake of law** means that there was an error in your understanding of the law.

A mistake of fact can be an defense under two circumstances:

1. The statute making the act a crime specifically provides for the defense
2. A mistaken belief of fact provides for a justification [as discussed in **8.2** above]

A mistake of law is generally no defense, unless the mistake is due to some official version of the law (statutes, high court decisions, administrative interpretations such as by the state AG's office) that is incorrect.

Mistakes of law other than the existence or interpretation of a specific statute *can* be used to disprove specific culpable metal states.

### c. Intoxication (§5-2-207)

Because it interferes with the ability to make rational choices and thus limits culpability, **intoxication** can be a defense, but only if the intoxication is involuntary. *Voluntary drunkenness is no defense.*

---

**§ 5-2-207. Intoxication**

(a) Intoxication that is not self-induced is an affirmative defense to a prosecution if at the time a person engages in the conduct charged to constitute the offense he lacks capacity to conform his conduct to the requirements of the law or to appreciate the criminality of his conduct.

(b) For the purposes of this section:

(1) "Intoxication" means a disturbance of mental or physical capacities resulting from the introduction of alcohol, drugs, or other substances into the body;

(2) "Self-induced intoxication" means intoxication caused by a substance which the actor knowingly introduces into his body, the tendency of which to cause intoxication he knows or ought to know.

---

### d. Duress (§ 5-2-208)

**Duress** means that you were forced to do something. Duress works as a defense under the theory that if someone forced you to commit a criminal act, then the guilty mind was theirs and not yours. Under AR law, it is an affirmative defense "that the actor engaged in the conduct charged ... because he reasonably believed he was compelled to do so by the threat or use of unlawful force against his person or the person of another that a person of ordinary firmness in the actor's situation would not have resisted." The statute stipulates that the defense is not available in circumstances where actors put themselves *recklessly* in a situation where the duress was reasonably foreseeable.

### e. Entrapment (§ 5-2-209)

This section makes **entrapment** an affirmative defense. Entrapment occurs when an agent of the state induces the commission of an offense by using persuasion likely to cause a normally law-abiding person to commit the offense. The statute specifically states that conduct "merely affording a person an opportunity to commit an offense" does not meet this standard. For it to be entrapment, the officer must "talk the person into" committing the crime.

### f. Mental Disease or Defect

The defense of mental disease or defect is a complicated issue and extensively involves the professional services of mental health professionals on both sides. This defense is governed by the following statutes:

§ **5-2-301.** Definitions
§ **5-2-302.** Lack of fitness to proceed generally
§ **5-2-303.** Admissibility of evidence to show mental state
§ **5-2-304.** Notice requirement
§ **5-2-305.** Mental health examination of defendant
§ **5-2-306.** Access to defendant by examiners of his choice
§ **5-2-309.** Determination of fitness to proceed
§ **5-2-310.** Lack of fitness to proceed -- Procedures subsequent to finding
§ **5-2-312.** Lack of capacity -- Affirmative defense
§ **5-2-314.** Acquittal – Examination of defendant – Hearing

# Chapter 9: Criminal Homicide

## (9.1) Criminal Homicide in General

Homicide means the killing of another human being. Not all homicides are criminal, such as those that are justified. Arkansas statutes make six separate varieties of homicide illegal. They are, arranged from greatest culpability to least, as follows:

1. Capital Murder
2. First Degree
3. Second Degree
4. Manslaughter
5. Negligent Homicide
6. Physician-assisted Suicide

## (9.2) Capital Murder (5-10-101)

Capital murder is considered to be the most culpable and is eligible for the death penalty. According to various USSC decisions, it can be concluded that murders generally need some aggravating circumstance to make them death penalty eligible. Arkansas recognizes 10 different aggravating circumstances in the capital murder statute.

### a. Aggravating Circumstance One

The first[57] death penalty eligible act listed concerns deaths occurring during the commission or attempted commission of specific serious felonies:

1. Terrorism (§5-54-205)
2. Rape (§5-14-103)
3. Kidnapping (§5-11-102)
4. Vehicular Piracy (§5-11-105)
5. Robbery (§5-12-103)
6. Burglary (§5-39-201)
7. Violations of the Uniform Controlled Substance Act (§5-64-101)
8. First Degree Escape (§5-54-110)

In addition to the commission of attempt to commit the serious felony, the person must

"In the course of and in furtherance of the felony or in immediate flight therefrom, he or she or an accomplice causes the death of any person under circumstances manifesting extreme indifference to the value of human life."

---

[57] §5-10-101(a)(1)

The language "manifesting extreme indifference to the value of human life" makes it clear that an inadvertent killing in the course of a felony will *not* establish liability under this section. According to the Arkansas courts, "extreme indifference is established by actions that evidence a mental state on the part of the accused to engage in some life-threatening activity against the victim."[58]

### b. Aggravating Circumstance Two

This section[59] specifies that a person who causes the death of any person (or who is an accomplice of a person causing such a death) during the commission or attempted commission of an arson is eligible for the death penalty.

### c. Aggravating Circumstance Three

This section[60] is designed to enhance the penalty for the murder of public servants in the line of duty. The statute specifies that if, with *premeditation and deliberation*, a person kills a

1. law enforcement officer
2. jailer
3. prison official
4. firefighter
5. judge or other court official
6. probation officer
7. parole officer
8. any military personnel
9. teacher or school employee

when that person is *acting in the line of duty*, then that person commits a capital murder.

### d. Aggravating Circumstance Four

This section[61] blurs the line between capital and first-degree murder by providing the death penalty for the premeditated killing of any person. The statute provides that a person is guilty of capital murder if, with the *premeditated* and *deliberated* purpose of causing the death of another person, he or she causes the death of *any* person.

### e. Aggravating Circumstance Five

This section[62] specifies that a person is guilty of capital murder if, with the premeditated and deliberated purpose of causing the death of the holder of any public office filled by election or appointment or a candidate for public office, he or she causes the death of *any* person.

### f. Aggravating Circumstance Six

This section[63] provides the death penalty for persons who, while incarcerated in the DOC or the DCC, *purposely* cause the death of another person after premeditation and deliberation.

### g. Aggravating Circumstance Seven

This section[64] provides the death penalty for killing a person pursuant to an agreement (commonly called a "contract killing") that he or she cause the death of another person for anything of value.

---

[58] *Williams v. State*, 351 Ark. 215, 91 S.W.3d 54 (2002)
[59] §5-10-101(a)(2)
[60] §5-10-101(a)(3)
[61] §5-10-101(a)(4)
[62] §5-10-101(a)(5)
[63] §5-10-101(a)(6)

## h. Aggravating Circumstance Eight

While §5-10-101(a)(7) provides the death penalty for a contract killer, this section[65] provides the death penalty for the person soliciting the death. To be eligible for the death penalty, the person must actually be killed.

## i. Aggravating Circumstance Nine

This section[66] provides the death penalty for those who kill children (persons 14 years of age or under), provided that the defendant is 18 years of age or older at the time the murder was committed.

The statute provides an affirmative defense to those responsible for the care of the minor who cause the death of the child by failing to seek medical treatment in favor of "spiritual treatment" in accordance with an established religious denomination.

## j. Aggravating Circumstance Ten

This section[67] makes "drive-by" shootings resulting in death capital murder. The statute requires that the discharging of the weapon be purposeful, and that the person knows or has good reason to know that, if the target is an "occupiable structure," the structure is occupied by a person.

## k. Defense

The statute[68] makes it an affirmative defense to capital murder prosecutions for an offense where the defendant was not the only participant and that the defendant did not commit the homicidal act or in any way solicit, command, induce, procure, counsel, or aid in its commission.

## l. Punishment

Capital murder is punishable by death *or life imprisonment* without parole.

### *(9.3) Murder in the First Degree (5-10-102)*

## a. Defining the Offense

*First degree murder* can be accomplished in three ways:

1. A person commits murder in the first degree if he commits or attempts to commit a felony, and in the course of and in the furtherance of the felony or in immediate flight therefrom, he or an accomplice causes the death of any person under circumstances manifesting extreme indifference to the value of human life.

2. A person commits murder the first degree if he, with the purpose of causing the death of another person, he causes the death of another person.

3. A person commits murder in the first degree if he knowingly causes the death of a person 14 years of age or younger at the time the murder was committed.

The statute[69] also provides an affirmative defense to a defendant who was not the only participant and who can show *all* of the following:

---

[64] §5-10-101(a)(7)
[65] §5-10-101(a)(8)
[66] §5-10-101(a)(9)
[67] §5-10-101(a)(10)
[68] §5-10-101(b)
[69] §5-10-102(b)

- He or she did not commit the homicidal act or in any way solicit, command, induce, procure, counsel, or aid its commission
- He or she was not armed with a deadly weapon
- He or she reasonably believed that no other participant was armed with a deadly weapon
- He or she reasonably believed that no other participant intended to engage in conduct which could result in death or serious physical injury

Murder in the first degree is a Class Y felony.

### *(9.4) Murder in the Second Degree (§5-10-103)*

*Murder in the second degree* can be accomplished in two ways:

1. A person is guilty of murder in the second degree if he *knowingly* causes the death of another person under circumstances manifesting extreme indifference to the value of human life.

2. A person is guilty of murder in the second degree if, with the *purpose* of causing serious physical injury to another person, he causes the death of any person.

Murder in the second degree is a Class B felony.

### *(9.5) Manslaughter (§5-10-104)*

#### a. Defining the Offense

*Manslaughter* can be accomplished in four ways:

1. A person commits manslaughter if he or she causes the death of another person under circumstances that would be murder, except that he causes the death under the influence of extreme emotional disturbance for which there is reasonable excuse.

2. A person commits manslaughter if he or she purposely causes or aids another person to commit suicide.

3. A person commits manslaughter if he or she recklessly causes the death of another person.

4. A person commits manslaughter if he or she commits or attempts to commit a felony and in the course of and in furtherance of the felony or in immediate flight therefrom, (a) the person or an accomplice negligently causes the death of any person, or (b) another person who is resisting such offense or flight causes the death of any person.

#### b. Defense

It is an affirmative defense that (in cases of negligent death during the commission of a felony under section 4 above[70]) the defendant was not the only participant and can show the following:

1. He or she did not commit the homicidal act or in any way solicit, command, induce, procure, counsel, or aid its commission
2. He or she was not armed with a deadly weapon
3. He or she reasonably believed that no other participant was armed with a deadly weapon
4. He or she reasonably believed that no other participant intended to engage in conduct which could result in death or serious physical injury

---

[70] 5-10-104(a)(4)

### c. Punishment

Manslaughter is a Class C felony[71].

### *(9.6) Negligent Homicide (§5-10-105)*

*Negligent homicide* can be accomplished in two ways:

1. A person commits negligent homicide when he or she *negligently* causes the death of another person because of operating a vehicle, aircraft, or a watercraft: (1) While intoxicated, or (2) While the person's BAC is 0.08 or higher. A person who commits negligent homicide in this way is guilty of a Class C Felony.

2. A person also commits negligent homicide if he or she negligently causes the death of any person. A person who commits negligent homicide in this way is guilty of a Class A Misdemeanor.

### *(9.7) Physician Assisted Suicide (5-10-106)*

This section criminalizes the act, by a health care provider, of helping anyone under their care to commit suicide. The statute makes this offense a Class C felony.

---

[71] 5-10-104(c)

# Chapter 10: Criminal Sexual Conduct

## (10.1) Sexual Offenses in General

This chapter brings together several types of offenses. These serious offenses come from Chapter 14 of the *Code*, entitled "Sexual Offenses." These include rape, sexual assault, and sexual crimes against children. Not all crimes that can logically be considered crimes of a sexual nature are considered here. The distribution of child pornography over the internet, for example, is considered in the discussion on computer crimes.

Sexual offenses require the use of a vocabulary of terms that, while known to everyday language, take on specific legal meanings in the context of the criminal code. Consult the textbox that follows for the terms of art described in §5-14-101.

## (10.2) Rape (§5-14-103)

### a. Rape in General

At common law, rape was defined as the unlawful carnal knowledge of a woman by a man, not her husband, without her consent. Modern law has made several changes to this outdated definition. According to the common law, it was a legal impossibility for a man to rape his wife. The marriage exception has largely been done away with. The two key elements in every rape statute are the presence of sex and the lack of consent. The presence of sex is rarely contested. Most criminal defenses hinge on the idea of consent.

Traditionally, consent was equated with force. That is, if a woman did not consent to sex, then she would resist and force would have to be employed by the rapist. Thus, rape prosecutions up to recent times required the prosecution to show that force was used, such as by bruises and cuts on the victim.

While physical evidence makes things easier for the prosecution, it is by no means required. In addition to forcible compulsion, most state statutes now recognize that certain categories of people are not able to consent in a valid way. These special categories, when applicable, amount to rape when they are coupled with sex. The most commonly discussed of these is when sex occurs with a girl under a certain age, which is known as statutory rape. The logic of criminalizing this type of sex is that girls under a certain age are not able to understand the quality of their action when consenting to sex.

### a. Defining the Modern Offense

Under current Arkansas law, a person commits *rape* if he or she[72] engages in sexual intercourse or deviate sexual activity with another person under four specific circumstances:

---

[72] Note that Arkansas law is progressive in that many states and the common law did not allow for the commission of rape by a female.

1. The first circumstance is "by forcible compulsion." This is what most people typically think of when the word *rape* is mentioned.

2. The second circumstance is when the victim is incapable of consent because he or she is physically helpless, mentally defective, or mentally incapacitated.

3. The third circumstance is when the victim is *less than* 14 years of age (It is an affirmative defense to prosecution under this subdivision that the actor was not more than three years older than the victim). This is commonly known as "statutory rape" because it is made rape by statute and not the common law definition.

4. The fourth circumstance raises the age of the victim to less than 18 years of age in cases if incest. The following relationships fit the statutory definition:

   - The perpetrator is the  victim's guardian
   - Is the victim's uncle, aunt, grandparent, step-grandparent, or grandparent by adoption
   - Is the victim's brother or sister of the whole or half blood or by adoption; or
   - Is the victim's nephew, niece, or first cousin.

It is an affirmative defense to prosecution under the incest prohibition that the actor was not more than 3 years older than the victim.

It is *no defense* to prosecution under subdivisions with age requirements that the victim consented to the conduct.

### b. Punishment

Rape is a Class Y felony.

### c. No Contact Order

A court may issue a permanent no contact order when a defendant pleads guilty or nolo contendere or all of the defendant's appeals have been exhausted and the defendant remains convicted.

> ### § 5-14-101. Definitions
>
> (1) "Deviate sexual activity" means any act of sexual gratification involving:
> (A) The penetration, however slight, of the anus or mouth of one person by the penis of another person; or
> (B) The penetration, however slight, of the labia majora or anus of one person by any body member or foreign instrument manipulated by another person;
>
> (2) "Forcible compulsion" means physical force or a threat, express or implied, of death or physical injury to or kidnapping of any person;
>
> (3) "Guardian" means a parent, stepparent, legal guardian, legal custodian, foster parent, or anyone who by virtue of a living arrangement is placed in an apparent position of power or authority over a minor.
>
> (4) (A) "Mentally defective" means that a person suffers from a mental disease or defect which renders the person:
> (i) Incapable of understanding the nature and consequences of sexual acts; or
> (ii) Unaware the sexual act is occurring.
>
> (B) A determination that a person is mentally defective shall not be based solely on the person's intelligence quotient;
>
> (5) "Mentally incapacitated" means that a person is temporarily incapable of appreciating or controlling the person's conduct as a result of the influence of a controlled or intoxicating substance:
>
> (A) Administered to the person without the person's consent; or
> (B) Which renders the person unaware the sexual act is occurring;
>
> (6) "Physically helpless" means that a person is:
>
> (A) (i) Unconscious; or
> (ii) Physically unable to communicate lack of consent; or
>
> (B) Rendered unaware the sexual act is occurring;
>
> (7) "Public place" means a publicly or privately owned place to which the public or substantial numbers of people have access;
>
> (8) "Public view" means observable or likely to be observed by a person in a public place;
>
> (9) "Sexual contact" means any act of sexual gratification involving the touching, directly or through clothing, of the sex organs, buttocks, or anus of a person or the breast of a female; and
>
> (10) "Sexual intercourse" means penetration, however slight, of the labia majora by a penis.

## (10.3) Sexual Indecency with a Child (§5-14-110)

A person can commit sexual indecency with a child in two ways:

1. Being 18 years old or older, the person solicits another person who is *less than* 15 years of age or who is represented to be less than 15 years of age to engage in sexual intercourse, deviate sexual activity, or sexual contact; or

2. With the purpose to arouse or gratify the sexual desires of himself or herself or those of any other person, the person purposefully exposes his or her sex organs to another person who is *less than* 15 years of age.

Note the phrase "or who is represented to be less than 15 years" in the first condition above. This language makes it possible for a LEO to pose as a child in an effort to apprehend violators of this section.

It is an affirmative defense if the person is within 3 years of age of the victim.

## b. Punishment

Sexual indecency with a child is a Class D felony.

### (10.4) Public Sexual Indecency (§5-14-111)

## a. Defining the Offense

A person commits *public sexual indecency* if he or she engages in any of the following three acts in a public place or in public view:

1. An act of sexual intercourse
2. An act of deviate sexual activity
3. An act of sexual contact

## b. Punishment

Public sexual indecency is a Class A misdemeanor.

### (10.5) Indecent Exposure (§5-14-112)

## a. Defining the Offense

A person commits indecent exposure if, with the purpose to arouse or gratify the sexual desire of the person or of any other person, he or she exposes his or her sex organs:

1. In a public place or in public view
2. Under circumstances in which the person knows the conduct is likely to cause affront or alarm

## b. Punishment

Indecent exposure is a Class A misdemeanor.

If the actor is age 18 or older and the exposure is committed against a person under the age of 15, then the statute stipulates that any second or subsequent such offense is a class D felony.

### (10.6) Bestiality (§5-14-122)

## a. Defining the Offense

Under the Arkansas statute, a person commits bestiality[73] if he or she "performs or submits to any act of sexual gratification with an animal involving the sex organs of the one and the mouth, anus, penis, or vagina of the other."

## b. Punishment

Bestiality is a Class A misdemeanor.

---

[73] This was formerly the sodomy statute. *Sodomy* (as a generic term) comes to us from common law usage where its meaning was analogous to "crimes against nature" and specifically criminalized homosexual sex. USSC decisions have severely curtailed the type of acts that states can prohibit; thus, the Arkansas General Assembly removed the unconstitutional elements of the sodomy statute with only bestiality remaining.

### (10.7) Exposing Another to HIV (§ 5-14-123)

> **§ 5-14-123. Exposing another person to human immunodeficiency virus**
>
> (a) A person with acquired immunodeficiency syndrome or who tests positive for the presence of human immunodeficiency virus antigen or antibodies is infectious to others through the exchange of body fluids during sexual intercourse and through the parenteral transfer of blood or blood products and under these circumstances is a danger to the public.
>
> (b) A person commits the offense of exposing another to human immunodeficiency virus if the person knows he or she has tested positive for human immunodeficiency virus and exposes another person to such viral infection through the parenteral transfer of blood or blood products or engages in sexual penetration with another person without first having informed the other person of the presence of human immunodeficiency virus.
>
> (c) As used in this section, "sexual penetration" means sexual intercourse, cunnilingus, fellatio, anal intercourse, or any other intrusion, however slight, of any part of a person's body or of any object into the genital or anal openings of another person's body, but emission of semen is not required.
>
> (d) Exposing another to human immunodeficiency virus is a Class A felony.

### (10.8) Sexual Assault (§§5-14-124, 125, 126, 127)

#### a. Sexual Assault in the First (§§5-14-124)

A person commits *sexual assault in the first degree* if the person engages in sexual intercourse or deviate sexual activity with another person[74], who is less than 18 years of age and the actor is employed with:

- The Department of Correction
- The Department of Community Correction
- The Department of Human Services
- Any city or county jail
- A juvenile detention facility

And the victim is in the custody of the above listed agencies or their contractors or agents.

Also, a person commits *sexual assault in the first degree* if the person is a professional[75] and is in a position of trust or authority over the victim and uses the position to engage in sexual intercourse or deviate sexual activity.

Also, a person commits *sexual assault in the first degree* if the person is an employee in the victim's school or school district, a temporary caretaker, or a person in a position of trust or authority over the victim.

It is an affirmative defense to prosecution under the school district employee section that the actor was not more than 3 years older than the victim.

It is *no defense* to prosecution under any provision of this section that the victim consented to the conduct.

Sexual assault in the first degree is a Class A felony.

#### b. Sexual Assault in the Second (§§5-14-125)

Second degree sexual assault is a "catch all" statute that prohibits several kinds of sexual conduct.

---

[74] the person's spouse is specifically excluded by the statute

[75] under § 12-12-507(b)

A person commits sexual assault in the second degree if they engage in sexual contact with a person by forcible compulsion, or a person who is incapable of consent because of physical helplessness, mental defect, or mental incapacitation.

In addition, sexual assault in the second degree prohibits anyone age 18 or over from engaging in sexual contact with a person who is less that 14 years of age. The age of the victim is *less than* 18 of the actor is in a position of power and authority over the victim. The consent of the minor is no defense to prosecution.

The statute also prohibits anyone *less than* 18 years of age from engaging in sexual contact with a person who is *less than* 14 years of age. It is a defense to this subsection that the actor was not more than three years older than the victim.

Finally, the statute prohibits public school teachers (K-12) from engaging in sexual contact with a student enrolled in the school and who is less than 21 years of age. If a person less than 18 years of age engages in sexual contact with a person less than 14 years of age, sexual assault in the second is a Class B Felony. Otherwise, it is a Class B felony.

### c. Sexual Assault in the Third (§5-14-126)

Sexual assault in the third degree prohibits a person in a position of power and authority over another from having sexual activity or intercourse with them.

It further prohibits a person under the age of 18 from engaging in sexual intercourse or deviate sexual activity with a person under the age of 14. It is an affirmative defense that the actor was not more than 3 years older than the victim.

It is no defense to prosecution under this section that the victim consented to the conduct.

Sexual assault in the third degree is a Class C felony.

### d. Sexual Assault in the Fourth (§5-14-127)

A person commits sexual assault in the fourth degree if, being 20 years of age or older, the person engages in sexual intercourse, deviate sexual activity, or sexual contact with a person under 16 years of age.

If the prohibited conduct consisted solely of sexual contact, then Sexual Assault in the Fourth is a Class A misdemeanor. Otherwise, it is a Class D felony.

## (10.9) Registered Offender Living Near School or Daycare (§5-14-128)

### a. Defining the Offense

This section makes it unlawful for a sex offender who has been assessed as Level 3 or Level 4 to reside within 2000 feet of any school or daycare[76].

### b. Punishment

A violation of this section is a Class D felony.

---

[76] This section does not apply to circumstances where the offender owned and occupied the property prior to the establishment of the school or daycare.

### (10.10) Registered Offender Working with Children (§5-14-129)

#### a. Defining the Offense

It is unlawful for a sex offender who is required to register under the *Sex Offender Registration Act of 1997*[77] and who has been assessed as a Level 3 or Level 4 offender to engage in an occupation or participate in a volunteer position that requires the sex offender to work or interact primarily and directly with a child under 16 years of age.

#### b. Punishment

Anyone who knowingly violates this section is guilty of a Class D felony.

---

[77] § 12-12-901

# Chapter 11: Crimes against People

## *(11.1) Crimes against People in General*

Nearly every society on Earth attempts to protect its members from pain, injury, or death at the hands of evildoers. Most of the crimes in this chapter developed very early on in the system of English common law, and were brought to America from England by the original colonists. Some of these crimes are unknown to the common law; they are recent inventions of the legislature that reflect growth and change within our society.

## *(11.2) Kidnapping (§5-11-102)*

### a. Kidnapping in General

In its earliest common law form, kidnapping was confined to the taking of persons from their own country to another country. In most jurisdictions today, the offense involves taking and conveying away a person against his or her will. This requirement of conveying or moving the person is known as an **asportation**. The taking of the person must generally be accomplished either by force, fraud, or intimidation.

A person legally in custody of another cannot generally be guilty of kidnapping that person. This usually applies to parents. A parent, however, may be guilty of kidnapping his or her own child if custody of the child has been given to another by court order. In most jurisdictions, when parents have separated without a custody order, one parent may take the child from the other (even by trick or deception) without committing the offense of kidnapping.

### b. Defining the Modern Offense

A person commits *kidnapping* if he or she restrains a person to interfere substantially with his or her liberty with any of six specified purposes. The prohibited purposes of the restraint are as follows:

1. Holding the person for ransom or reward or any other act performed or not performed for the person's release
2. Using the person as a shield or hostage
3. Facilitating the commission of any felony or flight thereafter
4. Inflicting injury on the person, engaging in sexual intercourse, deviant sexual activity, or sexual contact
5. Terrorizing the kidnapped person or another person
6. Interfering with the performance of any governmental or political function

---

**§ 5-11-101. Definitions**

As used in this chapter, unless the context otherwise requires:

(1) "Vehicle" means any craft or device designed for the transportation of people or property across land or water or through the air;

(2) "Restraint without consent" includes restraint by physical force, threat, or deception, or in the case of a person who is under the age of fourteen (14) years or incompetent, restraint without the consent of a parent, guardian, or other person responsible for general supervision of his welfare;

(3) "Incompetent" means that a person is unable to care for himself because of physical or mental disease or defect. The status embraced by this definition may or may not exist regardless of any adjudication concerning incompetency;

(4) "Sexual intercourse", "deviate sexual activity", and "sexual contact" have the meanings specified in § 5-14-101.

---

**§ 5-14-101. Definitions**

(1) "Deviate sexual activity" means any act of sexual gratification involving:

    (A) The penetration, however slight, of the anus or mouth of one person by the penis of another person; or

    (B) The penetration, however slight, of the labia majora or anus of one person by any body member or foreign instrument manipulated by another person;

    . . . .

(9) "Sexual contact" means any act of sexual gratification involving the touching, directly or through clothing, of the sex organs, buttocks, or anus of a person or the breast of a female; and

(10) "Sexual intercourse" means penetration, however slight, of the labia majora by a penis.

---

### c. Punishment

Kidnapping is a Class Y felony[78].

If the defendant can show by preponderance of the evidence that the victim was released alive and in a safe place prior to trial, then kidnapping is a Class B felony.

### (11.3) *False Imprisonment in the First (§5-11-103)*

#### a. Defining the Offense

A person commits this offense if, without consent or lawful authority, he or she knowingly restrains another person so as to interfere substantially with the person's liberty *in a manner that exposes that person to a substantial risk of serious physical injury.*

#### b. Punishment

False imprisonment in the first degree is a Class C felony[79].

---

[78] §5-11-102(b)
[79] §5-11-103(b)

### *(11.4) False Imprisonment in the Second (§5-11-104)*

#### a. Defining the Offense

A person commits this offense if, without consent or lawful authority, he or she knowingly restrains another person to *interfere substantially with the person's liberty.*

#### b. Punishment

False imprisonment in the second degree is a Class A misdemeanor.

### *(11.5) Vehicular Piracy (§5-11-105)*

#### a. Defining the Offense

A person commits *vehicular piracy* if, without lawful authority, seizes or exercises control, by force or threat of violence, over:
1.      Any aircraft occupied by an unconsenting person.
2.      Any other vehicle (a) Having a seating capacity of more than eight passengers, and (b) Operated by a common or contract carrier of passengers for hire, and (c) Occupied by an unconsenting person.

#### b. Punishment

If the vehicular piracy is of an aircraft, it is a Class B felony.  Otherwise, vehicular piracy is a Class C felony[80].

### *(11.6) Permanent Detention or Restraint (§5-11-106)*

#### a. Defining the Offense

This statute is designed to fill the gaps in the law to cover circumstances where then intent of the unlawful seizure of a person is intended to be permanent, such as when a couple takes a child with the intent of raising the child as their own.

A person commits the offense of *permanent detention or restraint* if, without consent and without lawful authority, he restrains a person with the purpose of holding or concealing him:

1.  Without ever releasing him; or
2.  Without ever returning him to the person or institution from whose lawful custody he was taken.

#### b. Punishment

Permanent detention or restraint is a Class B felony unless the person detained or restrained is the child of the defendant, in which case it is a Class D felony[81].

### *(11.7) School Bus Piracy (§5-11-107)*

#### a. Defining the Offense

A person commits school bus piracy if, without lawful authority, he possesses a deadly weapon as defined in § 5-1-102(4) and seizes or exercises control of a school bus and the vehicle is occupied by one (1) or more unconsenting persons.

---

[80] §5-11-105(b)
[81] §5-11-106(b)

---

**§ 5-11-107.**

(a) As used in this section, "school bus" means every motor vehicle owned by a public school district or a private school or a governmental agency and operated for the transportation of children to or from school or school-sponsored activities.

---

**§ 5-1-102(4)**

As used in this code, unless the context otherwise requires:

. . . .

(4) "Deadly weapon" means:
   (A) A firearm or anything manifestly designed, made, or adapted for the purpose of inflicting death or serious physical injury; or
   (B) Anything that in the manner of its use or intended use is capable of causing death or serious physical injury

---

### b. Punishment

School bus piracy is a Class A felony.

### (11.8) Robbery (§5-12-102)

### a. Defining the Offense

Robbery is often considered a crime against property because the most common objective is to gain property. But because the property is acquired through violent means, the most important factor is the violence against the victim.

In the context of robbery, physical force "means any bodily impact, restraint, or confinement or the threat thereof."[82]

A person commits *robbery* if, with the purpose of committing a felony or misdemeanor theft or resisting apprehension immediately thereafter, he employs or threatens to *immediately* employ *physical force* upon another.

### b. Punishment

Robbery is a Class B felony.

### (11.9) Aggravated Robbery (§5-12-103)

### a. Defining the Offense

A person commits *aggravated robbery* if he or she meets all of the requirements for robbery (**11.8** above) and in addition:

1. Is armed with a deadly weapon or represents by word or conduct that he is so armed; or
2. Inflicts or attempts to inflict death or serious physical injury upon another person

### b. Punishment

Aggravated robbery is a class Y felony[83].

---

[82] §5-12-101

*(11.10) Battery (§5-13-201, 202, 203)*

### a. Battery in the First (§5-13-201)

*Battery in the First Degree* covers can be accomplished by any of seven acts:

1.  Purposefully causing serious injury to any person with a deadly weapon.

2.  Purposefully (seriously and permanently) disfiguring another person or of destroying, amputating, or permanently disabling a member or organ of his body.

3.  Causing serious physical injury to another person under circumstances manifesting extreme indifference to the value of human life.

4.  Committing or attempts to commit a felony, and in the course of and in furtherance of the felony, or in immediate flight therefrom, either the person (or an accomplice) causes serious physical injury to any person under circumstances manifesting extreme indifference to the value of human life.  This also applies when another person who is resisting the offense or flight causes serious physical injury to any person.

The statute provides an affirmative defense where the defendant was not the only participant and that the defendant:

1.  Did not commit the battery or in any way solicit, command, induce, procure, counsel, or aid its commission
2.  Was not armed with a deadly weapon
3.  Reasonably believed that no other participant was armed with a deadly weapon
4.  Reasonably believed that no other participant intended to engage in conduct that could result in serious physical injury

5.  Causing physical injury to a pregnant woman in the commission of a felony or a Class A misdemeanor causing her to suffer a miscarriage or stillbirth as a result of that injury;
    *or*
Recklessly causes physical injury to a pregnant woman or causing physical injury to a pregnant woman under circumstances manifesting extreme indifference to the value of human life causing her to suffer a miscarriage or stillbirth as a result of that injury;
    *or*
Recklessly causing physical injury to a pregnant woman or causes physical injury to a pregnant woman under circumstances manifesting extreme indifference to the value of human life causing her to suffer a miscarriage or stillbirth as a result of that injury.

---

§ 5-13-201
(C) As used in this subdivision (a)(5), unless the context otherwise requires:

(i) "Physical injury" means the impairment of physical condition, including, but not limited to, the inability to complete a full-term pregnancy, as defined by the pregnant woman's physician, or the infliction of substantial pain;

(ii) "Miscarriage" means the interruption of the normal development of the fetus, other than by a live birth and which is not an induced abortion, resulting in the complete expulsion or extraction of a fetus from a pregnant woman. . . .

---

[83] §5-12-103(b)

6. Intentionally or knowingly (without legal justification) causing serious physical injury to one he knows to be 12 years of age or younger.

7. Purposefully causing physical injury to another person by means of a firearm. This also applies to "bad aim intent"—if *any* person is harmed.

Battery in the first degree is a Class B felony.

### b. Battery in the Second (§5-13-202)

A person can commits *battery in the second degree* in four ways:

1. Cause physical injury to *any* person with the intent to cause physical injury to a specific person.

2. Cause physical injury to *any* person with a deadly weapon other than a firearm with the intent to cause physical injury to a specific person.

3. Recklessly cause serious physical injury to another person by means of a deadly weapon.

4. Intentionally or knowingly causes physical injury to one he or she knows to be:

- A law enforcement officer, firefighter, or employee of a correctional facility while the officer, firefighter, or correctional facility employee is acting in the line of duty.
- A teacher or other school employee, while acting in the course of employment.
- An individual 60 years of age or older or 12 years of age or younger.
- An officer or employee of the state while the officer or employee is acting in the performance of his or her lawful duty.
- While performing medical treatment or emergency medical services or while in the course of other employment relating to his or her medical training:
    - A physician
    - A person certified as an emergency medical technician[84]
    - A licensed or certified health care professional
    - Any other health care provider
- An individual who is incompetent[85].

Battery in the second degree is a Class D felony.

### c. Battery in the Third (§5-13-203)

A person can commit *battery in the third degree* in four ways:

1. With the purpose of causing physical injury to another person, he causes physical injury to any person
2. He recklessly causes physical injury to another person
3. He negligently causes physical injury to another person by means of a deadly weapon
4. He purposely causes stupor, unconsciousness, or physical or mental impairment or injury to another person by administering to him, without his consent, any drug or other substance

---

[84] These shall include, but not be limited to: "EMT", "EMT-A", "EMT-Instructor", "EMT-Paramedic", and "EMS-Communications"

[85] "Incompetent" means any person unable to care for himself or herself because of physical or mental disease or defect. The status embraced by this definition may or may not exist regardless of any adjudication concerning incompetency

Battery in the third degree is a Class A misdemeanor.

### (11.11) Assault (§§5-13-204, 205, 206, 207)

#### a. Aggravated Assault (§5-13-204)

A person commits aggravated assault if under circumstances manifesting extreme indifference to the value of human life, he or she purposely:

1.  Engages in conduct that creates a substantial danger of death or serious physical injury to another person.
2.  Displays a firearm in such a manner that creates a substantial danger of death or serious physical injury to another person.

Aggravated assault is a Class D felony[86].

*The provisions of this section do not apply to law enforcement officers acting within the scope of their duty or to any person acting in self-defense or the defense of a third party[87].*

#### b. Assault in the First (§5-13-205)

A person commits assault in the first degree if he recklessly engages in conduct which creates a substantial risk of death or serious physical injury to another person.

Assault in the first degree is a Class A misdemeanor[88].

#### c. Assault in the Second (§5-13-206)

A person commits assault in the second degree if he recklessly engages in conduct that creates a substantial risk of physical injury to another person.

Assault in the second degree is a Class B misdemeanor[89].

#### d. Assault in the Third (§5-13-207)

A person commits assault in the third degree if he purposely creates apprehension of imminent physical injury in another person.

Assault in the third degree is a Class C misdemeanor[90].

### (11.12) Coercion (§5-13-208)

#### a. Defining the Offense

A person commits coercion if he compels or induces another person to engage in conduct from which the other person has a legal right to abstain, or to abstain from engaging in conduct in which he has a legal right to engage, by purposeful conduct designed to instill in the other person a fear that, if a demand is not complied with, the actor or another person will:

---

[86] 5-13-204(b)
[87] 5-13-204(c)
[88] 5-13-205(b)
[89] 5-13-206(b)
[90] 5-13-207(b)

- Cause physical injury to anyone
- Cause damage to property
- Subject anyone to physical confinement
- Accuse anyone of an offense or cause criminal proceedings to be instituted against anyone
- Expose a secret or publicize an asserted fact, whether true or false, tending to subject anyone to hatred, contempt, or ridicule.

### b. Punishment

Coercion is a Class A misdemeanor[91].

### (11.13) Abuse of Athletic Contest Officials (§5-13-209)

> § 5-13-209
>
> Any person, with the purpose of causing physical injury to another person, who shall strike or otherwise physically abuse an athletic contest official immediately prior to, during, or immediately following an interscholastic, intercollegiate, or any other organized amateur or professional athletic contest in which the athletic contest official is participating shall be guilty of a Class A misdemeanor.

### (11.14) Introduction of Controlled Substance to Another (§5-13-210)

It is unlawful for any person to inject any controlled substance as defined by the Uniform Controlled Substances Act[92] into the human body of another person. Of course, there is and exception when the controlled substance has been ordered for the by a licensed practitioner for a legitimate medical purpose.

It is also unlawful for any person to administer or cause to be ingested, inhaled, or otherwise introduced into the human body of another person a controlled substance as defined by the Uniform Controlled Substances Act.

Any person who violates this section with respect to:

1. A controlled substance in Schedules I or II, which is a narcotic drug, is guilty of a Class Y felony
2. Any other controlled substance in Schedules I, II, or III is guilty of a Class B felony
3. Any other controlled substance in Schedules IV, V, or VI is guilty of a Class C felony.

The provisions of this section "stack." That is, they can be charged in addition to any other sections of the code that may be applicable, especially the Uniform Controlled Substances Act.

It is no defense that the victim voluntarily participated.

The statute further stipulates that the introduction of a controlled substance into another for the purpose of sex is guilty of a Y felony.

### (11.15) Terroristic Threatening (§5-13-301)

### a. Terroristic Threatening in the First

A person can commit the offense of *terroristic threatening* in the first degree in two ways:

1. With the purpose of terrorizing another person, he threatens to cause death or serious physical injury or substantial property damage to another person.

---

[91] 5-13-208(b)
[92] § 5-64-101

2.  With the purpose of terrorizing another person, he threatens to cause physical injury or property damage to a teacher or other school employee acting in the line of duty.

Terroristic threatening in the first degree is a Class D felony.

### b. Terroristic Threatening in the Second

A person commits the offense of terroristic threatening in the second degree if, with the purpose of terrorizing another person, he threatens to cause physical injury or property damage to another person.

Terroristic threatening in the second degree is a Class A misdemeanor.

### c. No Contact Order

A judicial officer, upon pretrial release of the defendant, shall enter a no contact order in writing consistent with Rules 9.3 and 9.4 of the Arkansas Rules of Criminal Procedure and shall give notice to the defendant of penalties contained in Rule 9.5 of the Arkansas Rules of Criminal Procedure.

---

**Rule 9.3. Prohibition of wrongful acts pending trial.**

If it appears that there exists a danger that the defendant will commit a serious crime or will seek to intimidate witnesses, or will otherwise unlawfully interfere with the orderly administration of justice, the judicial officer, upon the release of the defendant, may enter an order:

(a) prohibiting the defendant from approaching or communicating with particular persons or classes of persons, except that no such order shall be deemed to prohibit any lawful and ethical activity of defendant's counsel;

(b) prohibiting the defendant from going to certain described geographical areas or premises;

(c) prohibiting the defendant from possessing any dangerous weapon, or engaging in certain described activities or indulging in intoxicating liquors or in certain drugs;

(d) requiring the defendant to report regularly to and remain under the supervision of an officer of the court.

**Rule 9.4. Notice of penalties.**

(a) When the conditions of the release of a defendant are determined or an order is entered under Rule 9.3, the judicial officer shall inform the defendant of the penalties for failure to comply with the conditions or terms of such order.

(b) All conditions of release and terms of orders under Rule 9.3 shall be recorded in writing and a copy given to the defendant.

**Rule 9.5. Violations of conditions of release.**

(a) A judicial officer shall issue a warrant directing that the defendant be arrested and taken forthwith before any judicial officer having jurisdiction of the charge for a hearing when the prosecuting attorney submits a verified application alleging that:

(i) the defendant has willfully violated the conditions of his release or the terms of an order under Rule 9.3; or

(ii) pertinent information which would merit revocation of the defendant's release has become known to the prosecuting attorney.

(b) A law enforcement officer having reasonable grounds to believe that a released defendant has violated the conditions of his release or the terms of an order under Rule 9.3 is authorized to arrest the defendant and to take him forthwith before any judicial officer having jurisdiction when it would be impracticable to secure a warrant.

(c) After a hearing, and upon finding that the defendant has willfully violated reasonable conditions or the terms of an order under Rule 9.3 imposed on his release, the judicial officer may impose different or additional conditions of release upon the defendant or revoke his release.

---

A terroristic act is a Class Y felony if the actor, with the purpose of causing physical injury to another person, causes serious physical injury or death to any person.

### (11.17) Domestic Battering (§5-26-303, 304, 305)

#### a. Domestic Battering in the First (§5-26-303)

Domestic battering in the first degree can be accomplished in three ways:

1. Purposely causing serious physical injury to a family or household member by means of a deadly weapon.

2. Purposely destroying, amputating, or permanently disabling a member or organ of a family or household member's body.

3. Causing serious physical injury to a family or household member under circumstances manifesting extreme indifference to the value of human life.

In addition, the section serves as a "third strike" law for those persons with 2 previous convictions for *any* act of battery against a family or household member as defined by the laws of Arkansas or by the equivalent laws of any other state or foreign jurisdiction.

Domestic battering in the first degree is a Class B felony.

However, domestic battering in the first degree is a Class A felony if the victim was a woman the actor knew or should have known was pregnant.

The Class A felony provision also applies to repeat offenders who have in the past 5 years committed the prior offense of
- Domestic battering in the first degree
- Domestic battering in the second degree[93]
- Domestic battering in the third degree[94]

This holds true for persons who have violated an equivalent penal law of this state or of another state or foreign jurisdiction.

### b. Domestic Battering in the Second (§5-26-304)

The elements of domestic battering in the second degree can be satisfied in three ways:

1. Purposely causing serious physical injury to a family or household member
2. Purposely causing injury to a family or household member by means of a deadly weapon
3. Recklessly causing serious physical injury to a family or household member by means of a deadly weapon

Domestic battering in the second degree is a Class C felony.

As with domestic battering in the first degree, the domestic battering in the second degree statute provides an enhanced penalty for repeat offenders and those who attack pregnant women.

### c. Domestic Battering in the Third (§5-26-305)

The elements of domestic battering in the third degree can be satisfied in four ways:

1. Purposely causing physical injury to a family or household member.
2. Recklessly causing physical injury to a family or household member.
3. Negligently causing physical injury to a family or household member by means of a deadly weapon.
4. Purposely causing stupor, unconsciousness, or physical or mental impairment or injury to a family or household member by administering to a family or household member, without the family or household member's consent, any drug or other substance.

---

[93] § 5-26-304
[94] § 5-26-305

Domestic battering in the third degree is a Class A misdemeanor. As with the other battering statutes, this section provides for an enhanced penalty when the batterer is a repeat offender or the victim is a pregnant woman.

### (11.18) Assault on Household Member (§5-26-306, 307, 308, 309)

#### a. Aggravated Assault on a Household Member (§5-26-306)

A person commits aggravated assault on a family or household member if, under circumstances manifesting extreme indifference to the value of human life, he *purposely* engages in conduct that creates a substantial danger of death or serious physical injury to a family or household member.

Aggravated assault on a family or household member is a Class D felony

#### b. First degree Assault on a Household Member (§5-26-307)

A person commits first degree assault on a family or household member if he *recklessly* engages in conduct which creates a substantial risk of death or serious physical injury to a family or household member.

First degree assault on a family or household member is a Class A misdemeanor.

#### c. Second Degree Assault on a Household Member (§5-26-308)

A person commits second degree assault on a family or household member if he *recklessly* engages in conduct which creates a substantial risk of physical injury to a family or household member.

Second degree assault on a family or household member is a Class B misdemeanor.

#### d. Third Degree Assault on a Household Member (§5-26-309)

A person commits third degree assault on a family or household member if he *purposely* creates apprehension of *imminent physical injury* to a family or household member.

Third degree assault on a family or household member is a Class C misdemeanor.

### (11.19) Endangering the Welfare of an Incompetent (§5-27-201, 202)

#### a. Endangering the Welfare of an Incompetent in the First (§5-27-201)

A person commits the offense of endangering the welfare of an incompetent person in the first degree if, being a parent, guardian, person legally charged with care or custody of an incompetent person, or a person charged with supervision of an incompetent person, he or she purposely deserts the incompetent person under circumstances creating a substantial risk of death or serious physical injury.

Endangering the welfare of an incompetent person in the first degree is a Class D felony.

#### b. Endangering the Welfare of an Incompetent in the Second (§5-27-202)

A person commits the offense of endangering the welfare of an incompetent person in the second degree if he knowingly engages in conduct creating a substantial risk of serious harm to the physical or mental welfare of one known by the actor to be an incompetent person.

Endangering the welfare of an incompetent person in the second degree is a Class A misdemeanor.

### (11.20) Endangering the Welfare of a Minor (§5-27-203, 204)

#### a. Endangering the Welfare of a Minor in the First (§5-27-203)

A person commits the offense of endangering the welfare of a minor in the first degree if, being a parent, guardian, person legally charged with care or custody of a minor, or a person charged with supervision of a minor, he or she purposely deserts a minor less than 10 years old under circumstances creating a substantial risk of death or serious physical injury.

Endangering the welfare of a minor in the first degree is a Class D felony.

#### b. Endangering the Welfare of a Minor in the Second ((§5-27-204)

A person commits the offense of *endangering the welfare of a minor* in the second degree if he *knowingly* engages in conduct creating a substantial risk of serious harm to the physical or mental welfare of one known by the actor to be a minor.

Endangering the welfare of a minor in the second degree is a Class A misdemeanor.

### (11.21) Contributing to the Delinquency of a Minor (§5-27-205)

A person commits the offense of *contributing to the delinquency of a minor* if, being an adult, he knowingly aids, causes, or encourages a minor to do any of the following:

- Any act prohibited by law.
- Any act that if done by an adult would render the adult subject to prosecution for an offense punishable by imprisonment.
- Habitually absent himself, without good or sufficient cause, from his home without the consent of his parent, stepparent, foster parent, guardian, or other lawful custodian.
- Habitually absent himself from school when required by law to attend school.
- Habitually disobey the reasonable and lawful commands of his parent, stepparent, foster parent, guardian, or other lawful custodian.

Contributing to the delinquency of a minor is a Class A misdemeanor.

### (11.22) Parental Responsibility for Student's Firearm (§5-27-206)

When a parent of a minor knows that the minor is in illegal possession of a firearm in or upon the premises of a public or private school, in or on the school's athletic stadium or other facility or building where school-sponsored events are conducted, or in a public park, playground, or civic center and the parent or guardian fails to prevent the possession or fails to report the possession to the appropriate school or law enforcement officials, the parent is guilty of a Class B misdemeanor.

### (11.23) Contributing to the Delinquency of a Juvenile ((§5-27-220)

Any person who willfully causes, aids, or encourages any person less than 18 years of age to do or perform any act which, if done or performed, would make such person less than 18 years of age a "delinquent juvenile" or "juvenile in need of supervision"[95] is guilty of a misdemeanor.

### (11.24) Permitting Abuse of a Minor (§5-27-221)

A person commits the offense of permitting abuse of a minor[96] if, being a parent, guardian, or person legally charged with the care or custody of a minor, he or she recklessly fails to take action to prevent the abuse of a minor.

---

[95] §§ 9-27-301 – 9-27-361

It is a defense to a prosecution for the offense of permitting abuse of a minor if the person takes immediate steps to end the abuse of the minor, including prompt notification of medical or law enforcement authorities, upon first knowing or having good reason to know that abuse has occurred.

Permitting abuse of a minor is a Class B felony if the abuse of the minor consisted of sexual intercourse or deviate sexual activity or caused serious physical injury or death to the minor, and is a Class D felony if the abuse of the minor consisted of sexual contact or caused physical injury to the minor.

### (11.25) Neglect of Minor Resulting in Delinquency (§5-27-222)

Any parent or person standing *in loco parentis* to a child under the age of eighteen (18) years whose gross neglect of parental duty with reference to the child proximately results in delinquency of the child or who, through gross neglect of parental duty with reference to the child, fails to correct the delinquency of the child is guilty of a misdemeanor.

### (11.26) Permitting Minors to Play in Saloons (§5-27-223)

This section is included only to note that it was repealed during the 2005 legislative session.

### (11.27) Permitting Minors to Play in Poolrooms (§5-27-224)

This section is included only to note that it was repealed during the 2005 legislative session.

### (11.28) Providing Minors with Tobacco Products (§5-27-227)

This section seeks to prevent minors from obtaining tobacco and tobacco paraphernalia. It provides offenses for minors in possession of tobacco as well as adults who supply these prohibited products to minors.

It is unlawful for any person to give, barter, or sell to a minor less than 18 years of age tobacco in any form or cigarette papers.

It is unlawful for any person under 18 years of age to use or possess[97] tobacco in any form, cigarette papers.

In addition it is unlawful for a minor to attempt to purchase tobacco in any form or cigarette papers.

It is also unlawful under this section for a minor to use a false identification or someone else's identification.

This section also provides specifications as to how minors may be used by law enforcement in conducting "sting" operations on businesses that sell tobacco.

*This section specifically prohibits arrest or search by any law enforcement officer merely on the grounds that the minor has or may have possession of tobacco or cigarette papers.*

### (11.29) Soliciting Money or Property from Incompetents (§5-27-229)

This section makes it unlawful for any person to solicit money or property from a person he knows or should have reason to know is an incompetent person or is a person with diminished mental capacity and to cause that incompetent person or person with diminished mental capacity to voluntarily surrender money or property in order to profit or secure gain by taking unfair advantage of the person's incompetency or diminished mental capacity.

Violating the provisions of this section is a Class D felony.

---

[96] "Minor" means a person under the age of eighteen (18) years
[97] "unless acting as an agent of the minor's employer within the scope of employment"

*(11.30) Exposing a Child to Chemical Substances or Meth (§5-27-230)*

Any adult who, with the intent to manufacture methamphetamine, knowingly causes or permits a child to be exposed to, ingest, inhale, or have any contact with a chemical substance or methamphetamine is guilty of a Class C felony. The penalty is enhanced to a Class B felony is the child suffers any physical harm.

---

**5-27-230. Exposing a child to a chemical substance or methamphetamine**

(a) For purposes of this section:

(1) (A) "Chemical substance" means a substance intended to be used as a precursor in the manufacture of methamphetamine, or any other chemical intended to be used in the manufacture of methamphetamine.

(B) Intent may be demonstrated by the substance's use, quantity, manner of storage, or proximity to other precursors or equipment used to manufacture methamphetamine;

(2) "Child" means any person under the age of eighteen (18) years; and

(3) "Methamphetamine" has the same meaning as provided in the Uniform Controlled Substances Act, § 5-64-101 et seq.

---

*(11.31) Sale or Possession of Child Pornography (§5-27-304)*

This section makes knowingly doing the following things in relation to the purpose of selling or distributing any visual or print medium depicting a child participating or engaging in sexually explicit conduct:

- Advertise for sale or distribution
- Sell
- Distribute
- Transport
- Ship
- Exhibit
- Display
- Receive

In addition, it is unlawful to knowingly

- Solicit
- Receive
- Purchase
- Exchange
- Possess
- View
- Distribute
- Control

any visual or print medium depicting a child participating or engaging in sexually explicit conduct.

Sale or possession of child pornography is a Class C felony for the first offense and a Class B felony for any subsequent offenses.

### *(11.32) Production of Child Pornography (§5-27-303)*

Any person who employs, uses, persuades, induces, entices, or coerces any child to engage in any sexually explicit conduct for the purpose of producing any visual or print medium depicting such conduct is guilty of a Class B Felony[98].

Any parent, legal guardian, or person having custody or control of a child who knowingly permits the child to engage in or to assist any other person to engage in sexually explicit conduct for the purpose of producing any visual or print medium depicting such conduct shall be guilty of a Class B felony for the first offense and a Class A felony for subsequent offenses.

### *(11.33) Transportation of Minors for Sexual Conduct (§5-27-305)*

This section makes it a Class C felony to transport, finance in whole or part the transportation of, or otherwise cause or facilitates the movement of any person under the age of 18 years if the person knows or has reason to know that prohibited sexual conduct will be commercially exploited by any person and the person intends that the minor be engaged in prostitution or prohibited sexual conduct.

### *(11.34) Adult Abuse (§5-28-103)*

This section makes it unlawful for any person or caregiver to abuse, neglect, or exploit any person under their care.

Penalties for this section are graduated based on the extent of the harm caused by the abuse.

### *(11.35) Death Threats to School Employees and Students (§5-17-101)*

#### a. Defining the Offense

A person commits the offense of communicating a death threat concerning a school[99] employee or student if:

1. The person communicates to any other person a threat to cause the death of a school employee or student.
2. The threat involves the use of a firearm or other deadly weapon.
3. A reasonable person would believe the person making the threat intends to carry out the threat.
4. The person making the threat purposely engaged in conduct that constitutes a substantial step in a course of conduct intended to culminate in the commission of the threatened act.
5. There is a close temporal relationship between the threatened act and the substantial step.

#### b. Punishment

Communicating a death threat concerning a school employee or student is a Class D felony.

---

[98] Any subsequent Conviction is a Class A Felony.
[99] "school" means any elementary school, junior high school, or high school technical institute or post-secondary vocational-technical school two-year or four-year college or university

# Chapter 12: Crimes against Habitations

## (12.1) Crimes Against Habitations in General

The title of this chapter is somewhat of a misnomer. Many of the crimes discussed are not, in fact, against habitations—they are against homes, businesses, and other property. If we examine these offenses carefully, we can see where this classification comes from. The most serious versions of these crimes are against habitations—the "dwelling house" so vigorously protected in the common law tradition. Crimes such as arson and burglary are most repugnant to our society when they invade the home.

## (12.2) Arson (§5-38-301)

### a. Defining the Offense

A person commits arson if he or she starts a fire or causes an explosion with the purpose of destroying or otherwise damaging any of the following:

- An occupiable structure or motor vehicle that is the property of another person
- Any property for the purpose of collecting any insurance
- Any property if the act thereby negligently creates a risk of death or serious physical injury to any person
- A vital public facility
- Any dedicated church property used as a place of worship
- Any public building or occupiable structure that is either owned or leased by the state or any of its political subdivisions

### b. Punishment

The Code established the classification of arson based on the value of the property destroyed or damaged.

| Classification of Arson Based on Value of Property Damaged ||
| --- | --- |
| Less than $500 | Class A Misdemeanor |
| $500 to $2,500 | Class D Felony |
| $2,500 to $5,000 | Class C Felony |
| $5,000 to $15,000 | Class B Felony |
| $15,000 to $100,000 | Class A Felony |
| More than $100,000 | Class Y Felony |

## (12.3) Reckless Burning (§5-38-302)

### a. Defining the Offense

A person commits the offense of *reckless burning* if he purposely starts a fire or causes an explosion, whether on his own property or that of another, and thereby recklessly does any of the following:

- Creates a substantial risk of death or serious physical injury to any person
- Destroys or causes substantial damage to an occupiable structure of another person
- Destroys or causes substantial damage to a vital public facility

### b. Punishment

Reckless burning is a Class D felony.

### *(12.4) Failure to Control or Report Dangerous Fire (§5-38-303)*

### a. Defining the Offense

A person commits the offense of *failure to control or report a dangerous fire* if he knows that a fire is unattended and is endangering the life, physical safety, or a substantial amount of property of another person, and he does either of the following:

- Fails to act in a reasonable manner to put out or control the fire when he can do so without substantial risk to himself.
- Fails to act in a reasonable manner to report the fire.

### b. Punishment

Failure to control or report a dangerous fire is a Class B misdemeanor.

### *(12.5) Unlawful Burnings – Miscellaneous Misdemeanors (§5-38-310)*

### a. Defining the Offense

This section prohibits several acts related to burning:

- Setting on fire or causing or procuring to be set on fire any forest, brush, or other inflammable vegetation on lands not his own.
- Allowing fire to escape from the control of the person building or having charge of the fire, or to spread to the lands of any person other than the builder of the fire.
- Burning any brush, stumps, logs, rubbish, fallen timber, grass, stubble, or debris of any sort, whether on his own land or that of another, without taking necessary precaution both before lighting the fire and at all times thereafter to prevent escape[100].
- Building a camp fire upon lands not one's own, without cleaning the ground immediately around it free from material which will carry fire, or leaving thereon a camp fire to spread thereon or by throwing away a lighted cigar, match, cigarette or by the use of firearms or in any other manner starting a fire in forest material not his own and leaving the fire unextinguished
- Defacing or destroying fire warning notices.
- Failure by any employee of the State Forestry Commission or any officer charged with the duties of enforcing criminal laws to attempt to secure the arrest and conviction of any persons against whom he has or can secure evidence of violating the fire laws.

### b. Punishment

The above acts are misdemeanors and are punishable by a fine of not less than $25.00 and not more than $300 or a jail sentence of not more than 1 year, or both fine and imprisonment.

---

[100] The escape of fire to adjoining timber, brush, or grasslands shall be prima facie evidence that necessary precautions were not taken

*(12.6) Unlawful Burnings – Miscellaneous Felonies (§5-38-311)*

### a. Defining the Offense

This section prohibits several acts related to burning that are not classifiable as arsons:

- Purposely or willfully or maliciously setting on fire the lands of another
- Starting a fire on one's own lands or lands which he has leased or are under his control with the intent of letting it escape to the lands of another
- The destruction or injuring of, or theft of, any telephone lines, towers, buildings, tools, or equipment used in the detection, reporting, or suppression of fires

### b. Punishment

These acts are felonies and are punishable by a fine of not less than $1,000 and not more $10,000 or not less than 1 year in the penitentiary and not more than 10 years, or both fine and imprisonment.

*(12.7) Burglary and Other Intrusions – Definitions (§5-39-101)*

§ 5-39-101. Definitions

As used in this chapter, unless the context otherwise requires:

(1) "Residential occupiable structure" means a vehicle, building, or other structure:

(A) Where any person lives; or

(B) Which is customarily used for overnight accommodation of persons whether or not a person is actually present. Each unit of a residential occupiable structure divided into separately occupied units is itself a residential occupiable structure.

(2) "Commercial occupiable structure" means a vehicle, building, or other structure:

(A) Where any person carries on a business or other calling; or

(B) Where people assemble for purposes of business, government, education, religion, entertainment, or public transportation.

(3) "Premises" means occupiable structures and any real property.

(4) "Enter or remain unlawfully" means to enter or remain in or upon premises when not licensed or privileged to do so. A person who enters or remains in or upon premises that are at the time open to the public does so with license and privilege, regardless of his purpose, unless he defies a lawful order not to enter or remain personally communicated to him by the owner of the premises or some other person authorized by the owner. A license or privilege to enter or remain in or upon premises only part of which are open to the public is not a license or privilege to enter or remain in a part of the premises not open to the public. A person who enters or remains upon unimproved and apparently unused land not fenced or otherwise enclosed in a manner designed to exclude intruders does so with license and privilege unless notice not to enter or remain is personally communicated to him by the owner or some person authorized by the owner, or unless notice is given by posting in a conspicuous manner.

(5) "Vehicle" means any craft or device designed for the transportation of people or property across land or water or through the air.

### b. Punishment

Breaking or entering is a Class D felony.

*(12.10) Criminal Trespass in a Vehicle or Structure (§5-39-203)*

### a. Defining the Offense

A person commits criminal trespass if he purposely enters or remains unlawfully in or upon a vehicle or the premises of another person.

### b. Punishment

Criminal trespass is a Class B misdemeanor if the vehicle or premises involved is an occupiable structure. Otherwise, it is a Class C misdemeanor.

*(12.11) Forcible Possession of Land (§5-39-210)*

### a. Defining the Offense

This section prohibits the taking or keeping control of land by armed force or threat of armed force against a person legally entitled to control of it.

### b. Punishment

Forcible possession of land is a misdemeanor punishable by a fine of not less than $50 and a term of imprisoned not to exceeding 1 year.

*(12.12) Cemeteries (§§5-39-211, 212)*

### a. Mining

It is unlawful for any corporation, company, or individual to:

- Mine, extract, or remove coal or any other mineral or substance from under or beneath any cemetery, graveyard, or burying place in this state
- Make, place, or drive any slope, pit, or entry of any kind into, under, through, or across any cemetery, graveyard, or other burying place in this state

A violation of this section is a felony punishable by a fine of not less than $1,000 and not more than $5,000 and by a term of imprisonment of not less than 1 year and not more than 5 years.

### b. Access, Debris, and Disturbances

It is unlawful for any person, firm, corporation, partnership, or association to construct any fence on any property in such manner as to enclose any cemetery unless suitable access by automobile to the cemetery is provided by gate or otherwise.

A violation of this section is a misdemeanor punishable by a fine of not less than $10 and not more than $100

*Every day that the violation exists constitutes a separate offense.*

*(12.13) Leaving Open Enclosure of Another (§5-39-301)*

If any person shall pull down or break the fence or open the gate and fail to close the gate of the farm, plantation, or other enclosed ground of another, the offending party shall be guilty of a Class A misdemeanor.

*(12.14) Unlawful Entry (§5-39-302)*

### a. Defining the Offense

This section makes it unlawful for any person to enter upon any enclosed grazing land except by way of a gate, gap, or other opening.

## b. Punishment

The statute makes unlawful entry a misdemeanor punishable by a fine of not less than $100 for the first offense and nor less than $250 for the second offense.

### (12.15) Criminal Trespass on Land (§5-39-305)

### a. Defining the Offense

This section prohibits any person from entering upon another person's property (located outside the boundaries of any city or town) without written permission of the owner or lessee if that land is either

- lawfully posted
- crop land
- enclosed with a fence[101]

*The posting of land is not a requirement under this section.*

### b. Punishment

The statute makes this offense a violation, subject to a fine of no more than $100 if the land was not lawfully posted. If the land was lawfully posted, then the offense is classified as a Class B misdemeanor.

### c. Defenses

It is an affirmative defense to a prosecution that:

- The person did not knowingly enter upon another person's property
- The person was a guest or invitee
- The person was required to enter upon the premises of another for business reasons or for health and safety reasons
- The person was authorized by law to enter upon the land
- The privately owned land was made open to the public

*This section shall not apply to a law enforcement officer in the line of duty.*

---

[101] sufficient under § 2-39-101

# Chapter 13: Crimes against Property

## (13.1) Crimes against Property in General

The category of crimes against property generally includes two groups of offenses:

1. Crimes in which property is destroyed
2. Crimes in which property is stolen or taken against the owner's will

Arson and vandalism are common examples of crimes involving the destruction of property. Arson is the purposeful burning of another person's property. In most states it is a crime to burn any building or structure, even if the person setting the fire is the owner.

There are several categories of crimes that involve taking property against the will of the owner. Larceny is the unlawful taking and carrying away of another person's property with the intent never to return it to the owner. Most states identify larceny as either grand or petty. Grand larceny (a felony) occurs when anything above a certain value is stolen. Petty larceny is a misdemeanor that involves the theft of anything of small value.

Burglary is the unlawful entry into any dwelling or structure with the intention to commit a crime. Under traditional classification systems, a person who is entrusted with property but then takes it unlawfully is guilty of embezzlement. Extortion, which is also called blackmail, takes place when one person uses threats to obtain another person's property. The threats may include harm to the victim's body, property, reputation, or loved ones.

Robbery is the taking of property from a person's possession by using force or threat of force. Because of the interpersonal violence inherent in this definition of burglary, it is treated as a crime against persons rather than a crime against property[102].

## (13.2) Theft Consolidation (§5-36-102)

As discussed in the previous section, property crime has traditionally been divided into many different offenses. Recently, many states have combined the various larcenous crimes into a single crime entitled *theft* in order to remove the technicalities which complicated the proof of the different crimes at common law. Arkansas is one of these progressive states. Under Current Arkansas law, the conduct previously constituting the separate offenses of larceny, embezzlement, false pretense, extortion, blackmail, fraudulent conversion, receiving stolen property, and other similar offenses are now more simply *theft*.

The theft consolidation statute also creates a presumption of law that *the knowing concealment (upon his or her person or the person of another) of store merchandise indicates that the actor took the merchandise with the purpose of depriving the owner, or another person having an interest in the merchandise.*

---

[102] See 11.8 for a more complete discussion of robbery.

The punishment for theft offenses is determined in large part by the value of the property taken. For legal purposes, the value involved in a theft is the highest value, by any reasonable standard, of the property or services which the actor obtained or attempted to obtain.

If several individual items are taken in one "scheme" or "course of conduct", then the value of the property may be added together in determining the grade of the offense.

### (13.3) Theft of Property (§5-36-103)

#### a. Defining the Offense

This section defines the offense of *Theft of Property* as knowingly coming into the possession of the property of another by any of the following means:

- Taking
- Exercising unauthorized control over
- Making an unauthorized transfer of an interest in
- Obtaining by deception or threat

Regardless of means, the actor must have the purpose of depriving the owner of the property.

#### b. Punishment

The punishment scheme for theft of property is rather complicated because it takes several factors into account beyond the value of the property taken.

The most serious grade of theft of property is classified as a Class B felony. Theft of property falls into this category when any of the following conditions are met:

- The value of the property exceeds $2,500
- The property is obtained by threat of serious physical injury to a person or the destruction of an occupiable structure
- The property is obtained by threat and the actor stands in a confidential or fiduciary relationship to the person threatened
- The property is obtained by threat, and the actor stands in a confidential or fiduciary relationship[103] to the person threatened.

Theft of property is a Class C felony if any of the following conditions are met:

- The value of the property is less than $2,500 but more than $500
- The property is obtained by threat
- The property is a firearm valued at less than $2,500
- The property is a:
    - Credit card or credit card account number
    - Debit card or debit card account number
- The property is livestock, and the value of the livestock is in excess of $200

Theft of property is a Class D felony if the value of the property is $500 or less and the property was unlawfully obtained during a criminal episode[104].

---

[103] A *fiduciary* is a person who occupies a position of trust in a relationship required to act for the latter's benefit within the scope of that relationship

Theft of property is a Class A misdemeanor if any of the following conditions are met:

- The value of the property is $500 or less
- The property has inherent, subjective, or idiosyncratic value to its owner or possessor even if the property has no market value or replacement cost

### c. Penalty Enhancement in a State of Emergency

Upon the proclamation of a *state of emergency* by the President of the United States or the Governor, or upon the declaration of a local emergency by the executive officer of any city or county and for a period of 30 days following that declaration, the penalty for theft of property shall be enhanced if the property is:
- A generator intended for use by:
  - A public facility
  - A nursing home or hospital
  - An airport
  - A public safety device
  - A communication tower or facility
  - A public utility
  - A water system or sewer system
  - A public safety agency
  - Any other facility or use providing a vital service
- Any other equipment used in the transmission of electric power or telephone service

The *mandatory* penalty under the state of emergency penalty enhancement is a fine of at least $5,000 and not more than $50,000. If the theft would have been classified as a Class A misdemeanor, it will be classified as a Class D felony under this penalty enhancement section.

### (13.4) Theft of Services (§5-36-104)

### a. Defining the Offense

A person commits *theft of services* if, with purpose to defraud he or she does any of the following:

- Purposely obtains services, which he or she knows to be available only for compensation, by deception, threat, or other means to avoid payment.
- Having control over the disposition of services to which he or she is not entitled, he or she purposely diverts such services to his or her own benefit or to the benefit of another person not entitled to them.

*In circumstances where payment is ordinarily made immediately upon the rendering of service, absconding without payment or offer to pay shall give rise to a presumption that the actor obtained the services with the purpose of avoiding payment.*

### b. Punishment

Theft of services is a Class B felony if any of the following conditions are met:

- The value of the services is $2,500 or more
- The services are obtained by the threat of serious physical injury to any person or destruction of the occupiable structure of another

---

[104] For the purposes of this subdivision, *criminal episode* means a series of thefts committed by the same person on 3 or more occasions within 3 days.

- The services are obtained by threat, and the actor stands in a confidential or fiduciary relationship to the person threatened
- The services involve theft of utility services which results in
    - o   Any contamination of the lines, pipes, waterlines, meters, or other utility property
    - o   Results in a spill, dumping, or release of any hazardous materials into the environment

Theft of services is a Class C felony if any of the following conditions are met:

- The value of the services is less than $2,500 but more than $500
- The services are obtained by threat

Theft of services is a Class A misdemeanor if it involves a theft of utility services which results in the destruction or damage to the lines, pipes, waterlines, meters, or any other property of the utility of less than $500 in value. In addition, all other theft of services is a Class A misdemeanor.

For offenses involving the theft of utility services (such as gas, electricity, water, telephone, or cable television), the statute stipulates that, in addition to the fines, the guilty party must make restitution to the utility company from which the services were obtained.

### (13.5) Theft of Property Lost or Delivered by Mistake (§5-36-105)

#### a. Defining the Offense

A person commits *theft of property lost, mislaid, or delivered by mistake* if he or she does the following:

1. Comes into control of property of another person.
2. Retains or disposes of such property when he knows it to have been lost, mislaid, or delivered under a mistake as to the identity of the recipient or as to the nature or amount of the property.
3. With the purpose of depriving anyone having an interest in the property, he fails to take reasonable measures to restore the property to a person entitled to it.

#### b. Punishment

Theft of property lost, mislaid, or delivered by mistake is a Class D felony if the value of the property is $1,000 or more.

Theft of property lost, mislaid, or delivered by mistake is a Class B misdemeanor if any of the following conditions are met:
- The value of the property is less than $1,000 but more than $500
- The property is a:
    - o   Credit card or credit card account number
    - o   Debit card or debit card account number

Otherwise, theft of property lost, mislaid, or delivered by mistake is a Class C misdemeanor.

### *(13.6) Theft by Receiving (§5-36-106)*

#### a. Defining the Offense

A person commits the offense of *theft by receiving*[105] if he or she receives, retains, or disposes of stolen property of another person, knowing that it was stolen or having good reason to believe it was stolen.

*The unexplained possession or control by a person of recently stolen property or the acquisition by a person of property for a consideration known to be far below its reasonable value shall give rise to a presumption that he or she knows or believes that the property was stolen.*

#### b. Punishment

Theft by receiving is a Class B felony if the value of the property is $2,500 or more.

Theft by receiving is a Class C felony if either of the following conditions is met:
- The value of the property is less than $2,500 but more than $500
- The property is a:
    o Credit card or credit card account number
    o Debit card or debit card account number
- The property is a firearm valued at less than $2,500

Otherwise, theft by receiving is a Class A misdemeanor.

#### c. Defenses

It is a defense to a prosecution for the offense of theft by receiving that the property is received, retained, or disposed of with the purpose of restoring it to the owner or other person entitled to it.

### *(13.7) Theft of Trade Secret (§5-36-107)*

> **§ 5-36-107.**
>
> (a) A person commits theft of trade secret if with purpose to deprive the owner of the control of a trade secret, he obtains or discloses to an unauthorized person a trade secret or, without authority, makes or causes to be made a copy or an article representing a trade secret.
>
> (b) Theft of a trade secret is a Class A misdemeanor.

### *(13.8) Theft of Rented or Entrusted Personal Property (§5-36-115)*

#### a. Defining the Offense

This section defines the following act as a theft:

Intentionally, fraudulently, or by false pretense take, carry, lead, drive away, destroy, sell, secrete, convert, or appropriate in any wrongful manner any personal property which is leased, rented, or entrusted to the person, or reports falsely of his wealth or mercantile credit and thereby fraudulently obtains possession of that personal property.

#### b. Punishment

See 13.3(b) above.

---

[105] *Receiving* means acquiring possession, control, or title or lending on the security of the property.

## *(13.9) Shoplifting (§5-36-116)*

### a. Detention of Suspects Concealing Merchandise

A person engaging in conduct giving rise to a presumption under §5-36-102(b)[106] may be detained in a reasonable manner and for a reasonable length of time by a *peace officer* or a *merchant* or a *merchant's employee*[107] in order that recovery of such goods may be effected. *The detention by a peace officer, merchant, or merchant's employee shall not render the peace officer, merchant, or merchant's employee criminally or civilly liable for false arrest, false imprisonment, or unlawful detention.*

### b. Detention of Subjects Activating Antishoplifting Devices

The activation of an antishoplifting or inventory control device[108] as a result of a person exiting the establishment or a protected area within the establishment shall constitute reasonable cause for the detention of the person so exiting by the owner or operator of the establishment or by an agent or employee of the owner or operator, provided sufficient notice has been posted to advise the patrons that such a device is being utilized.

Each such detention must be made only in a reasonable manner and only for a reasonable period of time sufficient for any inquiry into the circumstances surrounding the activation of the device or for the recovery of goods. Such detention by a peace officer, merchant, or merchant's employee shall not render such peace officer, merchant, or merchant's employee criminally or civilly liable for false arrest, false imprisonment, or unlawful detention.

### c. Warrantless Arrest Authorization

A peace officer may arrest without a warrant upon probable cause for believing the suspect has committed the offense of shoplifting. The peace officer, merchant, or merchant's employee who has observed the person accused of committing the offense of shoplifting must provide a written statement which serves as probable cause to justify the arrest. The accused must be brought before a magistrate as in other criminal cases.

## *(13.10) Theft of Motor Fuel (§5-36-120)*

### a. Defining the Offense

This section criminalizes gas station "drive offs." That is, it makes it illegal to leave a gas station without paying for fuel. The actor must have the intent to deprive the owner of the motor fuel and not pay for it.

### b. Punishment

Theft of motor fuel is a Class A misdemeanor.

In addition, a person guilty of theft of motor fuel will have his or her driver's license suspended by the court[109] for a period of not more than 6 months unless the person's license has previously been suspended for theft of motor fuel, in which case the court will suspend the person's license for not less than 1 year.

### c. Notice to the Public

Every place that sells motor fuel must prominently display on each face of a retail product dispenser a sign which contains the following:

---

[106] The knowing concealment (upon his or her person or the person of another) of store merchandise indicates that the actor took the merchandise with the purpose of depriving the owner, or another person having an interest in the merchandise.

[107] This language can be taken to mean store security or loss prevention.

[108] *Antishoplifting or inventory control device* means a mechanism or other device designed and operated for the purpose of detecting the removal from a mercantile establishment or similar enclosure or from a protected area within such an enclosure of specially marked or tagged merchandise.

[109] under § 27-16-907(a)

THEFT OF MOTOR FUEL IS A CLASS A MISDEMEANOR AND CARRIES A MAXIMUM PENALTY OF ONE (1) YEAR IN JAIL, $1000 FINE, AND A ONE (1) YEAR SUSPENSION OF YOUR DRIVER'S LICENSE.

### *(13.12) Theft of Public Benefits (5-36-202)*

A person commits theft of public benefits if he obtains or retains public benefits from the Department of Human Services or any other state agency administering the distribution of such benefits in any of the following ways:

* By means of any false statement, misrepresentation, or impersonation
* Through failure to disclose a material fact used in making a determination as to such person's qualifications to receive public benefits
* Receives, retains, or disposes of public benefits knowing or having reason to know that such public benefits were obtained in violation of this subchapter.

*Presentation of false or fictitious information or failure to disclose a material fact in the process of obtaining or retaining public benefits shall be prima facie evidence of intent to commit theft of public benefits.*

---

§ **5-36-203**. Penalties

(a) Theft of public benefits is a Class B felony if the value of the public benefit is two thousand five hundred dollars ($ 2,500) or more.

(b) Theft of public benefits is a Class C felony if the value of the public benefit is less than two thousand five hundred dollars ($ 2,500) but more than two hundred dollars ($ 200).

(c) Theft of public benefits is a Class A misdemeanor if the value of the public benefit is two hundred dollars ($ 200) or less.

---

### *(13.13) Forgery (§5-37-201)*

#### a. Defining the Offense

A person forges a written instrument if with purpose to defraud he draws, makes, completes, alters, counterfeits, possesses, or utters any written instrument that purports to be or is calculated to become or to represent if completed the act of a person who did not authorize that act.

A person commits *forgery in the first degree* if he forges a written instrument that is:

* Money, a security, a postage or revenue stamp, or other instrument issued by a government
* A stock, bond, or similar instrument representing an interest in property or a claim against a corporation or its property

A person commits *forgery in the second degree* if he forges a written instrument that is:

* A deed, will, codicil, contract, assignment, check, commercial instrument, credit card, or other written instrument that does or may evidence, create, transfer, terminate, or otherwise affect a legal right, interest, obligation, or status
* A public record, or an instrument filed or required by law to be filed, or one legally entitled to be filed in a public office or with a public servant
* A written instrument officially issued or created by a public office, public servant, or government agent

### b. Punishment

Forgery in the first degree is a Class B felony.  Forgery in the second degree is a Class C felony.

### *(13.14) Fraudulent Use of a Credit Card or Debit Card (§5-37-207)*

### a. Defining the Offense

A person commits the offense of *fraudulent use of a credit card or debit card* if, with purpose to defraud, he or she uses a credit card, credit card account number, debit card, or debit card account number to obtain property or services with knowledge of any of the following:

- The card or account number is stolen
- The card or account number has been revoked or cancelled
- The card or account number is forged
- For any other reason his or her use of the card or account number is unauthorized by either the issuer or the person to whom the credit card or debit card is issued

### b. Punishment

Fraudulent use of a credit card or debit card is a Class C felony if the value of all money, goods, or services obtained during any six-month period exceeds $100.  Otherwise, it is a Class A misdemeanor.

### *(13.15) Criminal Impersonation (§5-37-208)*

### a. Criminal Impersonation in the First Degree

A person commits criminal impersonation in the first degree if, with the intent to induce a person to submit to pretended official authority for the purpose to injure or defraud the person, he:

- Pretends to be a law enforcement officer by wearing or displaying, without authority, any uniform or badge by which law enforcement officers are lawfully distinguished
- Uses a motor vehicle or motorcycle designed, equipped or marked so as to resemble a motor vehicle or motorcycle belonging to a federal, state or local law enforcement agency.

Criminal impersonation in the first degree is a Class D felony.

### b. Criminal Impersonation in the Second Degree

A person commits criminal impersonation in the second degree if he does an act in his pretended or assumed capacity or character with the purpose to injure or defraud another person and he:

- Assumes a false identity
- Pretends to be a representative of some person or organization
- Pretends to be an officer or employee of the government other than a LEO
- Pretends to have a handicap or disability

Criminal impersonation in the second degree is a Class A misdemeanor.

### *(13.16) Criminal Possession of a Forgery Device (§5-37-209)*

#### a. Defining the Offense

A person commits criminal possession of a forgery device if he makes or possesses any device capable of or adaptable to a use in forging written instruments with the purpose to use it himself, or to aid or permit another to use it, to commit forgery.

#### b. Punishment

Criminal possession of a forgery device is a Class C felony.

### *(13.17) Unlawfully Using Slugs (§5-37-212)*

#### a. Defining the Offense

A person commits the offense of unlawfully using slugs if he or she does either of the following:

- With purpose to defraud, he or she obtains property or a service sold or offered by means of a coin machine by inserting, depositing, or using a slug in that machine.
- He or she makes, possesses, or disposes of a slug with purpose to enable a person to use it fraudulently in a coin machine.

#### b. Punishment

Unlawfully using slugs is a Class C felony if the value of the property or slugs exceeds $100. Otherwise, it is a Class A misdemeanor.

### *(13.18) Criminal Simulation (§5-37-213)*

#### a. Defining the Offense

A person commits criminal simulation if, with purpose to defraud or injure, he or she does either of the following:

- Makes, alters, or represents any object in such fashion that it appears to have an antiquity, rarity, source or authorship, ingredient, or composition that it does not in fact have.
- Possesses or transfers an object so simulated with knowledge of its true character.

#### b. Punishment

Criminal simulation is a Class D felony if the value of the object simulated exceeds $100. Otherwise it is a Class A misdemeanor.

### *(13.19) Financial Identity Fraud (§5-37-227)*

#### a. Defining the Offense

A person commits financial identity fraud if, with the intent to unlawfully appropriate financial resources of another person to his or her own use or to the use of a third party, and without the authorization of that person, he or she does either of the following:

- Obtains or records identifying information that would assist in accessing the financial resources of the other person.
- Accesses or attempts to access the financial resources of the other person through the use of the identifying information.

### b. Definition of Identifying Information

*Identifying information*, as used in this section, includes social security numbers, driver's license numbers, checking account numbers, savings account numbers, credit card numbers, debit card numbers, personal identification numbers, electronic identification numbers, digital signatures, or any other numbers or information that can be used to access a person's financial resources.

### c. Punishment

Financial identity fraud is a Class D felony.

### (13.20) Worthless Checks (§5-37-302)

This rather wordy section prohibits the issuance of a worthless check with the intent to defraud. It also prohibits the withdrawal of money from an account that already has a check written against it.

### (13.21) Knowingly Issuing a Worthless Check (§5-37-307)

#### a. Defining the Offense

A person commits an offense if he or she issues or passes a check, order, draft, or any other form of presentment involving the transmission of account information for the payment of money knowing that the issuer does not have sufficient funds in or on deposit with the bank or other drawee for the payment in full of the check, order, draft, or any other form of presentment involving the transmission of account information, as well as all other checks, orders, drafts, or any other form of presentment involving the transmission of account information outstanding at the time of issuance.

An offense under this section is a violation[110].

### (13.22) Theft of Communication Services (§5-37-402)

This section criminalizes various types of thefts and theft related acts involving communication services. The mens rea element of this offense requires that the offender commit any of the several acts knowingly and with the intent to defraud a communication service provider.

The several prohibited acts can be summarized as follows:

- Obtaining or attempting to obtain a communication service without authorization from the service provider. For the purpose of this section, *authorization* generally means paying for the service.
- Tampering with, modifying, or maintaining a modification to a communication device installed by a service provider.
- Possession with intent to distribute any communication device primarily designed for the theft of communication services. This includes the interception of signals and defeating encryption. This subsection also prohibits the use of any device used with the intent to conceal the point of origin or the existence of any communication service with the intent to defraud that service.
- Tampering, interfering with, or connecting to a cable television service.
- Possession, use, manufacture, or development of unlawful access devices.
- Possession, use, development, or distribution of any plans for making an unlawful access device under circumstances evidencing intent to use the device or allow the device to be used. This subsection also prohibits the possession, sale, or distribution of materials with the knowledge that a third person will use those materials in the manufacture of an unlawful access device.

---

[110] punishable as provided in § 5-4-104

*(13.23) Causing a Catastrophe (§5-38-202)*

### a. Causing a Catastrophe

A person commits the offense of causing a catastrophe if he or she knowingly causes a catastrophe by explosion, fire, flood, avalanche, collapse of building, distribution of poison, radioactive material, bacteria, virus, or other dangerous and difficult to confine force or substance.

Causing a catastrophe is a Class Y felony.

### b. Threatening to Cause a Catastrophe

A person commits the offense of threatening to cause a catastrophe if he or she contacts any person, company, corporation, or governmental entity and threatens to cause a catastrophe by explosion, fire, flood, avalanche, collapse of building, release of poison, radioactive material, bacteria, virus, or other dangerous and difficult to confine force or substance unless paid a sum of money or any type of property, or unless the person, company, corporation, or governmental entity performs a requested act.

Threatening to cause a catastrophe is a Class D felony.

*(13.28) Criminal Mischief (§5-38-203, 204)*

### a. Criminal Mischief in the First (§5-38-203)

A person commits the offense of criminal mischief in the first degree if he purposely and without legal justification destroys or causes damage to:

- Any property of another
- Any property, whether his own or that of another, for the purpose of collecting any insurance.

Criminal mischief in the first degree is a Class C felony if the amount of actual damage is $500 or more. Otherwise, it is a Class A misdemeanor.

### b. Criminal Mischief in the Second (§5-38-204)

A person commits criminal mischief in the second degree if he does either of the following:

- Recklessly destroys or damages any property of another
- Purposely tampers with any property of another, thereby causing substantial inconvenience to the owner or some other person.

Criminal mischief in the second degree is a Class D felony if the amount of actual damage is $2,500 or more. Criminal mischief in the second degree is a Class A misdemeanor if the amount of actual damage is $1,000 but less than $2,500. Otherwise, it is a Class B misdemeanor.

# Chapter 14: Computer Crimes

## (14.1) Computer Crime in General

Computer Crime (a.k.a. Cybercrime, Electronic Crime, and Hi-Tech Crime) generally refers to criminal activity where a computer or network is the tool, target, or place of a crime. These categories cannot be considered exclusive. That is, many times, a computer or computer network (the largest being the Internet) will serve in more than one of these roles. Both the substantive and procedural aspects of the criminal law are constantly evolving in this area. As new technologies are developed, the courts and law makers must adapt the law to fit new offenses either created of facilitated by these new technologies. Some ancient common law crimes are given new life by computer technology, such as fraud and embezzlement. Other crimes, such as computer trespasses and the deletion of data are entirely new, only coming into existence with the advance of computer technology. These rapidly advancing areas of law create an important challenge to law enforcement to keep up with the law[111].

## (14.2) Sexually Explicit Conduct Involving a Child (§5-27-602)

### a. Defining the Offense

A person commits distributing, possessing, or viewing of matter depicting sexually explicit conduct involving a child if the person in any way obtains or transfers any material that depicts a child engaging in sexually explicit conduct. The Internet is specifically included in the statute. The statute also prohibits the mere possession or viewing of images of a child engaged in sexually explicit conduct. The image need not be of real children; it can be a "computer-generated image, video game, or any other reproduction."

### b. Punishment

Distributing, possessing, or viewing of matter depicting sexually explicit conduct involving a child is a Class C felony for the first offense and a Class B felony for any subsequent offense.

### c. Affirmative Defense

It is an affirmative defense to a prosecution under this section that the defendant in good faith reasonably believed that the child depicted in the matter was 17 years of age or older[112].

## (14.3) Computer Child Pornography (§5-27-603)

### a. Defining the Offense

A person commits computer child pornography if the person does either of the following:

---

[111] The website of the Department of Justice's Computer and Intellectual Property Section (http://www.cybercrime.gov) is an excellent resource for this purpose.

[112] Note that this is the opposite of statutory rape, which seems a conflict of legal logic. Logic seems to dictate that the value of protecting children from sexual harm merits a strict liability offense, or it does not.

- Knowingly compiles, enters into, or transmits by means of computer, makes, prints, publishes, or reproduces by other computerized means, knowingly causes or allows to be entered into or transmitted by means of computer or buys, sells, receives, exchanges, or disseminates any notice, statement, or advertisement or any child's name, telephone number, place of residence, physical characteristics, or other descriptive or identifying information for purposes of facilitating, encouraging, offering, or soliciting sexually explicit conduct of or with any child or another individual believed by the person to be a child, or the visual depiction of the conduct.
- Knowingly utilizes a computer online service, Internet service, or local bulletin board service to seduce, solicit, lure, or entice or attempt to seduce, solicit, lure, or entice a child or another individual believed by the person to be a child, to engage in sexually explicit conduct.

Note the use of the phrase "or another individual believed by the person to be a child" in acts listed above. This phrase allows for adult LEOs to pose as children for the purposes of apprehending those who would violate this section.

### b. Punishment

Computer child pornography is a Class B felony.

## (14.4) Failure to Report Computer Child Pornography (§5-27-604)

### a. Defining the Offense

A person commits failure to report computer child pornography if the person:

Is the owner, operator, or employee of a computer on-line service, Internet service, or bulletin board service the person knowingly fails to notify law enforcement officials that a subscriber is using the service to commit Computer Child Pornography (Section 14.3 above).

### b. Punishment

Failure to report computer child pornography is a Class A misdemeanor.

## (14.5) Computer Exploitation of Children (§5-27-605)

### a. Computer Exploitation of a Child in the First

A person commits computer exploitation of a child in the first degree if the person causes or permits a child to engage in sexually explicit conduct if the person knows, has reason to know, or intends that the prohibited conduct may be photographed, filmed, reproduced, or reconstructed in any manner, including on the Internet, or may be part of an exhibition or performance.

Computer exploitation of a child in the first degree is a Class B felony for the first offense, and a Class A felony for the second offense and subsequent offenses.

### b. Computer Exploitation of a Child in the Second

A person commits computer exploitation of a child in the second degree if the person photographs or films a child engaged in sexually explicit conduct or uses any device, including a computer, to reproduce or reconstruct the image of a child engaged in sexually explicit conduct.

Computer exploitation of a child in the second degree is a Class C felony.

> **§ 5-27-606. Jurisdiction**
>
> For the purpose of determining jurisdiction, a person is subject to prosecution in this state for any conduct proscribed by this subchapter, if the transmission that constitutes the offense either originates in this state or is received in this state.

## (14.6) Unlawful Computerized Communication (§5-41-108)

### a. Defining the Offense

A person commits the offense of *unlawful computerized communications* if, with the purpose to frighten, intimidate, threaten, abuse, or harass another person, the person sends a message:

- To the other person on an electronic mail or other computerized communication system and in that message threatens to cause physical injury to any person or damage to the property of any person.
- On an electronic mail or other computerized communication system with the reasonable expectation that the other person will receive the message and in that message threatens to cause physical injury to any person or damage to the property of any person.
- To another person on an electronic mail or other computerized communication system and in that message uses any obscene, lewd, or profane language.
- On an electronic mail or other computerized communication system with the reasonable expectation that the other person will receive the message and in that message uses any obscene, lewd, or profane language.

### b. Punishment

Unlawful computerized communications is a Class A misdemeanor.

## (14.7) Computer Fraud (§5-41-103)

### a. Defining the Offense

A person commits *computer fraud* if the person intentionally accesses or causes to be accessed any computer, computer system, computer network, or any part of a computer, computer system, or computer network for the purpose of *either*:

- Devising or executing any scheme or artifice to defraud or extort.
- Obtaining money, property, or a service with a false or fraudulent intent, representation, or promise.

### b. Punishment

Computer fraud is a Class D felony.

## (14.8) Computer Trespass (§5-41-104)

### a. Defining the Offense

A person commits *computer trespass* if the person intentionally and without authorization accesses, alters, deletes, damages, destroys, or disrupts any computer, computer system, computer network, computer program, or data.

### b. Punishment

Computer trespass is a:

- Class C misdemeanor if it is a first violation that does not cause any loss or damage.
- Class B misdemeanor if it is a:
    - Second or subsequent violation that does not cause any loss or damage

- o   Violation that causes loss or damage of less than $500
- Class A misdemeanor if it is a violation that causes loss or damage of $500 or more, but less than $2,500.
- Class D felony if it is a violation that causes loss or damage of $2,500 or more.

# Chapter 15: Crimes against Public Order and Morals

## *(15.1) In General*

This section contains a wide variety of criminal statutes that deal with public order and public morals. The public order sections deal mainly with acts against the function of government. These cover acts directly against the orderly function of government, such as obstructing government operations. In addition, there are several statutes that deal with the ethical conduct of public servants, such as bribery. Crimes against public morals is a general category that encompasses what are traditionally considered vice crimes: gambling, obscenity, and so forth. These are often controversial offenses because they are considered by many to be victimless crimes, and thus not worthy of legal regulation.

## *(15.2) Manufacture or Alteration of ID Documents (§5-27-502)*

### a. Defining the Offense

This section makes criminal the following three *acts*:

1. The manufacture or production of fraudulent personal identification documents
2. The alteration of personal identification documents
3. The sale or distribution of such fraudulent personal identification documents

In addition, the *purpose* the first two acts must be to provide a person under age 21 identification which can be used for the purpose of purchasing alcoholic beverages or other substances or materials restricted for adult purchase or possession.

### b. Punishment

A person who violates this section is guilty of a Class C felony.

A *second or subsequent* violation of this section is a Class B felony.

## *(15.3) Possession of Fraudulent Identification Documents (§5-27-503)*

### a. Defining the Offense

This section prohibits the possession of fraudulent or altered personal identification documents for the purposes of one of the following:

- For another person *providing* a person under age 21 identification that can be used for the purpose of obtaining materials restricted for adults.
- For a person under 21 to *possess* such identification for such a purpose.
- For a person under 21 to *attempt to use* such identification for such a purpose.

## b. Punishment

A person who violates this section shall be deemed guilty of a Class B misdemeanor.

A second or subsequent violation of this section shall be a Class A misdemeanor.

### *(15.4) Video Voyeurism (§5-16-101)*

## a. Defining the Offense

This section makes it unlawful to use any:
- Camera
- Videotape
- photo-optical
- photo-electric
- or any other image recording device

for the purpose of *secretly*
- observing
- viewing
- photographing
- filming *or*
- videotaping

a person present in a
- residence
- place of business
- school *or*
- other structure (or any room or particular location within that structure)

where that person is
1. in a private area out of public view
2. has a reasonable expectation of privacy, and
3. has not consented to the observation.

## b. Punishment

A violation of this section is a Class D felony.

## c. Exemptions

The provisions of this section shall not apply to *any* of the following:

- Video recording or monitoring conducted pursuant to a court order from a court of competent jurisdiction.
- Security monitoring operated by or at the direction of an occupant of a residence.
- Security monitoring operated by or at the direction of the owner or administrator of a place of business, school, or other structure.
- Security monitoring operated in motor vehicles used for public transit.
- Security monitoring and observation associated with correctional facilities, regardless of the location of the monitoring equipment.
- Video recording or monitoring conducted by law enforcement officers within the official scope of their duties.

- Videotaping pursuant to § 12-12-508(b)[113].

### (15.5) *Public Servant Bribery (§5-52-103)*

#### a. Defining the Offense

A person commits *public servant bribery* if he or she does either of the following:

1. He offers, confers, or agrees to *confer any benefit* upon a public servant *as consideration* for the recipient's decision, opinion, recommendation, vote, or other exercise of discretion as a public servant.
2. He solicits, accepts, or agrees to *accept any benefit*, the conferring of which is prohibited by this section.

#### b. Punishment

Public servant bribery is a Class D felony.

### (15.6) *Abuse of Office (§5-52-107)*

#### a. Defining the Offense

A person commits the offense of abuse of office if,
1. being a *public servant*
2. with the *purpose* of benefiting in a pecuniary[114] fashion himself or another person
   OR
   harming another person
3. he *knowingly* commits an unauthorized act which purports to be an act of his office
   OR
   omits to perform a duty imposed on him by law or clearly inherent in the nature of his office

#### b. Punishment

Abuse of office is a Class B misdemeanor[115].

### (15.7) *Soliciting Unlawful Compensation (§5-52-104)*

#### a. Defining the Offense

A person commits the offense of soliciting unlawful compensation if he requests a benefit for the performance of an official action as a public servant knowing that he is required to perform that action without compensation, other than authorized salary or allowances, or at a level of compensation lower than that requested.

#### b. Punishment

Soliciting unlawful compensation is a Class A misdemeanor[116].

### (15.8) *Attempting to Influence a Public Servant (§5-52-105)*

#### a. Defining the Offense

A person commits the offense of attempting to influence a public servant if he
1. threatens violence or economic reprisal against *any* person

---

[113] Provides that "Hospitals and clinics may make videotapes which may be probative as to the existence or extent of child maltreatment"
[114] i.e., making a profit
[115] §5-52-107(b)
[116] §5-52-104(b)

OR

uses deceit

2.  with the purpose to alter or affect the public servant's decision, vote, opinion, or action concerning any matter which is afterwards to be considered or performed by him or the agency or body of which he is a member.

### b. Punishment

Attempt to influence a public servant is a Class A misdemeanor[117].

## (15.9) Obstructing Government Operations (§5-54-102)

### a. Defining the Offense

A person commits the offense of *obstructing governmental operations* if the person does *any* of the following:

*   Knowingly obstructs, impairs, or hinders the performance of any governmental function.
*   Knowingly refuses to provide information requested by an employee of a governmental agency relating to the investigation of a case brought under Title IV-D of the Social Security Act and is the physical custodian of the child in the case.
*   Fails to submit to court-ordered scientific testing by a noninvasive procedure to determine the paternity of a child in a case brought under Title IV-D of the Social Security Act.
*   Falsely identifies himself or herself to a law enforcement officer.

### b. Punishment

Obstructing governmental operations by using or threatening to use physical force is a Class A misdemeanor.

Otherwise, obstructing governmental operations is a Class C misdemeanor.

### c. Exceptions

This section does not apply to:

*   Unlawful flight by a person charged with an offense; or
*   Refusal to submit to arrest[118]; or
*   Any means of avoiding compliance with the law not involving affirmative interference with governmental functions unless specifically set forth in this section[119]; or
*   The obstruction, impairment, or hindrance of unlawful action by a public servant.

## (15.10) Resisting Arrest (§5-54-103)

### a. Resisting Arrest

A person commits the offense of *resisting arrest* if he knowingly resists a person known by him to be a law enforcement officer effecting an arrest.

**Resists** (used in context of resisting arrest) means using or threatening to use physical force or any other means that creates a substantial risk of physical injury to any person.

---

[117] §5-52-105(b)

[118] This conduct is better charged under §5-54-103.  See **15.10**.

[119] Such conduct is covered by several other statutes and contempt.

**Caveat**: It is *no defense* to a prosecution under this subsection that the law enforcement officer *lacked legal authority* to make the arrest, provided he was acting under color of his official authority.

Resisting arrest is a Class A misdemeanor.

### b. Refusal to Submit to Arrest

A person commits the offense of *refusal to submit to arrest* if he knowingly refuses to submit to arrest by a person known by him to be a law enforcement officer effecting an arrest.

**Refusal** means both active and passive refusals.

Refusal to submit to arrest is a Class B misdemeanor.

## (15.11) Interference with a LEO (§5-54-104)

### a. Defining the Offense

A person commits the offense of interference with a law enforcement officer if he knowingly employs or threatens to employ physical force against a law enforcement officer engaged in performing his official duties.

### b. Punishment

Interference with a law enforcement officer is a Class C felony if the person uses or threatens to use deadly physical force or the person is assisted by one or more other persons and physical injury to the officer results.

Otherwise, interference with a law enforcement officer is a Class A misdemeanor.

## (15.12) Hindering Apprehension or Prosecution (§5-54-105)

The mental element of this offense is that the person have the purpose to hinder the action of the criminal justice system (apprehension, prosecution, conviction, or punishment) *of another* for an offense.

The criminal act can be satisfied in any of the following ways:

1. Harbor or conceal the person.
2. Provide or aid in providing the person with a weapon, money, transportation, disguise, or other means of avoiding apprehension, discovery, or effecting escape.
3. Prevent or obstruct anyone from performing an act which might aid in the discovery, apprehension, or identification of the person by means of force, intimidation, or the threat of such, or by means of deception.
4. Conceal, alter, destroy, or otherwise suppresses the discovery of any facts, information, or other things related to the crime which might aid in the discovery, apprehension, or identification of the person.
5. Warn the person of impending discovery, apprehension, or identification.
6. Volunteer false information to a law enforcement officer.
7. Purposefully lie or attempt to purposefully provide erroneous information, documents or other instrumentalities which he knows to be false to a certified law enforcement officer that would distract from the true course of the investigation or inhibit the logical or orderly progress of the investigation.

### b. Punishment

Hindering apprehension uses a more complex punishment scheme which is more lenient on persons related[120] to the perpetrator. Hindering is classified according to the following table:

---

[120] "in the relation of parent, child, brother, sister, corresponding steprelationships of the preceding, husband, or wife"

| Hindering is Classified As: | | |
|---|---|---|
| **Classification of Original Crime** | **Relation** | **Not a Relation** |
| **Y** or **A** Felony | D Felony | B Felony |
| **B** Felony | C Felony | C Felony |
| **C** Felony | D Felony | D Felony |
| **D**[121] or Unclassified Felony | A Misdemeanor | A Misdemeanor |
| **A** Misdemeanor | B Misdemeanor | B Misdemeanor |
| **B** Misdemeanor | C Misdemeanor | C Misdemeanor |
| **C** Misdemeanor | D Misdemeanor | D Misdemeanor |

*(15.13) Aiding the Consummation of an Offense (§5-54-106)*

### a. Defining the Offense

A person commits an offense under this section if he knowingly aids another by safeguarding or securing the proceeds of an offense or by converting the proceeds of an offense into negotiable funds.

### b. Punishment

A person violating any provision of this section is guilty of a Class D felony if the conduct of the person aided in violation of this section constitutes a felony of any class.

Otherwise, a violation of this section is a Class A misdemeanor.

*(15.14) Compounding (§5-54-107)*

### a. Defining the Offense

A person commits the offense of *compounding* if he commits *any* of the following acts:

- Solicits, accepts, or agrees to accept any pecuniary benefit as consideration for refraining from reporting to law enforcement authorities the commission or suspected commission of any offense or information relating to an offense.
- Offers, confers, or agrees to confer a benefit, the receipt of which is prohibited by this section.

### b. Punishment

Compounding is a:

- Class B felony if the offense concealed is a Class Y felony.
- Class C felony if the offense concealed is a Class A felony.
- Class D felony if the offense concealed is a Class B, C, D, or unclassified felony.
- Class B misdemeanor if the offense concealed is a misdemeanor of any class.

*(15.15) Escape (§5-54-110,111,112)*

### a. First Degree Escape (§5-54-110)

A person commits the offense of first degree escape if, at any time from the point of departure from confinement to the return to confinement, aided by another person actually present, he or she *uses or threatens to use physical force* in escaping from:

---

[121] If the person was assisting in escape from correctional custody after a felony conviction, then it is a D felony.

- Custody
- A correctional facility
- A juvenile detention facility
- A youth services facility

OR

At any time from the point of departure from confinement to the return to confinement, he or she uses or threatens to use a deadly weapon in escaping from:

- Custody
- A correctional facility
- A juvenile detention facility
- A youth services facility

First degree escape is a Class C felony.

### b. Second Degree Escape (§5-54-111)

A person commits the offense of *second degree escape* if he or she commits *any* of the following acts:

- At any time from the point of departure from confinement to the return to confinement, uses or threatens to use physical force in escaping from custody.
- Having been found guilty of a felony, escapes from custody.
- Escapes from a correctional facility.
- Escapes from a juvenile detention facility.
- Escapes from a youth services facility.

Second degree escape is a Class D felony.

### c. Third Degree Escape (§5-54-112)

A person commits the offense of *third degree escape* if he escapes from custody.

Third degree escape is a Class A misdemeanor.

It is a defense that the person escaping was in custody pursuant to an unlawful arrest.

### (15.16) Permitting Escape (§5-54-13)

### a. Permitting Escape in the First (§5-54-113)

A public servant responsible for supervision of persons detained in correctional facilities or in custody commits the offense of *permitting escape in the first degree* if he *knowingly* permits the escape of a person known to be detained in a correctional facility or in custody pursuant to an arrest for, or a charge or conviction of, a felony of any class.

Permitting escape in the first degree is a Class C felony[122].

---

[122] 5-54-113(b)

### b. Permitting Escape in the Second (§5-54-114)

A public servant responsible for supervision of persons detained in correctional facilities or in custody commits the offense of *permitting escape in the second degree* if he *recklessly* permits a person so detained to escape.

Permitting escape in the second degree is a Class A misdemeanor.

## (15.17) Aiding an Unauthorized Departure (§5-54-116)

### a. Defining the Offense

A person commits the offense of *aiding an unauthorized departure* if, *not being* an inmate in a juvenile detention facility, a youth services facility, or the Arkansas State Hospital, he knowingly aids another person in making or attempting to make an unauthorized departure from a juvenile detention facility, a youth services facility, or the Arkansas State Hospital.

### b. Punishment

Aiding an unauthorized departure is a Class C felony if the person aiding an unauthorized departure uses physical force or uses or threatens to use a deadly weapon.

Otherwise, it is a Class A misdemeanor.

## (15.18) Furnishing Implements for Escape (§5-54-117)

### a. Defining the Offense

A person commits the offense of *furnishing an implement for escape* if, with the purpose of facilitating escape, he does any of the following:

- Introduces such an implement into a correctional facility.
- Provides an inmate in a correctional facility with such an implement.
- Provides a person in custody with such an implement.

### b. Punishment

Providing an implement for escape is a Class C felony if the implement provided is a deadly weapon.

Otherwise, it is a Class D felony.

## (15.19) Furnishing Implement for Unauthorized Departure (§ 5-54-118)

### a. Defining the Offense

A person commits *furnishing an implement for unauthorized departure* if, with the purpose of facilitating an unauthorized departure, he does *either* of the following:

- Introduces such an implement into the Arkansas State Hospital or a juvenile training school.
- Provides a person detained in the Arkansas State Hospital or a juvenile training school with such an implement.

### b. Punishment

Furnishing an implement for unauthorized departure is a Class C felony, if the implement furnished is a deadly weapon.

Otherwise, it is a Class A misdemeanor.

### (15.20) Furnishing Prohibited Articles (§5-54-119)

#### a. Defining the Offense

A person commits the offense of *furnishing a prohibited article* if he *knowingly* does either of the following:

- Introduces a prohibited article into a correctional facility, the Arkansas State Hospital, or a juvenile training school.
- Provides a person confined in a correctional facility, the Arkansas State Hospital, or a juvenile training school with a prohibited article.

#### b. Punishment

Furnishing or providing a

- Weapon
- intoxicating beverage
- controlled substance
- moneys
- any other items that would facilitate an *escape* or *violence* within a facility

is a Class B felony.

Otherwise furnishing a prohibited article is a Class C felony.

This section does not apply to a religious official who supplies sacramental wine to an inmate in the Arkansas Department of Correction for the sole purpose of approved religious services.

### (15.21) Failure to Appear (§5-54-120)

#### a. Defining the Offense

A person commits the offense of *failure to appear* if that person fails to appear without reasonable excuse after having been:

1. Cited or summonsed as an accused
2. Lawfully set at liberty upon condition that he appear at a specified time, place, and court

#### b. Punishment

Failure to appear is a Class C felony if the required appearance was to answer a charge of felony or for disposition of any such charge.

Failure to appear is a Class A misdemeanor if the required appearance was to answer a charge of misdemeanor or for disposition of any such charge.

Failure to appear is a Class C misdemeanor if the required appearance was to answer a violation.

### (15.22) Tampering With A Public Record (§5-54-121)

#### a. Defining the Offense

A person commits *tampering with a public record* if, with the *purpose* of impairing the verity, legibility, or availability of a public record, he knowingly does *any* of the following:

- Makes a false entry in or falsely alters any public record.
- Erases, obliterates, removes, destroys, or conceals a public record.

#### b. Punishment

Tampering with a public record is a Class C felony if the public record is a court record.

Tampering with a public record is a Class B felony if the public record is a court record and the person broke into any building or structure with the intent of tampering with a court record located therein.

Otherwise, tampering with a public record is a Class D felony.

### (15.23) Filing a False Report with LE (§5-54-122)

#### a. Defining the Offense

A person commits *filing a false report* if he files a report with any law enforcement agency or prosecuting attorney's office of any alleged criminal wrongdoing on the part of another knowing that such report is false.

#### b. Punishment

Filing a false report is a Class D felony if *any* of the following is true:

- The crime is a capital offense, Class Y felony, Class A felony, or Class B felony.
- The agency or office to whom the report is made has expended in excess of five hundred dollars $500 in order to investigate said report, including the costs of labor.
- Physical injury results to any person as a result of the false report.
- The false report is made in an effort by the person filing said false report to conceal his own criminal activity.
- The false report results in another person being arrested.

Otherwise, filing a false report is a Class A misdemeanor.

### (15.24) Fleeing (5-54-125)

#### a. Defining the Offense

If a person knows that a law enforcement officer is attempting his immediate arrest or detention, it is the lawful duty of such person to refrain from fleeing.

#### b. Punishment

Fleeing on foot is a Class C misdemeanor, except under the following conditions:

1. If the defendant has been previously convicted of fleeing on foot anytime within the past one-year period, subsequent fleeing on foot offenses shall be Class B misdemeanors.

2. Where property damage occurs as a direct result of the fleeing on foot, the offense shall be a Class A misdemeanor.

3. Where serious physical injury occurs to any person as a direct result of the fleeing on foot, the offense shall be a Class D felony.

4. Fleeing by means of any vehicle or conveyance shall be considered a Class A misdemeanor.

5. Fleeing by means of any vehicle or conveyance shall be considered a Class D felony if, under circumstances manifesting extreme indifference to the value of human life, a person purposely operates the vehicle or conveyance in such a manner that creates a substantial danger of death or serious physical injury to another person or persons.

6. Where serious physical injury to any person occurs as a direct result of fleeing by means of any vehicle or conveyance, the offense shall be a Class C felony.

7. If the defendant is under the age of 21 and has not been previously convicted of fleeing, the offense is a Class C misdemeanor.

### (15.25) Killing LEO Animals (§5-54-126)

Any person who, without just cause, purposely kills or injures any animal owned by or used by a law enforcement agency or any search and rescue dog is guilty of a Class D felony.

### (15.26) Failure to Execute Process (§5-54-127)

If any LEO willfully and corruptly fails or refuses to execute any lawful process whatever, which by law it is his duty to execute, requiring the apprehension or confinement of any person charged with a criminal offense, whereby such person shall escape, the offending officer shall be punished in the same manner as persons aiding or assisting an escape.

### (15.27) Absconding (§5-54-131)

#### a. Defining the Offense

A person commits the offense of *absconding* if the person knowingly does *either* of the following:

- Leaves a designated residence while under house arrest ordered as a condition of the person's release on a criminal offense by a court of competent jurisdiction.
- Leaves a designated area while wearing an electronic monitoring device ordered as a condition of the person's release on a criminal offense by a court of competent jurisdiction or a sheriff or his designee.

#### b. Punishment

Absconding is a Class D felony[123].

### (15.28) Projecting a Laser Light on a LEO (§5-54-132)

#### a. Defining the Offense

This section makes it unlawful for any person to *knowingly* cause a laser light beam, colored light beam or other targeting, pointing, or spotting light beam to be projected, displayed or shined on a law enforcement officer while in the performance of his duties.

#### b. Punishment

A violation of this provision is a Class A misdemeanor.

---

[123] §5-54-131(b)

## (15.29) Abuse of a Corpse (§5-60-101)

### a. Defining the Offense

A person commits abuse of a corpse if, except as authorized by law, he knowingly does any of the following:

- Disinters, removes, dissects, or mutilates a corpse.
- Physically mistreats a corpse in a manner offensive to a person of reasonable sensibilities.

### b. Punishment

Abuse of a corpse is a Class D felony.

## (15.30) Misconduct on a Bus (§5-60-112)

### a. Defining the Offense

It is unlawful for any person to do any of the following while on a bus:

- Threaten a breach of the peace or use any obscene, profane, or vulgar language.
- Be under the influence of alcohol or the influence of a controlled substance.
- Ingest or have in his possession any controlled substance.
- Drink intoxicating liquor, except a chartered bus.
- Fail to obey a reasonable request or order of a bus driver or company representative.

If any person violates any above provision, the driver of the bus or person in charge may stop it at the place where the offense is committed or at the next convenient stopping place and require the person to leave the bus.

### b. Punishment

A violation of this provision is a Class C misdemeanor.

## (15.31) Using Abusive Language to a School Bus Driver (§5-60-113)

### a. Defining the Offense

This provision makes it unlawful for any person or persons to threaten, curse, or use abusive language to a school bus driver in the presence of students in this state.

### b. Punishment

A person who violates this provision is guilty of a misdemeanor, punishable by fine of not less than $25 nor more than $100.

## (15.32) Breathing Intoxicating Compounds (§5-60-116)

### a. Defining the Offense

No person shall breathe, inhale, or drink any compound, liquid, or chemical containing any gasoline or similar substance for the purpose of inducing a condition of intoxication, stupefaction, depression, giddiness, paralysis, or irrational behavior or in any manner changing, distorting, or disturbing the auditory, visual, or mental processes.

For the purposes of this section, any condition so induced shall be deemed an intoxicated condition.

This section does not apply to legitimate medical treatments.

### b. Punishment

Breathing intoxicating compounds is a misdemeanor and upon is subject to a fine of not less than $100 an no more than $200 or imprisonment for not less than 30 and no more than 6 months, or both fine and imprisonment.

## (15.33) Motion Pictures Shown on Sunday (§5-60-119)

This section makes it *lawful* to show motion pictures on Sunday for profit.

## (15.34) Interception and Recording (§6-60-120)

### a. Defining the Offense

This section makes it unlawful for a person to intercept any of the following types of communications:

- Wire
- Landline
- Oral
- Telephonic
- Or wireless communication

It also makes it an offense to record or possess a recording of such communication.

### b. Exceptions

An exception to this prohibition is that the person is a party to the communication or 1 of the parties to the communication has given prior consent to such interception and recording.

The prohibition does not apply to LEOs acting under color of law. In addition, it does not apply to communication company employees acting to aid LE.

The statute does not affect licensed radio operators or anyone operating a police scanner who is intercepting communications "for pleasure."

### c. Punishment

A violation of this section shall be a Class A misdemeanor.

## (15.35) Laser Lights – Minors (§§5-60-121, 122)

### a. Sale of Laser Light to Minor (§5-60-121)

This section makes it unlawful to sell a hand-held laser pointer to a person under 18 years of age.

Sale of a laser light to a minor is a violation and is punishable by a fine of $100.

### b. Possession of Laser Light by Minor (§5-60-122)

This section makes it unlawful for a person less than 18 years of age to possess a hand-held laser pointer without the supervision of a parent, guardian, or teacher. It also directs LEOs to finding minors in possession of such a device to seize the device as contraband.

### (15.36) Cruelty to Animals (§5-62-101)

#### a. Defining the Offense

A person commits the offense of *cruelty to animals* if, except as authorized by law, he or she *knowingly* does *any* of the following:

- Abandons any animal.
- Subjects any animal to cruel mistreatment.
- Subjects any animal in his or her custody to cruel neglect.
- Kills or injures any animal belonging to another without legal privilege or consent of the owner.

#### b. Punishment

Cruelty to animals is a Class A misdemeanor.

### (15.37) Prevention of Cruelty to Animals (§5-62-111)

This section provides authority for any officer, agent, or member of a society that is incorporated for the prevention of cruelty to animals to interfere to prevent the perpetration of any act of cruelty upon any animal in his presence.

Obstruction of a person acting under this section is an unclassified misdemeanor.

### (15.38) Authority to Take Charge of Animals (§5-62-114)

> **§ 5-62-114. Authority to Take Charge of Animals**
>
> When any person arrested is, at the time of arrest, in charge of any vehicle drawn by or containing any animal, any agent of a society for the prevention of cruelty to animals may take charge of the animal and the vehicle and its contents and deposit them in a safe place of custody, or deliver them into the possession of the police or sheriff of the county or place wherein the arrest was made, who shall thereupon assume the custody thereof.

### (15.39) Dog Fighting (§5-62-120)

#### a. Dog Fighting in the First

A person commits the offense of *unlawful dog fighting in the first degree* if he *knowingly* does *any* of the following:

- Promotes, engages in, or is employed at dog fighting.
- Receives money for the admission of another person to a place kept for dog fighting.
- Sells, purchases, possesses, or trains a dog for dog fighting.

Unlawful dog fighting in the first degree is a Class D felony.

#### b. Dog Fighting in the Second

A person commits the offense of *unlawful dog fighting in the second degree* if he *knowingly* does *any* of the following:

- Purchases a ticket of admission to or is present at a dog fight.
- Witnesses a dog fight if it is presented as a public spectacle.

Unlawful dog fighting in the second degree is a Class A misdemeanor.

*LEOs may seize all dogs in the custody of persons arrested under this section.*

### (15.40) Permitting Livestock to Run at Large (§5-62-122)

A person commits the offense of *permitting livestock to run at large* if being the owner or person charged with the custody and care of livestock he *knowingly* permits such livestock to run at large.

Unless the livestock in question is a hog, permitting livestock to run at large is a violation. Any person who allows any hog to run at large is guilty of a misdemeanor and upon conviction shall be subject to a fine not to exceed five hundred dollars $500.

### (15.42) Lottery (§5-66-118)

The AR courts have defined a lottery as "as a scheme for the distribution of prizes by chance among persons who have paid or agreed to pay a valuable consideration for the chance to obtain a prize."[124] Accordingly, "raffles" appear to count as lotteries for legal purposes.

It is unlawful for any person to do *any* of the following:

- Keep an office, room, or place for the sale or disposition of lottery, policy, and gift concert tickets or slips or like devices.
- Vend, sell, or otherwise dispose of any lottery, policy, or gift concert ticket, slip, or like device.
- Possess any lottery, policy, or gift concert ticket or slip or like device, except a lottery ticket issued in another state where a lottery is legal.
- Be interested either directly or indirectly in the sale or disposition of any lottery, policy, or gift concert ticket or slip or like device.

This section does not prohibit the printing or manufacture of lottery related products for use in otherwise legal lotteries, such as those of other states.

Contrary to popular belief, ***there is no exception for lotteries that benefit charitable organizations***[125].

#### b. Punishment

A violation if this section is a misdemeanor and is punishable by a fine not less than $50.00 and no more than $500.

### (15.43) Advertising Signs Generally (§5-67-101)

#### a. Defining the Offense

This section makes it unlawful for any persons, firms, or corporations to place any advertising signs on the highway right-of-way in this state, excepting signs placed under direction of the State Highway Commission.

#### b. Punishment

A violation of this section is a misdemeanor and is punishable by fine in any sum not less than $25.00 and not more than $100.

---

[124] *Burks v. Harris*, 91 Ark. 205, 120 S.W. 979 (1909)
[125] *State v. Bass*, 224 Ark. 976, 277 S.W.2d 479 (1955).

### (15.44) *False or Misleading Signs (§5-67-102)*

#### a. Defining the Offense

This section makes it unlawful for any person, firm, or corporation to erect or cause to be erected or maintained, on or within one hundred yards (100 yds.) of the right-of-way of any state highway, any sign or billboard which has:

- Words or figures calculated to cause the traveling public of this state or tourists from other states to abandon state highways and travel any public road to any town, city, or destination in this state.
- Words or figures which give to the traveling public any false or misleading information pertaining to the highways of this state.

#### b. Punishment

Any person, firm, or corporation violating the provisions of this section is guilty of a misdemeanor punishable by fine in any sum not less $25.00 and no more than $100.

### (15.45) *Violation of Posted Bridge Prohibitions (§5-67-104)*

#### a. Defining the Offense

This section makes it unlawful for any person owning or operating a motor vehicle which in any way exceeds or violates any properly posted limitations, regulations, or restrictions governing the use of a bridge to use the bridge as long as such use violates any of the posted prohibitions.

#### b. Punishment

*Violation of Posted Bridge Prohibitions* is a misdemeanor punishable by fine of not more than $200.

The person is liable for the costs to restore the damage and injury to the structure.

### (15.46) *Use of Spotlights (§5-67-106)*

#### a. Defining the Offense

This section makes it unlawful to use a spotlight from any public road, street, or highway except for use by any of the following persons:

- A law enforcement officer, game and fish officer, emergency service worker, or utility company employee in the performance of his duties.
- A person or his employee to examine real or personal property or livestock owned or rented by the person.
- A person to assist in the repair or removal of a motor vehicle or other property.

*This section does not apply within the boundaries of a city of the first class or a city of the second class.*

#### b. Punishment

A violation of this section shall be a Class C misdemeanor.

### (15.47) *Solicitation on a Highway (§5-67-107)*

#### a. Defining the Offense

It is unlawful for any person to solicit a donation or offer to sell any item or service in any of the following places:

- On a state highway.
- Within ten feet of a state highway, if there is not a sidewalk along the highway.
- Between the highway and a sidewalk, if there is a sidewalk within ten feet (10') of the highway.

### b. Punishment

A violation of this section is a Class C misdemeanor.

### (15.48) Exhibition of Obscene Figures (§5-68-201)

### a. Defining the Offense

This section makes it unlawful for a person publicly exhibiting any obscene figures.

### b. Punishment

A violation of this section is a misdemeanor punishable by fine of $50.

### (15.49) Literature Rejected by the U.S. Mail (§5-68-202)

---

**§ 5-68-202. Sale or possession of literature rejected by U.S. mails**

(a) It shall be unlawful for any person, firm, or corporation to sell or to offer for sale, or to have in possession, any magazine, paper, or other literature or printed book, picture, or matter, the shipment or transportation of which has been refused and rejected from the United States mails, or which literature or literature of like character the Government of the United States will not permit to be sold, shipped, or handled.

(b) Any violation of the provisions of this section shall constitute a misdemeanor and, upon conviction, shall subject the offender to a fine of any sum not less than fifty dollars ($ 50.00) nor more than one hundred dollars ($ 100), and each day that this section shall be violated shall constitute a separate offense.

---

### (15.50) Obscene Films (§5-68-203)

### a. Defining the Offense

It is unlawful for any person *knowingly* to exhibit, sell, offer to sell, give away, circulate, produce, distribute, attempt to distribute, or have in his possession any obscene film.

### b. Punishment

A violation of this section, *other than mere possession*, is a felony and is punishable by fine not more than $2,000 or be imprisonment for a period not less than 1 year and no more than 5 years, or be both. Mere possession on an obscene film is a misdemeanor punishable by a fine of no more than $1,000 or imprisonment in the county jail for a period not to exceed 1 year, or both.

> **§ 5-68-203(b)**
>
> (b) As used in this section:
>
> (1) "Person" means any individual, partnership, firm, association, club, corporation, or other legal entity;
>
> (2) "Obscene" means that to the average person, applying contemporary community standards, the dominant theme of the material taken as a whole appeals to prurient interest;
>
> (3) "Film" means motion picture film, still picture film, slides, and movie film of any type.

## (15.51) Nudism (§5-68-204)

### a. Defining the Offense

This section makes the following acts unlawful:

- For any person, club, camp, corporation, partnership, association, or organization to advocate, demonstrate, or promote nudism.
- For any person to rent, lease, or otherwise permit his land, premises, or buildings to be used for the purpose of advocating, demonstrating, or promoting nudism.

**Nudism** is defined to be the act or acts of a person or persons congregating or gathering with his, her, or their private parts exposed in the presence of 1 or more persons of the opposite sex as a form of social practice.

### b. Punishment

A violation of this section a misdemeanor and upon punishable by a fine not less than $50.00 and not more than $1,000 or imprisoned for not less than 30 days and not more than 6 months, or both.

### c. Exceptions

This section does not apply to these acts when:

- The purpose of the person committing the act or acts is to render medical or surgical treatment by a licensed doctor or nurse.
- When the persons are married legally one to another.

## (15.52) Public Display of Obscenity (§5-68-205)

### a. Defining the Offense

A person commits the offense of *publicly displaying an obscenity* when the person *knowingly* causes an obscenity to be displayed in a manner that is readily visible to the public and its content or character is distinguishable by normal vision.

For this section, **obscenity** means an obscene sticker, painting, decal, emblem, or other device which is or contains an obscene writing, description, photograph, or depiction.

### b. Punishment

Publicly displaying an obscenity is a Class B misdemeanor.

This section makes it unlawful to publicly display obscene material on any motor vehicle or wearing apparel, which is a Class C Misdemeanor.

## (15.53) Obscenity Definitions (§5-68-302)

### § 5-68-302. Definitions

(1) "Advertising purposes" means purpose of propagandizing in connection with the commercial sale of a product or type of product, the commercial offering of a service, or the commercial exhibition of an entertainment;

(2) "Hard-core sexual conduct" means patently offensive acts, exhibitions, representations, depictions, or descriptions of:

(A) Intrusions, however slight, actual or simulated, by any object, any part of an animal's body, or any part of a person's body into the genital or anal openings of any person's body; or
(B) Cunnilingus, fellatio, anilingus, bestiality, lewd exhibitions of genitals, or excretory functions, actual or simulated;

(3) "Live public show" means a public show in which human beings, animals, or both appear bodily before spectators or customers;

(4) "Obscene material" means that material which:

(A) Depicts or describes in a patently offensive manner sadomasochistic abuse, sexual conduct, or hard-core sexual conduct;
(B) Taken as a whole, appeals to the prurient interest of the average person, applying contemporary statewide standards; and
(C) Taken as a whole, lacks serious literary, artistic, political, or scientific value;

(5) "Obscene performance" means a play, motion picture, dance, show, or other presentation, whether pictured, animated, or live, performed before an audience and which in whole or in part depicts, or reveals, sexual conduct, hard-core sexual conduct, or sadomasochistic abuse, or which includes explicit verbal descriptions or narrative accounts of sexual conduct or hard-core sexual conduct, and which:

(A) Depicts or describes in a patently offensive manner, sadomasochistic abuse, sexual conduct, or hard-core sexual conduct;
(B) Taken as a whole, appeals to the prurient interest of the average person, applying contemporary statewide standards; and
(C) Taken as a whole, lacks serious literary, artistic, political, or scientific value;

(6) "Promote" means to produce, direct, perform in, manufacture, issue, sell, give, provide, lend, mail, deliver, transfer, publish, distribute, circulate, disseminate, present, exhibit, or advertise, for consideration, or to offer or agree to do any of these things for consideration;

(7) "Public show" means any entertainment or exhibition advertised or in some other fashion held out to be accessible to the public or member of a club, regardless of whether an admission or other charge is levied or collected and regardless of whether minors are admitted or excluded;

(8) "Sadomasochistic abuse" means flagellation, mutilation, or torture by or upon a person who is nude or clad in undergarments or in revealing or bizarre costume, or the condition of being fettered, bound, or otherwise physically restrained on the part of one so clothed, in a sexual context;

(9) "Sexual conduct" means human masturbation or sexual intercourse.

## (15.54) Promoting Obscene Materials (§5-68-303)

### a. Defining the Offense

A person commits *promoting obscene materials*[126] if he knowingly promotes, or has in his possession with intent to promote, any obscene material.

### b. Punishment

Promoting obscene materials is a Class D felony.

## (15.55) Promoting Obscene Performances (§5-68-304)

### a. Defining the Offense

A person commits *promoting an obscene performance* if he or she knowingly does *any* of the following:

- Directs, manages, finances, or presents an obscene performance.

---

[126] Except as otherwise provided in § 5-68-308

- Promotes any obscene performance, as owner, producer, director, manager, or performer.

### b. Punishment

Promoting an obscene performance is a Class D felony.

### (15.56) Obscene Performance at a Live Public Show (§5-68-305)

#### a. Defining the Offense

A person commits an *obscene performance at a live public show* if he *knowingly* does *any* of the following:

- Engages in an obscene performance of sadomasochistic abuse, hard-core sexual conduct, or sexual conduct in a live public show.
- Directs, manages, finances, or presents an obscene performance at a live public show in which the participants engage in sadomasochistic abuse, hard-core sexual conduct, or sexual conduct.

#### b. Punishment

Committing an obscene performance at a live public show is a Class C felony.

### (15.57) Public Display of Hard Core Sexual Conduct (§5-68-307)

#### a. Defining the Offense

A person commits a *public display of hard-core sexual conduct* if he knowingly engages in hard-core sexual conduct in an open public place.

#### b. Punishment

Engaging in hard-core sexual conduct in an open public place is a Class D felony.

### (15.58) Selling or Loaning Pornography to Minors (§5-68-502)

#### a. Defining the Offense

This section makes it unlawful for any person to *knowingly* do *any* of the following:

- Display material which is harmful to minors in such a way that minors, as a part of the invited general public, will be exposed to view such material.
- Sell, furnish, present, distribute, allow to view, or otherwise disseminate to a minor, with or without consideration, any material which is harmful to minors.
- Present to a minor or participate in presenting to a minor, with or without consideration, any performance which is harmful to a minor.

A person *does not* displayed material harmful to minors if the lower two-thirds of the material is not exposed to view and segregated in a manner that physically prohibits access to the material by minors.

#### b. Punishment

A violation of this section is a misdemeanor punishable by a fine of not less than $100 and not more than five hundred dollars $500 or imprisonment of not less than 3 months and no more than 6 months, or both[127]

---

[127] §5-68-503

*(15.59) Prostitution (§5-70-102)*

### a. Defining the Offense

A person commits *prostitution* if in return for or in expectation of a fee he or she engages in or agrees or offers to engage in sexual activity with any other person.

### b. Punishment

Prostitution is a Class B misdemeanor for the first offense and a Class A misdemeanor for second and subsequent offenses.

*(15.60) Patronizing a Prostitute (§5-70-103)*

### a. Defining the Offense

A person commits the offense of *patronizing a prostitute* if he or she pays or agrees to pay a fee to another person on an understanding that in return that person or a third person will engage in sexual activity with him or her or solicits or requests another person to engage in sexual activity with him or her in return for a fee.

### b. Punishment

Patronizing a prostitute is a Class B misdemeanor for the first offense and a Class A misdemeanor for second and subsequent offenses.

*(15.61) Promoting Prostitution (5-70-104, 105, 106)*

### a. Promoting Prostitution in the First (§5-70-104)

A person commits the offense of *promoting prostitution in the first degree* if he *knowingly* does *either* of the following:

- Advances prostitution by compelling a person by physical force or intimidation to engage in prostitution, or profits from such coercive conduct by another.
- Advances prostitution, or profits from prostitution, of a person less than 18 years old.

Promoting prostitution in the first degree is a Class D felony.

### b. Promoting Prostitution in the Second (§5-70-105)

A person commits the offense of promoting prostitution in the second degree if he knowingly advances prostitution or profits from prostitution by managing, supervising, controlling, or owning, either alone or in association with others, a house of prostitution or a prostitution enterprise involving 2 or more prostitutes.

Promoting prostitution in the second degree is a Class A misdemeanor.

### c. Promoting Prostitution in the Third (§5-70-106)

A person commits the offense of *promoting prostitution in the third degree* if he or she does *either* of the following:

- Having a possessory or proprietary interest in premises that he knows are being used for prostitution, he fails to make reasonable effort to halt or abate such use.
- He knowingly advances prostitution or profits from prostitution.

Promoting prostitution in the third degree is a Class B misdemeanor.

## (15.62) Riot (§5-71-201)

### a. Defining the Offense

A person commits the offense of riot if, with 2 or more other persons, he *knowingly* engages in tumultuous or violent conduct that creates a substantial risk of *any* of the following:

- Causing public alarm.
- Disrupting the performance of a governmental function.
- Damaging or injuring property or persons.

### b. Punishment

Riot is a Class A misdemeanor.

## (15.63) Aggravated Riot (§5-71-202)

### a. Defining the Offense

A person commits the offense of *aggravated riot* if he commits the offense of riot when he or she *knowingly* possesses a deadly weapon and *knows* that others involved also possess a deadly weapon.

### b. Punishment

Aggravated riot is a Class D felony.

## (15.64) Unlawful Assembly (§5-71-205)

### a. Defining the Offense

A person commits the offense of *unlawful assembly* if he assembles with 2 or more other persons, and he has the purpose of engaging in conduct constituting a riot.

### b. Punishment

Unlawful assembly is a Class C misdemeanor.

## (15.65) Failure to Disperse (§5-71-206)

### a. Defining the Offense

A person commits the offense of *failure to disperse* if, during a riot or an unlawful assembly, he refuses or *knowingly* fails to disperse when ordered to do so by a law enforcement officer or other person engaged in enforcing or executing the law.

### b. Defense

It is a defense to a prosecution under this section that the actor was a news reporter or other person observing or recording the events on behalf of the news media not knowingly obstructing efforts by a law enforcement officer or other person engaged in enforcing or executing the law to control or abate the riot or unlawful assembly.

### c. Punishment

Failure to disperse is a Class C misdemeanor.

*(15.66) Disorderly Conduct (§5-71-207)*

### a. Defining the Offense

A person commits the offense of *disorderly conduct* if, with the purpose to cause public inconvenience, annoyance, or alarm or recklessly creating a risk thereof, he or she does *any* of the following:

- Engages in fighting or in violent, threatening, or tumultuous behavior.
- Makes unreasonable or excessive noise.
- In a public place, uses abusive or obscene language, or makes an obscene gesture, in a manner likely to provoke a violent or disorderly response.
- Disrupts or disturbs any lawful assembly or meeting of persons.
- Obstructs vehicular or pedestrian traffic.
- Congregates with 2 other persons in a public place and refuses to comply with a lawful order to disperse of a law enforcement officer or other person engaged in enforcing or executing the law.
- Creates a hazardous or physically offensive condition.
- In a public place, mars, defiles, desecrates, or otherwise damages a patriotic or religious symbol that is an object of respect by the public or a substantial segment thereof.
- In a public place, exposes his private parts.

### b. Punishment

Disorderly conduct is a Class C misdemeanor.

*(15.67) Harassment (§5-71-208)*

### a. Defining the Offense

A person commits the offense of *harassment* if, with *purpose* to harass, annoy, or alarm another person, without good cause, he or she does *any* of the following:

- Strikes, shoves, kicks, or otherwise touches a person, subjects him to offensive physical contact or attempts or threatens to do so.
- In a public place, directs obscene language or makes an obscene gesture to or at another person in a manner likely to provoke a violent or disorderly response.
- Follows a person in or about a public place.
- In a public place repeatedly insults, taunts, or challenges another in a manner likely to provoke a violent or disorderly response.
- Engages in conduct or repeatedly commits acts that alarm or seriously annoy another person and that serve no legitimate purpose.
- Places the person under surveillance by remaining present outside his or her school, place of employment, vehicle, other place occupied by the person, or residence, other than the residence of the defendant, for no purpose other than to harass, alarm, or annoy.

### b. Punishment

Harassment is a Class A misdemeanor.

*(15.68) Harassing Communication (§5-71-209)*

### a. Defining the Offense

A person commits the offense of *harassing communications* if, with the *purpose* to harass, annoy, or alarm another person, he or she does *any* of the following:

- Communicates with a person, anonymously or otherwise, by telephone, telegraph, mail, or any other form of written communication, in a manner likely to harass, annoy, or cause alarm.
- Makes a telephone call or causes a telephone to ring repeatedly, with no purpose of legitimate communication, regardless of whether a conversation ensues.
- Knowingly permits any telephone under his control to be used for any purpose prohibited by this section.

### b. Punishment

Harassing communications is a Class A misdemeanor.

### c. Jurisdiction

Offenses involving use of telephones may be prosecuted in the county in which the defendant was located when he used a telephone, or in the county in which the telephone made to ring by the defendant was located.

### (15.69) Communicating a False Alarm (5-71-210)

#### a. Defining the Offense

A person commits the offense of *communicating a false alarm* if he or she *purposely* initiates or circulates a report of a present, past, or impending bombing, fire, offense, catastrophe, or other emergency while knowing that the report is false or baseless and knowing that it is likely to do *any* of the following:

- To cause action of any sort by an official or volunteer agency organized to deal with emergencies.
- To place any person in fear of physical injury to himself or herself or another person or of damage to his or her property or that of another person.
- To cause total or partial evacuation of any occupiable structure, vehicle, or vital public facility.

#### b. Punishment

- Communicating a false alarm is a Class C felony if physical injury to a person results.
- Communicating a false alarm is a Class D felony if it results in damage to property or the false alarm communicates a present or impending bombing and is made to or about a public or private educational institution.
- If there is no resulting physical injury or damage to property, communicating a false alarm is a Class A misdemeanor.

A second or subsequent offense that would otherwise be a Class A misdemeanor is a Class D felony.

### (15.70) Threatening A Fire or Bomb (§5-71-211)

#### a. Defining the Offense

A person commits the offense of *threatening a fire or bombing* if he *purposely* threatens damage or injury to the person or property of another by bombing, fire, or other means, in a manner likely to place another person in reasonable apprehension of physical injury to himself or another or of damage to his property or to the property of another, or to create public alarm.

#### b. Punishment

Threatening a fire or bombing is a Class D felony if physical injury to a person results. Otherwise, it is a Class A misdemeanor.

### (15.71) Public Intoxication – Drinking in Public (§5-71-212)

#### a. Defining the Offenses

A person commits the offense of *public intoxication* if he appears in a public place manifestly under the influence of alcohol or a controlled substance to the degree and under circumstances such that he is likely to endanger himself or other persons or property, or that he unreasonably annoys persons in his vicinity.

A person commits the offense of *drinking in public* if that person consumes any alcoholic beverages in any public place, on any highway, or street, or upon any passenger coach, streetcar, or in or upon any vehicle commonly used for the transportation of passengers, or in or about any depot, platform, waiting station or room, or other public place other than a place of business licensed to sell alcoholic beverages for consumption on the premises.

#### b. Punishment

Public intoxication and drinking in public are both Class C misdemeanors.

#### c. Exception

The provisions of this section do not prohibit or restrict the consumption of alcoholic beverages when consumed as a part of a recognized religious ceremony or ritual.

### (15.72) Loitering (§5-71-213)

A person commits the offense of *loitering* if he or she does *any* of the following:

- Lingers, remains, or prowls in a public place or the premises of another without apparent reason and under circumstances that warrant alarm or concern for the safety of persons or property in the vicinity and, upon inquiry by a law enforcement officer, refuses to identify himself and give a reasonably credible account of his presence and purpose.
- Lingers, remains, or prowls in or near a school building, not having any reason or relationship involving custody of or responsibility for a student and not having written permission from anyone authorized to grant permission.
- Lingers or remains in a public place or on the premises of another for the purpose of begging.
- Lingers or remains in a public place for the purpose of unlawful gambling.
- Lingers or remains in a public place for the purpose of engaging or soliciting another person to engage in prostitution or deviate sexual activity.
- Lingers or remains in a public place for the purpose of unlawfully buying, distributing, or using a controlled substance.
- Lingers or remains in a public place for the purpose of unlawfully buying, distributing, or consuming an alcoholic beverage.
- Lingers or remains on or about the premises of another for the purpose of spying upon or invading the privacy of another.
- Lingers or remains on or about the premises of any off-site customer-bank communication terminal without any legitimate purpose.

#### b. Circumstantial Evidence

Among the circumstances that may be considered in determining whether a person is loitering are that the person:

1. Takes flight upon the appearance of a law enforcement officer.
2. Refuses to identify himself.
3. Manifestly endeavors to conceal himself or any object.

### c. LE Requirements

Unless flight by the actor or other circumstances make it impracticable, a LEO must, prior to an arrest for an offense under this section, afford the actor an opportunity to dispel any alarm that would otherwise be warranted by requesting him to identify himself and explain his presence and conduct.

It is a defense to a prosecution under this section that the law enforcement officer did not afford the defendant an opportunity to identify himself and explain his presence and conduct or if it appears at trial that an explanation given by the defendant to the officer was true and, if believed by the officer at that time, would have dispelled the alarm.

### d. Punishment

Loitering is a Class C misdemeanor.

## (15.73) Obstruction of a Highway (§5-71-214)

### a. Defining the Offense

A person commits the offense of *obstructing a highway* or other public passage if, having no legal privilege to do so and acting alone or with other persons, he renders any highway or other public passage impassable to pedestrian or vehicular traffic.

### b. Punishment

Obstructing a highway or other public passage is a Class C misdemeanor.

## (15.74) Defacing Objects of Public Respect (§5-71-215)

### a. Defining the Offense

A person commits the offense of *defacing objects of public respect* if he or she purposely does *any* of the following:

- Defaces, mars, or otherwise damages any public monument.
- Defaces, mars, or otherwise damages a work of art on display in any public place.
- Defaces, mars, desecrates, or otherwise damages any place of worship, cemetery, or burial monument.

### b. Punishment

- Defacing objects of public respect is a Class A misdemeanor if the value of repairing or replacing the damaged objects does not exceed $500.
- Defacing objects of public respect is a Class D felony if the value of repairing or replacing the damaged objects exceeds $500, but does not exceed $2,500.
- Defacing objects of public respect is a Class C felony if the value of repairing or replacing the damaged objects exceeds $2,500.

## (15.75) Defacing Public Buildings (§5-71-216)

### a. Defining the Offense

A person commits the offense of *defacing a public building* if he or she *purposely* defaces, mars, or otherwise damages a public building.

### b. Punishment

Defacing a public building is a Class A misdemeanor.

*(15.76) Picketing Before a Private Residence (§5-71-225)*

### a. Defining the Offense

It is unlawful for any person to engage in demonstrations of any type or picketing before or about any residence or dwelling place of any individual.

### c. Punishment

This offense is punishable by fine of not more than $200, imprisonment for not more than 6 months, or both.

*(15.77) Disrupting Campus Activities (§5-71-226)*

### a. Defining the Offense

It is unlawful for any group composed 2 or more persons to act jointly with one another, or attempt any action in conjunction with one another to do *any* of the following at the public, private, or parochial schools and colleges of this state:

- Obstruct or bar any hallway or door of any campus building or facility.
- Seize control of buildings or campus facilities.
- Prevent the meeting of or cause the disruption of any classes.
- Erect any type of barricades aimed at obstructing the orderly passage of persons or vehicles onto or off of campus grounds.

### b. Punishment

A violation of this section is a misdemeanor punishable by a fine of not less $200 or imprisonment in the county jail for a period of not less than 6 months, or both.

*Nothing in this section applies to the activities of any labor organization or teachers' organization.*

*(15.78) Obstructing Sporting Devices (§5-71-228)*

### a. Defining the Offense

It is unlawful for any person to willfully obstruct or impede the participation of any individual in the lawful activity of shooting, hunting, fishing, or trapping.

### b. Punishment

A violation of this section is a misdemeanor punishable by a fine of not less than $100 and no more than $500, or imprisonment for a period not to exceed 30 days, or both.

If such person holds an Arkansas hunting, fishing, or trapping license at the time of conviction, such license shall be revoked.

*Nothing in this section shall prohibit a landowner or lessee from exercising his or her lawful right to prohibit hunting, fishing, or trapping on his or her land, or from exercising any other legal right.*

*(15.79) Stalking (§5-71-229)*

### a. Stalking on the First Degree

A person commits *stalking in the first degree* if he purposely engages in a course of conduct that harasses another person and makes a terroristic threat with the intent of placing that person in imminent fear of death or serious bodily injury or placing that person in imminent fear of the death or serious bodily injury of his or her immediate family and he or she does any of the following:

- Does so in violation of *any* other order issued by any court protecting the same victim or victims
- Has been convicted within the previous 10 years of any of the following:
    - Stalking in the second degree
    - Terroristic threatening[128]
    - Terroristic act[129]
    - Stalking or threats against another person's safety under the statutory provisions of any other state jurisdiction
- Is armed with a deadly weapon or represents by word or conduct that he is so armed

### b. Stalking in the Second Degree

A person commits *stalking in the second degree* if he or she purposely engages in a course of conduct that harasses another person and makes a terroristic threat with the intent of placing that person in imminent fear of death or serious bodily injury or placing that person in imminent fear of the death or serious bodily injury of his or her immediate family.

### c. Definitions

**Course of conduct** means a pattern of conduct composed of 2 or more acts separated by at least 36 hours, but occurring within 1 year. (Constitutionally protected activity is not included within the meaning of "course of conduct".)

**Harasses** means acts of harassment as defined by § 5-71-208.

**Immediate family** means any spouse, parent, child, any person related by consanguinity or affinity within the second degree, or any other person who regularly resides in the household or who, within the prior 6 months, regularly resided in the household.

### d. Punishment

Stalking in the first degree is a Class B felony.
Stalking in the second degree is a Class C felony.

*For both degrees of stalking, the judge will issue a no contact order.*

### (15.80) *Possessing Instruments of Crime (§5-73-102)*

### a. Defining the Offense

A person commits the offense of *possessing an instrument of crime* if he possesses any instrument of crime with a purpose to employ it criminally.

### b. Punishment

Possessing an instrument of crime is a Class A misdemeanor.

---

[128] §5-13-301
[129] §5-13-310

*(15.81) Possession of Firearms by Certain Persons (§5-73-103)*

### a. Defining the Offense

No person[130] shall possess or own any firearm who has been:

- Convicted of a felony.
- Adjudicated mentally ill.
- Committed involuntarily to any mental institution.

### b. Punishment

A person who violates this section commits a Class B felony if any of the following apply:

- He or she has a prior violent felony conviction.
- His or her current possession of a firearm involves the commission of another crime.
- He or she has been previously convicted under this section or a similar provision from another jurisdiction.

A person who violates this section commits a Class D felony, if he or she has been previously convicted of a felony and his or her present conduct or the prior felony conviction does not fall within the Class B felony description above.

Otherwise, he or she commits a Class A misdemeanor.

*(15.82) Criminal Use of Prohibited Weapons (§5-73-104)*

### a. Defining the Offense

A person commits the offense of *criminal use of prohibited weapons* if, except as authorized by law, he uses, possesses, makes, repairs, sells, or otherwise deals in any bomb, machine gun, sawed-off shotgun or rifle, firearm specially made or specially adapted for silent discharge, metal knuckles, or other implement for the infliction of serious physical injury or death which serves no common lawful purpose.

### b. Punishment

Criminal use of prohibited weapons is a Class B felony if the weapon is a bomb, machine gun, or firearm specially made or specially adapted for silent discharge. Otherwise, it is a Class D felony.

### c. Defenses

The statute provides 2 defenses to prosecution under this section:

1. The person was a law enforcement officer, prison guard, or member of the armed forces acting in the course and scope of his duty at the time he used or possessed the prohibited weapon
2. The defendant used, possessed, made, repaired, sold, or otherwise dealt in any of the above enumerated articles under circumstances negating any likelihood that the weapon could be used unlawfully.

*(15.83) Defacing a Firearm (§5-73-106, 107)*

### a. Defacing a Firearm

A person commits the offense of *defacing a firearm* when he knowingly removes, defaces, mars, covers, alters, or destroys the manufacturer's serial number or identification mark of a firearm.

---

[130] There are several rare instances, such as a pardon by the Governor, that will allow specific persons immunity to this statute.

### b. Possession of a Defaced Firearm

A person commits the offense of *possession of a defaced firearm* if he knowingly possesses a firearm with a manufacturer's serial number or other identification mark required by law which has been removed, defaced, marred, altered, or destroyed.

### c. Defense

It is a defense to a prosecution under this section that the person reported such possession to the police or other governmental agency prior to arrest or the issuance of an arrest warrant or summons.

### d. Punishment

Defacing a firearm is a Class D felony.

Possession of a defaced firearm is a Class D felony.

If the manufacturer's serial number or other identification mark required by law is merely covered or obstructed, but still retrievable, then possession of a defaced firearm is a Class A misdemeanor.

## (15.84) *Criminal Possession of Explosives (§5-73-108)*

### a. Defining the Offense

A person commits the offense of *criminal possession of explosives* when he or she sells, possesses, manufactures, or transports an explosive substance or incendiary device under any of the following conditions:

- If he has the *purpose* of using that substance or device to commit an offense.
- If he *knows* or *should know* that some other person intends to use that substance or device to commit an offense.

### b. Punishment

Criminal possession of explosives is a Class B felony.

## (15.85) *Furnishing a Deadly Weapon to a Minor (§5-73-109)*

### a. Defining the Offense

A person commits the offense of *furnishing a deadly weapon to a minor* when he sells, barters, leases, gives, rents, or otherwise furnishes a firearm or other deadly weapon to a minor without the consent of a parent, guardian, or other person responsible for general supervision of his welfare.

### b. Punishment

Furnishing a deadly weapon to a minor is a Class A misdemeanor.
This offense is a Class B felony of the weapon is any of the following:

- A handgun
- A sawed-off or short-barrelled shotgun, as defined in § 5-1-102(21)[131]
- A sawed-off or short-barrelled rifle, as defined in § 5-1-102(22)[132]

---

[131] "Sawed-off or short-barrelled shotgun" means a shotgun having 1 or more barrels less than eighteen inches (18") in length and any weapon made from a shotgun, whether by alteration, modification, or otherwise, if such weapon, as modified, has an overall length of less than twenty-six inches (26");

- A firearm that has been specially made or specially adapted for silent discharge
- A machine gun
- An explosive or incendiary device, as defined in § 5-71-301
- Metal knuckles
- A defaced firearm, as defined in § 5-73-107 (**15.83**)
- Other implement for the infliction of serious physical injury or death that serves no common lawful purpose

---

**§ 5-71-301. Definitions**

(2) "Explosive or incendiary device" includes:
  (A) Dynamite and all other forms of high explosives;
  (B) Any explosive bomb, grenade, missile, or similar device;
  (C) Explosive materials, meaning:
    (i) Explosives;
    (ii) Blasting agents; and
    (iii) Detonators; and
  (D) Any incendiary bomb or grenade, fire bomb, or similar device, and including any device which consists of or includes a breakable container containing a flammable liquid or compound and a wick composed of any material which, when ignited, is capable of igniting such flammable liquid or compound, and can be carried or thrown by one (1) individual acting alone. . .

---

### *(15.86) Disarming Minors and Irresponsible Persons (§5-73-110)*

#### a. Seizure Authority of LE

Subject to constitutional limitation, nothing in this section shall be construed to prohibit a law enforcement officer from disarming, without arresting, a minor or person who reasonably appears to be mentally defective or otherwise mentally irresponsible, when that person is in possession of a deadly weapon.

#### b. Disposition of Seized Property

Property seized pursuant to this section may be:

- Returned to the parent, guardian, or other person entrusted with care and supervision of the person so disarmed; or
- Delivered to the custody of a court having jurisdiction to try criminal offenses.

### *(15.87) Handgun Possession by a Minor or at Schools (§5-73-119)*

#### a. Defining the Offense

It is unlawful for any person under the age of 18 to possess a handgun[133].

*No person* in this state shall possess a firearm in any of the following places:

- Upon the developed property of the public or private schools, K-12.
- In or upon any school bus.

---

[132] "Sawed-off or short-barrelled rifle" means a rifle having one (1) or more barrels less than sixteen inches (16") in length and any weapon made from a rifle, whether by alteration, modification, or otherwise, if such weapon, as modified, has an overall length of less than twenty-six inches (26").

[133] A "handgun" is a firearm, capable of firing rimfire ammunition or centerfire ammunition, which is designed or constructed to be fired with one (1) hand.

- At a designated bus stop as identified on the route lists published by school districts each year.

It is unlawful for *any person* to possess a handgun upon the property of any private institution of higher education or the publicly supported institutions of higher education in this state on or about his person, in a vehicle occupied by him, or otherwise readily available for use with a purpose to employ it as a weapon against a person.

The above section does not apply in its broadest sense to persons who can show valid concealed carry permits. According to the attorney general's office, a

> concealed handgun permit carrier may carry a handgun onto a college or university campus if the licensed carrier does not carry the handgun into any college or university "event" (whether the event is held inside a campus building or not), and if the carrier does not carry the handgun into any of the campus buildings. However, if the institution in question has elected to prohibit the carrying of concealed handguns into its property by the posting of signs to that effect, no handguns may be carried in any property of the institution, even by licensed handgun carriers. (It should be noted that these conclusions do apply to situations in which the handgun carrier is attending a firearms-related activity.)[134]

### b. Defenses

The statute offers 10 defenses for the possession of a handgun in a prohibited place:

1. The person is in his or her own dwelling or place of business or on property in which he or she has a possessory or proprietary interest.
2. The person is a law enforcement officer, prison guard, or member of the armed forces acting in the course and scope of his or her official duties.
3. The person is assisting a law enforcement officer, prison guard, or member of the armed forces acting in the course and scope of his or her official duties pursuant to the direction or request of the law enforcement officer, prison guard, or member of the armed forces.
4. The person is a licensed security guard acting in the course and scope of his or her duties.
5. The person is hunting game with a handgun or firearm which may be hunted with a handgun or firearm under the rules and regulations of the Arkansas State Game and Fish Commission or is en route to or from a hunting area for the purpose of hunting game with a handgun or firearm.
6. The person is a certified law enforcement officer.
7. The person is on a journey, unless the person is 18 years old or less.
8. The person is participating in a certified hunting safety course sponsored by the commission or a firearm safety course recognized and approved by the commission or by a state or national nonprofit organization qualified and experienced in firearm safety.
9. The person is participating in a school-approved educational course or sporting activity involving the use of firearms.
10. The person is a minor engaged in lawful marksmanship competition or practice or other lawful recreational shooting under the supervision of his parent, legal guardian, or other person 21 years of age or older standing in loco parentis or is traveling to or from this activity with an unloaded handgun or firearm accompanied by his parent, legal guardian, or other person 21 years of age or older standing in loco parentis.

### b. Punishment

Generally, possession of a handgun by a minor is a Class A misdemeanor.

---

[134] Opinion No. 2003-372 (2003 Ark. AG LEXIS 407)

Possession of a handgun by a minor is a Class D felony if the person has previously:

- Been adjudicated delinquent for a violation of this section
- Been adjudicated delinquent for any offense which would be a felony if committed by an adult
- Pleaded guilty or nolo contendere to, or been found guilty of, a felony in circuit court while under the age of 18 years.

Possession of a firearm in prohibited places as described above is a Class D felony.

### (15.88) Carrying a Weapon (§5-73-120)

#### a. Defining the Offense

A person commits the offense of *carrying a weapon* if he possesses a handgun, knife, or club on or about his person, in a vehicle occupied by him, or otherwise readily available for use with a purpose to employ it as a weapon against a person.

#### b. Definitions

As used in this section, unless the context otherwise requires:

**Handgun** means any firearm with a barrel length of less than twelve inches (12") that is designed, made, or adapted to be fired with one (1) hand.

**Knife** means any bladed hand instrument that is capable of inflicting serious physical injury or death by cutting or stabbing. It includes a dirk, sword or spear in a cane, razor, ice pick, and a throwing star, switchblade, and butterfly knife.

**Club** means any instrument that is specially designed, made, or adapted for the purpose of inflicting serious physical injury or death by striking, including a blackjack, billie, and sap.

#### c. Defenses

It is a defense to a prosecution under this section that at the time of the act of carrying a weapon:

- The person is in his or her own dwelling, place of business, or on property in which he or she has a possessory or proprietary interest.
- The person is a law enforcement officer, prison guard, or member of the armed forces acting in the course and scope of his or her official duties.
- The person is assisting a law enforcement officer, prison guard, or member of the armed forces acting in the course and scope of official duties pursuant to the direction or request of the law enforcement officer, prison guard, or member of the armed forces.
- The person is carrying a weapon when upon a journey, unless the journey is through a commercial airport when presenting at the security checkpoint in the airport or is in the person's checked baggage and is not a lawfully declared weapon.
- The person is a licensed security guard acting in the course and scope of his or her duties.
- The person is hunting game with a handgun which may be hunted with a handgun under rules and regulations of the Arkansas State Game and Fish Commission or is en route to or from a hunting area for the purpose of hunting game with a handgun.
- The person is a certified law enforcement officer.
- The person is in a motor vehicle and the person has a license to carry a concealed weapon pursuant to § 5-73-301[135].

---

[135] The Concealed Handgun License Laws

#### d. Punishment

Any person who carries a weapon into an establishment that sells alcoholic beverages guilty of a misdemeanor and subject to a fine of not more than $2,500, or imprisonment for not more than 1 year, or both.

Otherwise, carrying a weapon is a Class A misdemeanor.

### (15.89) Carrying a Knife as a Weapon (§5-73-121)

#### a. Defining the Offense

A person who carries a knife as a weapon, except when upon a journey or upon his own premises, shall be punished as provided by § 5-73-123(b)[136].

If a person carries a knife with a blade three and one-half inches (3 1/2") long or longer, this fact shall be prima facie proof that the knife is carried as a weapon.

This section does not apply to officers whose duties include making arrests or keeping and guarding prisoners, nor to persons summoned by the officers to aid in the discharge of their duties while actually engaged in the discharge of their duties.

*There is a consensus among the LE community that this is bad law for a number of reasons, including the fact that there is currently no statutory punishment for it. Many prefer the charge* Carrying a Weapon *(see 15.88 above).*

### (15.90) Carrying Firearms in a Publicly Owned Building (§5-73-122)

#### a. Defining the Offense

This section makes it unlawful for any person other than a LEO (or a security guard employed by the state) or any city or county, or any state or federal military personnel, to knowingly carry or possess a loaded firearm or other deadly weapon in any publicly owned building or facility or on the State Capitol grounds.

In addition, it is unlawful for any person other than a LEO, or any state or federal military personnel, to knowingly carry or possess a firearm, whether loaded or unloaded, in the State Capitol Building or the Justice Building in Little Rock.

Furthermore, the provisions of this subsection shall not apply to persons carrying or possessing firearms or other deadly weapons in a publicly owned building or facility or on the State Capitol grounds for the purpose of participating in shooting matches or target practice under the auspices of the agency responsible for the building or facility or grounds or if necessary to participate in trade shows, exhibits, or educational courses conducted in the building or facility or on the grounds.

#### b. Definitions

As used in this section, "facility" means municipally owned or maintained parks, football fields, baseball fields, soccer fields, and other similar municipally owned or maintained recreational structures and property.

#### c. Punishment

Any person other than a law enforcement officer, officer of the court, or bailiff, acting in the line of duty, or any other person authorized by the court, who possesses a handgun in the courtroom of any court of this state is guilty

---

[136] This section was repealed by the General Assembly in 2005.

of a Class D felony. Any person otherwise violating the provisions of this section is guilty of a Class A misdemeanor.

## (15.91) Metal Knuckles and Canes (§5-73-123)

### a. Defining the Offense

This section was repealed by the General Assembly in 2005. Only the Punishment section is presented here because it is referenced in other offenses.

### b. Punishment

"Any person convicted of a violation of any of the provisions of this section shall be punishable by a fine of not less than fifty dollars ($ 50.00) nor more than two hundred dollars ($ 200) or by imprisonment in the county jail for not less than thirty (30) days nor more than three (3) months, or by both fine and imprisonment."

## (15.92) Tear Gas – Pepper Spray (§5-73-124)

### a. Defining the Offense

This section is constructed to make the possession of tear gas or pepper spray unlawful in general. Several exceptions, however, are provided. In addition, any "weapon" designed for the discharge of these chemicals is also prohibited.

It *is* lawful for a person to possess or carry, and use, a small container of tear gas or pepper spray to be used for self-defense purposes only, but the capacity of the cartridge or container may not exceed one hundred fifty cubic centimeters (150 cc).

The provisions of this section obviously do not apply to any LEO. In addition, bank employees may be armed with pepper spray or tear gas for the purpose of securing bank funds.

### b. Punishment

Any person convicted of a violation of the provisions of this section shall be punished by a fine of not less than $50.00 and not more than $200 or by imprisonment in the county jail for not less than 30 days and not more than three 3 months, or by both fine and imprisonment.

The use of pepper spray on a LEO acting under color of office is a Class A misdemeanor.

## (15.93) Booby Traps (§5-73-126)

### a. Defining the Offense

This section makes it unlawful for any person to install or maintain a booby trap upon his own property or any other person's property.

### b. Definitions

A *booby trap* is a device designed to cause death or serious physical injury to a person.

### c. Punishment

Any person who pleads guilty or nolo contendere or who is found guilty of violating this section shall be guilty of a Class D felony.

*(15.95) Public Schools (§5-73-128)*

This section provides for the suspension of driving privileges for anyone convicted of a weapons charge on school property or a school bus.

*(15.96) Furnishing Prohibited Weapons to a Felon (§5-73-129)*

### a. Defining the Offense

A person commits the offense of furnishing a handgun to a felon if he sells, barters, leases, gives, rents, or otherwise furnishes a handgun (or other implement for the infliction of serious physical injury or death that serves no common lawful purpose) to a person who he knows has been found guilty of, or who has pleaded guilty or nolo contendere to, a felony.

### b. Punishment

Furnishing a handgun or a prohibited weapon to a felon is a Class B felony.

*(15.97) Sale or Transfer to Prohibited Person (§5-73-132)*

### a. Defining the Offense

A person shall not sell, rent, or transfer a firearm to any person who he or she knows is prohibited by state or federal law from possessing the firearm.

Generally, a violation of this section is a Class A misdemeanor. If, however, the weapon is found in the following list, then it is a Class B felony:

- A handgun
- A sawed-off or short-barrelled shotgun[137],
- A sawed-off or short-barrelled rifle[138]
- A firearm that has been specially made or specially adapted for silent discharge
- A machine gun
- An explosive or incendiary device[139]
- A defaced firearm[140]
- Other implement for the infliction of serious physical injury or death that serves no common lawful purpose

*(15.98) Engaging in a Continuing Criminal Gang (§5-74-104)*

### a. Engaging in a Continuing Criminal Gang in the First Degree

A person commits the offense of engaging in a continuing criminal gang, organization, or enterprise in the first degree if he or she does *both* of the following:

- Commits or attempts to commit or solicits to commit a felony predicate criminal offense.
- That offense is part of a continuing series of 2 or more predicate criminal offenses which are undertaken by that person in concert with 2 or more other persons with respect to whom that person occupies a position of organizer, a supervisory position, or any other position of management.

---

[137] As defined in § 5-1-102(21)
[138] as defined in § 5-1-102(22)
[139] as defined in § 5-71-301(2)
[140] as defined in § 5-73-107

A person who engages in a continuing criminal gang, organization, or enterprise in the first degree is guilty of a felony 2 classifications higher than the classification of the highest underlying predicate offense.

### b. Engaging in a Continuing Criminal Gang in the Second Degree

A person commits the offense of engaging in a continuing criminal gang, organization, or enterprise in the second degree if he does *both* of the following:

- Commits or attempts to commit or solicits to commit a felony predicate criminal offense.
- That offense is part of a continuing series of 2 or more predicate criminal offenses which are undertaken by that person in concert with 2 or more other persons, but with respect to whom that person does not occupy the position of organizer, a supervisory position, or any other position of management.

A person who engages in a continuing criminal gang, organization, or enterprise in the second degree is guilty of a felony 1 classification higher than the classification of the highest underlying offense.

A person who engages in a continuing criminal gang, organization, or enterprise where the underlying predicate offense is a Class A or Class Y felony is guilty of a Class Y felony.

Any sentence of imprisonment imposed pursuant to this section *is in addition to* any sentence imposed for the violation of a predicate criminal offense.

### (15.99) Possession of Both Guns and Drugs (§5-74-106)

#### a. Defining the Offense

This section penalizes those who commit felony drug offenses while possessing a firearm. In addition, the prohibition extends beyond firearms to "Any implement or weapon which may be used to inflict serious physical injury or death, and which under the circumstances serves no apparent lawful purpose."

#### b. Punishment

Any person who violates this section is guilty of a Class Y felony.

#### c. Defenses

This section *does not* be applied to misdemeanor drug offenses. It is a defense to this section that the defendant was in his home and the firearm was not readily accessible for use.

### (15.100) Discharge of a Firearm from a Vehicle (§5-74-107)

#### a. Discharge of a Firearm from a Vehicle in the First Degree

A person commits unlawful discharge of a firearm from a vehicle in the first degree if he *knowingly* discharges a firearm from a vehicle and thereby causes death or serious physical injury to another person.

Any person who is guilty of unlawfully discharging a firearm from a vehicle in the first degree commits a Class Y felony.

#### b. Discharge of a Firearm from a Vehicle in the Second Degree

A person commits unlawful discharge of a firearm from a vehicle in the second degree if he *recklessly* discharges a firearm from a vehicle in a manner that creates a substantial risk of physical injury to another person or property damage to a home, residence, or other occupiable structure.

Any person who is guilty of unlawfully discharging a firearm from a vehicle in the second degree commits a Class B felony.

### (15.101) Violent Criminal Group Activity (§5-74-108)

#### a. Defining the Offense

This section subjects any person who violates any provision of Arkansas law which is a crime of violence while acting in concert with two (2) or more other persons to enhanced penalties.

#### b. Punishment

Upon conviction of a crime of violence committed while acting in concert with 2 or more other persons, the classification and penalty range shall be increased by 1 classification.

*The fact that the group was not a criminal gang, organization, or enterprise is not a defense to prosecution under this statute.*

### (15.102) Gang Recruitment (§5-74-203)

#### a. Defining the Offense

This section prohibits any person from causing a minor to become or to remain a member of any group which the actor knows to be a criminal gang, organization, or enterprise by duress or intimidation.

#### b. Punishment

Gang recruitment is a Class C felony for the first offense, and a Class B felony for second and subsequent offenses.

### (15.103) Operating a Motorboat While Intoxicated (§5-76-102)

No person shall operate any motorboat on the waters of this state while either of the following is true:

- The person is Intoxicated.
- There is an alcohol concentration[141] in the person's breath or blood of eight-hundredths (0.08) or more.

#### b. Probable Cause

In the case of a motorboat or device, only where the certified law enforcement officer has probable cause to believe that the operator of the motorboat is operating while intoxicated or operating while there is an alcohol concentration of eight-hundredths (0.08) in the person's breath or blood, the law enforcement officer is authorized to administer and may test the operator at the scene by using a portable breath-testing instrument or other approved method to determine if the operator may be operating a motorboat or device in violation of this section.

*The consumption of alcohol or the possession of open containers aboard a vessel shall not in and of itself constitute probable cause.*

#### c. Punishment

For a first offense, a person violating this section will be punished by imprisonment in the county or municipal jail for not more than 1 year or by a fine of not less than dollars $250 and not more than $1,000 or by both fine and imprisonment. In addition, the court will order the person not to operate a motorboat for a period of 90 days.

---

[141] based upon the definition of breath, blood, and urine concentration in § 5-65-204

For a second offense within a three-year period, a person violating this section will be punished by a fine of not less than $500 and not more than $2,500 and by imprisonment in the county or municipal jail for not more than 1 year. The statute makes 48 hours in jail or 20 days of community service mandatory. In addition, the court will order the person not to operate a motorboat for a period of 1 year.

For a third or subsequent offense within a three-year period, a person violating this section will be punished by a fine of not less than $1,000 and not more than $5,000 and by imprisonment in the county or municipal jail for not less than 60 days and not more than one 1 year, to include a minimum of 60 days which will be served in the county or municipal jail and which cannot be probated or suspended. In addition, the court will order[142] the person not to operate a motorboat for a period of 3 years.

### d. Evidentiary and Procedural Provisions

A person who has been arrested for violating this section may not be released from jail, under bond or otherwise, until the alcohol concentration is less than eight-hundredths (0.08) in the person's breath or blood and the person is no longer intoxicated.

In any criminal prosecution of a person charged with violating this section, the amount of alcohol in the defendant's blood at the time of or within 2 hours of the alleged offense, as shown by chemical analysis of the defendant's blood, urine, breath, or other bodily substance, shall give rise to the following:

- If there was at that time an alcohol concentration of four-hundredths (0.04) or less in the defendant's blood, urine, breath, or other bodily substance, it shall be presumed that the defendant was not under the influence of intoxicating liquor.
- If there was at that time an alcohol concentration in excess of four-hundredths (0.04) but less than eight-hundredths (0.08) in the defendant's blood, urine, breath, or other bodily substance, this fact shall not give rise to any presumption that the defendant was or was not under the influence of intoxicating liquor, but this fact may be considered with other competent evidence in determining the guilt or innocence of the defendant.

The above provisions should not be construed as limiting the introduction of any other relevant evidence bearing upon the question of whether or not the defendant was intoxicated.

The fact that any person charged with violating this section is or has been legally entitled to use alcohol or a controlled substance does not constitute a defense against any charge of violating this section.

*Neither reckless operation of a motorboat nor any other boating or water safety infraction is a lesser included offense under a charge in violation of this section.* This means that the safety infractions can be charged along with this offense.

### (15.104) Blue Lights (§5-77-201)

### a. Defining the Offense

This section makes it unlawful to sell a blue light or blue lens cap to any person other than a law enforcement officer or a county coroner.

In addition, it is unlawful for a person other than a law enforcement officer or a county coroner to buy a blue light or blue lens cap.

---

[142] Any person who operates a motorboat on the waters of this state in violation of a court order shall be imprisoned for ten (10) days.

This section further requires that, before selling a blue light or blue lens cap, the seller must require the buyer to provide identification that legally demonstrates that the buyer is a law enforcement officer or a county coroner. In addition, each sale of a blue light or blue lens cap shall be reported to the Department of Arkansas State Police on a form prescribed by the department.

### b. Punishment

A violation of this section is a Class D felony.

### c. Definitions

*Blue light* means an operable blue light which is designed for use by an emergency vehicle, or is similar in appearance to a blue light designed for use by an emergency vehicle and can be operated by use of the vehicle's battery, the vehicle's electrical system, or a dry cell battery.

### (15.105) LE Insignia Sales (§5-77-202)

#### a. Defining the Offense

This section makes it unlawful to sell official law enforcement insignia to any person other than a law enforcement officer.

In addition, it is unlawful for a person other than a law enforcement officer to buy official law enforcement insignia.

Before selling official law enforcement insignia, the seller must require the buyer to provide identification that legally demonstrates that the buyer is a law enforcement officer.

#### b. Punishment

A violation of this section shall be a Class A misdemeanor.

#### c. Definitions

The term *official law enforcement insignia* means those items relating to the performance of a person's duty as a law enforcement officer when the items are formally sanctioned by the law enforcement agency employing the person.

### (15.106) Tobacco (§5-78-101,102)

This section makes it unlawful for a person under 18 years of age (unless acting as an agent of his or her employer within the scope of employment) to possess, purchase, or use any cigarettes or other tobacco products.

Persons under 18 years of age may be enlisted to assist an authorized agent or representative of a state or local law enforcement authority, the Arkansas Tobacco Control Board, the Department of Health, or other state governmental agency in testing compliance with laws relating to the prohibition of the sale of tobacco in any form or cigarette papers to minors, provided the following 2 conditions are met:

1. The testing is conducted under the direction or supervision of an authorized agent or representative of a state or local law enforcement authority, the Arkansas Tobacco Control Board, the Department of Health, or other governmental agency monitoring illegal sales of tobacco to minors.
2. Written parental or legal guardian's consent has been provided after the consenting parent or guardian has received from the testing entity written information about the duties which such persons under 18 years of age will be asked to perform and the methods and procedures to be employed in carrying out such duties.

### (15.107) Criminal Possession of Body Armor (§5-79-101)

#### a. Defining the Offense

No person may possess body armor if that person has been found guilty of or has pleaded guilty or nolo contendere to any of the following offenses: Capital murder[143], Murder in the first degree[144], Murder in the second degree[145], Manslaughter[146], Aggravated robbery[147], Battery in the first degree[148], or Aggravated assault[149].

#### b. Definitions

*Body armor* means any material designed to be worn on the body and to provide bullet penetration resistance.

#### c. Punishment

A violation of this section is a Class A misdemeanor.

---

[143] §5-10-101
[144] §5-10-102
[145] §5-10-103
[146] §5-10-104
[147] §5-12-103
[148] §5-13-201
[149] §5-13-204

# Chapter 16: Drug Enforcement

## *(16.1) Controlled Substance Act in General*

Exactly what drugs fall into what schedule are not codified in the *Arkansas Code*. The scheduling of drugs in Arkansas is done by administrative regulation. Specifically, they are published annually by the Director of the Arkansas Department of Health. For a copy of the most recent drug schedules, consult the Arkansas Department of Health[150].

## *(16.2) Obtaining Drugs by Fraud*

It is criminal to knowingly or intentionally acquire a controlled substance by misrepresentation, fraud, forgery, deception, subterfuge, or theft[151].

## *(16.3) Drug Paraphernalia*

It is also criminal to possess, use, sell, advertise for sale, or manufacture drug paraphernalia[152].

## *(16.4) Manufacture & Delivery of a Controlled Substance (§5-64-401)*

§5-64-401 is the meat of the Controlled Substance Act. It provides criminal penalties for the unlawful *manufacture, delivery*, and *possession with the intent* to manufacture or deliver a controlled substance. This section is particularly difficult to understand because of the several elements of each violation. The schedule of the drug, the weight of the drugs involved, and other factors involved must be considered.

Note that this section prohibits the *delivery* of a controlled substance, not its sale[153].

Generally, if actual delivery can be shown, then there can be no question as to the intent[154].

---

[150] See http://www.healthyarkansas.com/rules_regs/controlled_substances_list_2006.pdf for the 2006 list.
[151] A.C.A. §5-64-403(a)(2)
[152] A.C.A. §5-64-403(c)
[153] *Higgs v. State*, 313 Ark. 272, 854 S.W.2d 328 (1993)
[154] *Moser v. State*, 266 Ark. 200, 583 S.W.2d 15 (1979)

| Penalties for Violations of §6-64-401(a) | | | | | |
|---|---|---|---|---|---|
| **Description** | **Weight** | **Min. Sentence** | **Max. Sentence** | **Max. Fine** | **Felony Class** |
| Schedule 1 or 2 (Narcotic / Meth) | < 28 grams | 10 Years | 40 Years (or life) | $25,000 | Y |
| Schedule 1 or 2 (Narcotic / Meth) | ≥28 grams < 200 grams | 15 Years | 40 Years (or life) | $50,000 | Y |
| Schedule 1 or 2 (Narcotic / Meth) | ≥200 grams < 400 grams | 20 Years | 40 Years (or life) | $100,000 | Y |
| Schedule 1 or 2 (Narcotic / Meth) | ≥400 grams | 40 Years | Life | $250,000 | Y |
| Schedule 1,2, 3 | < 28 grams | 5 Years | 20 Years | $15,000 | B |
| Schedule 1,2, 3 | ≥28 grams < 400 grams | 10 Years | 40 Years (or life) | $50,000 | B |
| Schedule 1,2, 3 | ≥400 grams | 15 Years | 40 Years (or life) | $100,000 | B |
| Schedule 4 or 5 | < 200 grams | 3 Years | 10 Years | $10,000 | C |
| Schedule 4 or 5 | ≥200 grams < 400 grams | 10 Years | 40 Years (or life) | $50,000 | C |
| Schedule 4 or 5 | ≥400 grams | 15 Years | 40 Years (or life) | $100,000 | C |
| Schedule 6 | > 10 pounds | 4 Years | 10 Years | $25,000 | C |
| Schedule 6 | > 10 pounds < 100 pounds | 5 Years | 20 Years | $50,000 | B |
| Schedule 6 | ≥100 pounds | 6 Years | 30 Years | $100,000 | A |

## (16.5) Counterfeit Substances

In addition to real drugs, Arkansas law makes it illegal to create, deliver, or possess with the intent to deliver a counterfeit substance[155] (drug).

The possession of 100 doses of a counterfeit substance creates a rebuttable presumption that the person has intent to deliver the substance.

The penalty is based on the schedule of the drug that the counterfeit substance purports to be.

| **Schedule Purported** | **Penalty** |
|---|---|
| 1 or 2 (Narcotic) | Class B Felony |
| 1, 2, or 3 | Class C Felony |
| 4 | Class C Felony |
| 5 | Class C Felony |
| Not Classified | Class D Felony |

## (16.6) Possession of a Counterfeit or Controlled Substance

The statute governing mere possession of a controlled substance also penalizes the possession of a counterfeit substance. Most drug possession charges are penalized based on the number of prior offenses, not the schedule of the drug. *Schedule I and II drugs are always a class C felony.* Otherwise, the penalty is according to the following table:

| **Offense** | **Classification** |
|---|---|
| First | A Misdemeanor |
| Second | D Felony |
| Third or More | C Felony |

---

[155] see §5-64-101(e) for a definition of *counterfeit substance*

*(16.7) Rebuttable Presumption of Intent to Deliver*

Possession by any person of a quantity of any controlled substance that is more than listed in the table below creates a presumption that that person had the intent to deliver the substance[156]:

| Intent to Deliver Presumption Amounts | |
|---|---|
| **Drug** | **Weight** |
| Heroin | 100 milligrams |
| Opium | 3 grams |
| Cocaine | 1 gram |
| Codeine | 300 milligrams |
| Pethidine | 300 milligrams |
| Hydromorphine Hydrochloride | 16 milligrams |
| Methadone | 100 milligrams |
| Marijuana | 1 ounce |
| Hashish | 6 grams |
| Lysergic Acid Diethylamide (LSD) | 100 micrograms |
| Unlisted Depressant Drugs | 20 hypnotic dosage units |
| Unlisted Stimulant Drugs | 200 milligrams |
| Unlisted Hallucinogenic Drugs | 10 dosage units |

*(16.8) Presumption on Attempt to Manufacture Methamphetamine*

The presumption of attempted[157] methamphetamine production can be created in either of two ways:

1. Simultaneous possession of drug paraphernalia and a drug precursor appropriate for use to manufacture methamphetamine.
2. possession of drug paraphernalia appropriate for use to manufacture methamphetamine that tests positive for methamphetamine residue.

*(16.9) Distribution near Certain Facilities (§5-64-411)*

This section provides for enhanced penalties for those selling, delivering, possessing with intent to deliver, dispensing, manufacturing, transporting or administering a controlled substance near certain types of facilities. Specifically, an additional term of 10 years can be added to a sentence if it was determined that the act took place within 1,000 feet of

- A city or state park
- A school or college
- A skating rink, Boys Club, Girls Club, YMCA, YWCA, or other community or recreation center
- A publicly funded and administered multifamily housing development
- A drug or alcohol treatment center
- A church
- A shelter

---

[156] A.C.A. §5-64-101(d)
[157] § 5-3-201

# Chapter 17: DWI Enforcement

## (17.1) Driving While Intoxicated in General

Many states differentiate between a driver impaired by alcohol and one impaired by other substances. The Arkansas Code combines these dangerous offenses under one DWI heading. At the core of the violation is simply driving while intoxicated—this intoxication can come from alcohol or controlled substances, or a combination of the two. The statute is sometimes confusing because there are provisions for determining "intoxication" and provisions for determining if blood alcohol levels are beyond the legal limit. The Arkansas Supreme court has stated that these two provisions are "two different ways of proving a single violation[158]."

## (17.2) DWI Definitions (§ 5-65-102)

*Intoxicated* means influenced or affected by the ingestion of alcohol, a controlled substance, any intoxicant, or any combination thereof, to such a degree that the driver's reactions, motor skills, and judgment are substantially altered and the driver, therefore, constitutes a clear and substantial danger of physical injury or death to himself and other motorists or pedestrians.

*Controlled substance* means a drug, substance, or immediate precursor in Schedules I through VI. The fact that any person charged with a violation of this act is or has been entitled to use that drug or controlled substance under the laws of this state shall not constitute a defense against any charge of violating this act.

*Victim impact statement* means a voluntary written or oral statement of a victim, or relative of a victim, who has sustained serious injury due to a violation of this act.

*Sworn report* means a signed, written statement of a certified law enforcement officer, under penalty of perjury, on a form provided by the Director of the Department of Finance and Administration.

## (17.3) Defining the Offense (§ 5-65-103)

The offense can be demonstrated in two ways:

1. It is unlawful for any person who is intoxicated to operate or be in actual physical control of a motor vehicle.
2. It is unlawful for any person to operate or be in actual physical control of a motor vehicle if at that time the alcohol concentration in the person's breath or blood was eight-hundredths (0.08) or more[159].

## (17.4) Seizure, Suspension, and Revocation of License (§5-65-104)

At the time of arrest for operating or being in actual physical control of a motor vehicle while intoxicated or while there was an alcohol concentration of eight-hundredths (0.08) or more in the person's breath or blood, the arrested

---

[158] *Stephens v. State*, 320 Ark. 426 (1995)
[159] Based on the definition of breath, blood, and urine concentration in §5-65-204

person shall immediately surrender his or her license, permit, or other evidence of driving privilege to the arresting law enforcement officer[160].

The Office of Driver Services of the Revenue Division of the Department of Finance and Administration or its designated official will suspend or revoke the driving privilege of an arrested person or will suspend any nonresident driving privilege of an arrested person[161]. The suspension or revocation will be based on the number of previous offenses as follows:

- Suspension for 120 days for the first offense of operating or being in actual physical control of a motor vehicle while intoxicated or while there was an alcohol concentration of at least eight hundredths (0.08) but less than fifteen hundredths (0.15) by weight of alcohol in the person's blood or breath.
- Suspension for 6 months for the first offense of operating or being in actual physical control of a motor vehicle while intoxicated by the ingestion of or by the use of a controlled substance
- Suspension for 180 days for the first offense of operating or being in actual physical control of a motor vehicle while intoxicated and while there was an alcohol concentration of fifteen hundredths (0.15) or more by weight of alcohol in the person's blood or breath.

*If the court orders issuance of an ignition interlock restricted license[162], the interlock restricted license will be available immediately.*

A second offense will result in a suspension for 24 months for a second offense, if within 5 years of the first offense. If the court orders issuance of an ignition interlock restricted license, the suspension period for which no restricted license will be available will be a minimum of 1 year.

A third offense will result in suspension for 30 months, if the offense occurred within 5 years of the first offense. If the court orders issuance of an ignition interlock restricted license, the suspension period for which no restricted license will be available will be a minimum of 1 year.

A fourth and subsequent conviction within 5 years of the first offense will result in a revocation for 4 years, during which no restricted permits may be issued.

### (17.5) Operation during Period of License Suspension or Revocation (§ 5-65-105)

Any person whose privilege to operate a motor vehicle has been suspended or revoked under the provisions of this act and who still operates a motor vehicle in this state during the period of such suspension or revocation, will be imprisoned for 10 days and may be assessed a fine of not more than $1,000.

### (17.6) Refusal to submit (§5-65-205)

If a person under arrest refuses upon the request of a law enforcement officer to submit to a chemical test[163] designated by the law enforcement agency, none may be given. The person's motor vehicle operator's license must be seized by the LEO, and the officer must immediately deliver to the person from whom the license was seized a temporary driving permit[164].

The Office of Driver Services of the Revenue Division of the Department of Finance and Administration will then proceed to suspend or revoke the driving privilege of the arrested person. The suspension shall be as follows: Suspension for 180 days for the first offense of refusing to submit to a chemical test of blood, breath, or urine for

---

[160] As provided in §5-65-402
[161] As provided in §5-65-402
[162] Under §5-65-118
[163] As provided in § 5-65-202
[164] As provided by § 5-65-402

the purpose of determining the alcohol or controlled substance contents of the person's blood or breath. However, if the court orders issuance of an ignition interlock restricted license[165], the interlock restricted license will available immediately[166].

- Suspension for 2 years, during which no restricted permits may be issued, for a second offense of refusing to submit to a chemical test of blood, breath, or urine for the purposes of determining the alcohol or controlled substance contents of the person's blood or breath within 5 years of the first offense.

- Revocation for 3 years, during which no restricted permits may be issued, for the third offense of refusing to submit to a chemical test of blood, breath, or urine for the purpose of determining the alcohol or controlled substance contents of the person's blood within 5 years of the first offense.

- Lifetime revocation, during which no restricted permit may be issued, for the fourth or subsequent offense of refusing to submit to a chemical test of blood, breath, or urine for the purpose of determining the alcohol or controlled substance contents of the person's blood or breath within 5 years of the first offense.

---

[165] Under §5-65-118

[166] The restricted driving permit provision of § 5-65-120 does not apply to this suspension.

# Chapter 18: Traffic Law

### (18.1) Traffic Law in General

Traffic law is a lengthy and complex topic under Arkansas law. This chapter provides a very brief overview of the most commonly encountered traffic violations.

Traffic Law is governed by Title 27 of the Arkansas Code. These statutes can be found in the code, as well as in a book published under the authority of the State Highway and Transportation Department and the Department of Finance and Administration every two years.

| Traffic Violations Classified as Offenses | |
|---|---|
| Racing on a highway | Class A misdemeanor |
| Reckless driving | Class B misdemeanor |
| Driving with lights off to avoid detection | Class B misdemeanor |
| Hazardous driving | Class C misdemeanor |
| Leaving the scene of an accident involving property damage only | Class C misdemeanor |
| Wrong way on a one-way street | Class C misdemeanor |
| Speeding in excess of 15 m.p.h. over the posted speed limit | Class C misdemeanor |
| Using nitrous oxide in a motor vehicle | Class C misdemeanor |
| More than 3 violations in a twelve-month period | Class C misdemeanor |

Any *moving* traffic law violation not enumerated in the table above is a violation[167], and shall be punishable as provided under § 5-4-201.

---

[167] as defined in Arkansas Criminal Code, §§ 5-1-105 and 5-1-108

---

**§ 5-4-201. Fines -- Limitations on amount**

(c) A defendant convicted of a violation may be sentenced to pay a fine:

(1) Not exceeding one hundred dollars ($100) if the violation is defined by the Arkansas Criminal Code or defined by a statute enacted subsequent to January 1, 1976, that does not prescribe a different limitation on the amount of the fine; or

(2) In accordance with a limitation of the statute defining the violation if that statute prescribes limitations on the amount of the fine.

(d) (1) Notwithstanding a limit imposed by this section, if the defendant has derived pecuniary gain from commission of an offense, then upon conviction of the offense the defendant may be sentenced to pay a fine not exceeding two (2) times the amount of the pecuniary gain.

(2) As used in this subsection, "pecuniary gain" means the amount of money or the value of property derived from the commission of the offense, less the amount of money or the value of property returned to the victim of the crime or seized by or surrendered to a lawful authority prior to the time sentence is imposed.

(e) An organization convicted of an offense may be sentenced to pay a fine authorized by subsection (d) of this section or not exceeding two (2) times the maximum fine otherwise authorized upon conviction of the offense by subsections (a), (b), or (c) of this section.

---

### (18.2) Fraudulent Applications (§ 27-14-303)

Any person who fraudulently uses a false or fictitious name or address in any application for the registration of a vehicle or a certificate of title or knowingly makes a false statement or knowingly conceals a material fact or otherwise commits a fraud in any application will be punished by a fine of not more $1,000 or by imprisonment for not more than 1 year, or both.

### (18.3) Operation of Vehicles without License Plates (§ 27-14-304)

No person may operate, and no owner may knowingly permit to be operated, upon any highway any vehicle required to be registered under this chapter unless there is a valid license plate issued for that vehicle attached to it.

Any violation of this section is a misdemeanor.

### (18.4) Police Authority Generally (§ 27-14-405)

This section grants the Commissioner of Motor Vehicles (the Director of the Department of Finance and Administration) and his designated agents the following powers:

- Of peace officers for the purpose of enforcing the provisions of this chapter and of any other law regulating the operation of vehicles or the use of the highways.
- To make arrests upon view and without warrant for any violation committed in their presence of any of the provisions of this chapter or other law regulating the operation of vehicles or the use of the highways.
- When on duty, upon reasonable belief that any vehicle is being operated in violation of any provision of this chapter or of any other law regulating the operation of vehicles, to require the driver thereof to stop and exhibit his driver's or chauffeur's license and the registration certificate issued for the vehicle and submit to an inspection of the vehicle, the registration plates, and registration certificate thereon or to an inspection and test of the equipment of the vehicle.
- To inspect any vehicle of a type required to be registered under this chapter in any public garage or repair shop or in any place where such vehicles are held for sale or wrecking, for the purpose of locating stolen vehicles and investigating the title and registration thereof.

- To serve warrants relating to the enforcement of the laws regulating the operation of vehicles or the use of the highways.
- To investigate reported thefts of motor vehicles, trailers, and semitrailers.

### (18.5) Registration to Be Signed, Carried, and Exhibited (§ 27-14-714)

Every owner, upon receipt of a registration certificate, must write his signature on it, in ink in the space provided. Every such registration certificate must be, at all times, carried in the vehicle to which it refers or must be carried by the person driving or in control of such vehicle, who shall display it upon demand of a police officer or any officer or employee of the office.

*No person charged with violating this section will be convicted if he produces in a court a registration certificate for such vehicle which was issued prior to, and in effect at, the time of the arrest.*

*Possession of a photocopy of the license registration card or certificate is acceptable under the requirements of this section.*

### (18.8) Display of License Plates Generally (§ 27-14-716)

License plates issued for a motor vehicle (other than a motorcycle) must be attached to the vehicle, one in the front and the other in the rear. When one 1 plate is issued, it must be attached to the rear.

License plates for trucks of one ton capacity or larger may be displayed either on the front or rear of the vehicle.

The license plate issued for a motorcycle must be attached to the rear.

### (18.7) When to Obtain State Registration and License (§27-14-723)

Within 30 calendar days of becoming a resident, any person who is a resident of this state must obtain an Arkansas motor vehicle registration and license in order to operate the motor vehicle upon the streets and highways of this state.

Any nonresident who has been physically present in this state for a period of 6 months must obtain an Arkansas motor vehicle registration and license in order to operate the motor vehicle upon the streets and highways of this state.

### (18.8) Registration by Transferee – Title Retention Notes (§27-14-903)

The transferee of any new or used vehicle required by law to be registered must apply for, or cause to be applied for, the registration of the vehicle within 30 days after the date of the release of lien by a prior lienholder[168], or 30 days after the date of the transfer if no lien exists.

No vehicle may be operated upon a public street or highway for more than 30 days after the release of lien by a prior lienholder or 30 days after the transfer date if no lien exists, unless a valid registration plate is properly attached to the vehicle.

### (18.9) Unlawful taking of vehicle (§27-14-2207)

Any person who drives a vehicle, not his own, without the consent of the owner of that vehicle and with intent temporarily to deprive the owner of his possession of the vehicle, without intent to steal it, is guilty of a misdemeanor.

---

[168] As provided in § 27-14-909

The consent of the owner of a vehicle to its taking or driving will not in any case be presumed or implied because of the owner's consent on a previous occasion to the taking or driving of the vehicle by the same or a different person.

Any person who assists in, or is a party or accessory to or an accomplice in any such unauthorized taking or driving, is guilty of a misdemeanor.

### *(18.10) Use of vehicle without owner's consent (§27-14-2208)*

No chauffeur or other person may drive or operate any motor vehicle upon any street or highway in this state in the absence of the owner of the motor vehicle without the owner's consent.

Any person violating this section is guilty of a misdemeanor and upon conviction will be fined a sum not exceeding $200 or imprisoned in the county jail for a period not exceeding 6 months, or both.

### *(18.11) Penalties (§ 27-15-305)*

Any individual who provides false information in order to acquire or who assists an unqualified person in acquiring the special license plate or the special certificate and any person who abuses the privileges granted by this subchapter shall be deemed guilty of a Class A misdemeanor.

Any vehicle found to be parked in an area designated for the exclusive use of any person with a disability, including the access aisle on which is not displayed a special license plate, a special certificate, or an official designation of another state or which is found to be parked in an area designated for the exclusive use of any person with a disability, *if operated by a person who is not a person with a disability while not being used for the actual transporting of a person with a disability* will be subject to impoundment by the appropriate law enforcement agency.

In addition to impoundment, the owner of the vehicle will be subject to a fine of not less than $100 and not more than $500 for the first offense and not less than $250 and not more than $1,000 for the second and subsequent offenses, plus applicable towing, impoundment, and related fees as well as court costs.

Upon the second or subsequent conviction, the court will suspend the driver's license for up to 6 months.

### *(18.12) Unlawful Use of License (§27-16-302)*

It is a misdemeanor for any person:

- To display, or cause or permit to be displayed, or have in his possession any cancelled, revoked, suspended, fictitious, or fraudulently altered driver's license.
- To knowingly assist or permit any other person to apply for or obtain through fraudulent application or other illegal means any Arkansas driver's license.
- To lend his driver's license to any other person or knowingly permit its use by another.
- To display or represent as one's own any driver's license not issued to him.
- To fail or refuse to surrender to the office, upon its lawful demand, any driver's license which has been suspended, revoked, or cancelled.
- To use a false or fictitious name in any application for a driver's license, or to knowingly make a false statement, or to knowingly conceal a material fact or otherwise commit a fraud in any application.
- To permit any unlawful use of a driver's license issued to him.
- To do any act forbidden or fail to perform any act required by this act.

### (18.13) Driving While License Suspended or Revoked (§ 27-16-303)

Any person whose driver's license or driving privilege as a resident or nonresident has been cancelled, suspended, or revoked as provided in this act and who drives any motor vehicle upon the highways of this state while the license or privilege is cancelled, suspended, or revoked is guilty of a misdemeanor.

Upon conviction, an offender will be punished by imprisonment for not less than 2 days and not more than 6 months. In addition, there may be a fine imposed of not more than $500.

### (18.14) Permitting Unauthorized Person to Drive (§27-16-304)

No person may authorize or knowingly permit a motor vehicle owned by him or under his control to be driven upon any highway by any person who is not authorized under this chapter or is in violation of any of the provisions of this act.

### (18.15) Permitting a Minor to Drive (§27-16-305)

No person shall cause or knowingly permit his child or ward under the age of 18 years to drive a motor vehicle upon any highway when the minor is not authorized under this act or is in violation of any of the provisions of this act.

### (18.16) License to Be Carried and Exhibited On Demand (§27-16-601)

Every licensee shall have his driver's license in his immediate possession at all times when operating a motor vehicle and shall display the license upon demand of a justice of the peace, a peace officer, or an employee of the office.

*No person charged with violating this section will be convicted if he produces in court a driver's license issued to him and valid at the time of his arrest.*

### (18.17) Driver's License Required (§27-16-602)

No person, except those expressly exempted, shall drive any motor vehicle upon a highway in this state unless the person has a valid driver's license.

No person may receive a driver's license unless and until he surrenders to the office all valid driver's licenses in his possession issued to him by any other jurisdiction. All surrendered licenses shall be returned by the office to the issuing department together with information that the licensee is now licensed in the new jurisdiction.

No person may be permitted to have more than one valid driver's license at any time.

No person may drive a commercial motor vehicle as a commercial driver unless he holds a valid commercial driver's license.

No person may receive a commercial driver's license unless and until he surrenders to the office any noncommercial driver's license issued to him or an affidavit that he does not possess a noncommercial driver's license. Any person holding a valid commercial driver's license under this chapter need not procure a noncommercial driver's license.

### (18.18) Persons Exempted From Licensing (§27-16-603)

The following persons are exempt from licensing under this act:

- Any person while operating a motor vehicle in the service of the Army, Air Force, Navy, or Marine Corps of the United States.

- Any person while operating or driving any road machine, farm tractor, or implement of husbandry temporarily operated or moved on a highway.
- A nonresident who is at least 16 years of age and who has in his immediate possession a valid noncommercial driver's license issued to him in his home state or country may operate a motor vehicle in this state only as a noncommercial driver.
- A nonresident who is at least 18 years of age and who has in his immediate possession a valid commercial driver's license issued to him by his home state or country may operate a motor vehicle in this state either as a commercial or a noncommercial driver.
- Any nonresident who is at least 18 years of age whose home state or country does not require the licensing of noncommercial drivers may operate a motor vehicle as a noncommercial driver only, for a period of not more than 90 days in any calendar year, if the motor vehicle so operated is duly registered in the home state or country of the nonresident.

### *(18.19) Instruction Permits (§27-16-802)*

Any person who is at least 14 years of age may apply to the Office of Motor Vehicle for an instruction permit.

After the applicant has successfully passed all parts of the examination other than the driving test, the office may, in its discretion, issue to the applicant an instruction permit which will entitle the applicant while having the permit in his or her immediate possession to drive a motor vehicle upon the public highways for a period of 6 months when accompanied by a licensed driver who is at least 21 years of age and who is occupying a seat beside the driver, except in the event that the permittee is operating a motorcycle.

Any instruction permit may be renewed or a new permit issued for an additional period of 6 months as long as the permittee has remained free of a serious accident and conviction of a serious traffic violation for at least the last 6 months.

Any passengers riding in the motor vehicle while a permittee is driving shall wear seat belts at all times.

The office, upon receiving proper application may, in its discretion, issue a restricted instruction permit effective for a school year or a more restricted permit to an applicant who is enrolled in a driver education program which includes practice driving and which is approved by the office even though the applicant has not reached the legal age to be eligible for a noncommercial license.

The instruction permit will entitle the permittee when he or she has the permit in his or her immediate possession to operate a motor vehicle only on a designated highway or within a designated area but only when an approved instructor is occupying a seat beside the permittee.

### *(18.20) Restricted, Learner's, and Intermediate Licenses (§27-16-804)*

The Office of Motor Vehicle, upon issuing any driver's license, has the authority, whenever good cause appears, to impose restrictions suitable to the licensee's driving ability with respect to the type of or special mechanical control devices required on a motor vehicle which the licensee may operate or other restrictions applicable to the licensee as the office may determine to be appropriate to assure the safe operation of a motor vehicle by the licensee.

The office may either issue a special restricted license or may set forth such restrictions upon the usual license form.

The office may, upon showing of need, waive any age restriction set forth in this chapter. The waiver of the age restrictions for need is subject to review upon a complaint from certain officials[169].

All licensees who have a tested uncorrected visual acuity of less than 20/40 must be restricted to the operation of a motor vehicle, motorcycle, or motor-driven cycle only while they are wearing corrective lenses. No person may be allowed to operate a motor vehicle, motorcycle, or a motor-driven cycle if he or she has a tested corrected visual acuity of less than 20/50 or if he or she has a field of vision less than 140 degrees with 2 functioning eyes or less than 105 degrees with 1 functioning eye.

The office may, upon receiving satisfactory evidence of any violation of the restrictions of a license, suspend or revoke it, but the licensees will be entitled to a hearing.

*It is a misdemeanor for any person to operate a motor vehicle in any manner in violation of the restrictions imposed in a restricted license issued to him or her.*

The office shall have authority to issue a restricted driver's license, to be known as a "learner's license", to those persons under 16 years of age. The learner's license will be issued only to an applicant with a valid instruction permit who is at least 14 years of age, who has remained free of a serious accident and conviction of a serious traffic violation in the last 6 months, and who meets all other licensing examinations requirements. The driver with a learner's license shall operate the motor vehicle on the public streets and highways only when both of the following conditions are met:

- All passengers in the vehicle are wearing their seat belts at all times.
- The driver with a learner's permit is being accompanied by a driver over 21 years of age.

The office shall have authority to issue a restricted driver's license to those persons under 18 years of age called an intermediate driver's license. The intermediate driver's license shall be issued only to an applicant with a valid instruction permit or a learner's license who is at least 16 years of age, who has remained free of a serious accident and conviction of a serious traffic violation for at least the last 6 months, and who meets all other licensing examination requirements. The driver with an intermediate driver's license shall operate the motor vehicle on the public streets and highways only when all passengers in the vehicle are wearing their seat belts.

*No motor vehicle, nor the operator of a vehicle, nor the passengers of the vehicle shall be stopped, inspected, or detained solely to determine compliance with the requirement set out in this subchapter for wearing a seat belt.*

### (18.21) Standard Equipment Required (§ 27-20-104)

All *motor-driven cycles and all motorcycles* used upon the public streets and highways of this state must be equipped with the following standard equipment:

- At least 1, but not more than 2, headlights which, in the dark, must emit a white light visible from a distance of at least 500' in front
- A red reflector on the rear, which must be visible from a distance of 300' to the rear when directly in front of a lawful upper beam head lamp of a motor vehicle
- A lamp emitting a red light visible from a distance of 500' to the rear must be used in addition to the red reflector.
- Good hand or foot brakes
- A horn in good working order, but no bell, siren, or whistle shall be permitted

---

[169] Upon receiving a complaint from a prosecuting attorney, a city attorney, or a certified law enforcement officer, the office shall review the validity of any waiver of age restrictions based on need and any violations of restrictions placed on a license.

- A standard muffler
- Handholds and support for the passenger's feet when designed to carry more than 1 person, unless it is equipped with a sidecar

All passengers and operators of *motorcycles and motor-driven cycles* used upon the public streets and highways of this state shall be equipped with the following equipment under standards set forth by the Office of Motor Vehicle:

- Protective headgear unless the person is 21 years of age or older
- Protective glasses, goggles, or transparent face shields

*The provisions of this section do not apply to three-wheel motorcycles equipped with a cab and a windshield which do not exceed twenty horsepower (20 hp) when such motorcycles are used by municipal police departments.*

### (18.22) Operator's License Required – Special License (§27-20-106)

No person who is 16 years of age or older may operate a motorcycle, motor-driven cycle, or similarly classified motor vehicle which is subject to registration in this state upon the public streets and highways of this state unless the person holds a current valid motorcycle operator's license.

It is unlawful for any person to operate a motorcycle or motor-driven cycle in this state unless the person has a current valid motorcycle operator's license. However, any person 14 years of age or older who is under the lawful age to obtain a motorcycle operator's license may operate a motor-driven cycle if that person has obtained a special license.

Any person 14 years of age, but less than 16 years of age, may obtain a license to operate a motor-driven cycle if the motor of the motor-driven cycle displaces two hundred fifty cubic centimeters (250 cc) or less. This license shall expire upon the licensee's sixteenth birthday.

### (18.23) Penalty [Failure to be Insured] (§27-22-103)

Any person who operates a motor vehicle within this state will be subject to a mandatory fine of not less than $50.00 and not more than $250 unless the vehicle is covered by a certificate of self-insurance or an insurance policy[170].

Any person who operates a motor vehicle in violation of the insurance requirement will be fined not less than $250 and not more than $500 for the second offense, and the minimum fine will be mandatory.

Any person who operates a motor vehicle in violation in the state insurance requirement will be fined not less than $500 and not more than $1,000 or sentenced to 1 year in jail, or both, for the third offense or for any subsequent offenses.

Upon a showing that liability coverage required was in effect at the time of arrest, the judge may dismiss the charge imposed under this act, and the penalties will not be imposed.

### (18.24) Insurance Required – Minimum Coverage (§27-22-104)

It is unlawful for any person to operate a motor vehicle within this state unless the vehicle is covered by a certificate of self-insurance[171], or by an insurance policy issued by an insurance company authorized to do business in this state.

---

[170] as required under § 27-22-104(a)(1)
[171] Under the provisions of § 27-19-107

*Failure to present proof of insurance coverage at the time of arrest <u>and</u> a failure of the vehicle insurance database to show current insurance coverage at the time of the traffic stop create a rebuttable presumption that the motor vehicle is uninsured.*

The policy shall provide as a minimum the following coverage:

- Not less than $25,000 for bodily injury or death of 1 person in any one accident
- Not less than $50,000 for bodily injury or death of 2 or more persons in any 1 accident
- If the accident has resulted in injury to or destruction of property, not less than $25,000 for the injury to or destruction of property of others in any 1 accident

If the operator of the motor vehicle is unable to present proof of the vehicle's insurance coverage when requested by a law enforcement officer <u>or</u> if a check of the vehicle insurance database at the time of the traffic stop fails to show current insurance coverage, the operator must be issued, in addition to any traffic citation issued for a violation of this section, a notice of noncompliance with the provisions of this section on a form to be provided to the Department of Finance and Administration.

The officer must forward a copy of the notice of noncompliance to the department within 10 days of issuance. In addition, the officer must remove and impound the license plate attached to the vehicle. The license plate shall be returned to the Office of Driver Services or to the local revenue office. The law enforcement officer who removes and impounds the license plate must issue for attachment to the rear of the vehicle a temporary sticker denoting its use in lieu of an official license plate. The sticker must bear the date upon which it shall expire in written or stamped numerals or alphabetic characters not less than three inches (3") in height. This temporary sticker shall only be effective for a period of 10 days beginning from the day on which the license plate was taken. The temporary stickers shall be designed by the department and supplied at no cost to all law enforcement agencies authorized to enforce traffic laws in Arkansas. However, if the vehicle was insured at the time of the offense, the owner of the vehicle shall have 10 days to present proof of insurance coverage or other financial security in effect at the time of the offense, whereupon the license plate shall be returned at no cost to the owner of the vehicle.

### (18.25) Violations (§27-37-101)

It is a misdemeanor for any person to drive, or for the owner to cause or knowingly permit to be driven or moved, on any highway any vehicle, or combination of vehicles, which is in such unsafe condition as to endanger any person, or which does not contain those parts, or is not at all times equipped with equipment in proper condition and adjustment as required in this chapter or which is equipped in any manner in violation of this chapter, or for any person to do any act forbidden or fail to perform any act required under this chapter.

### (18.26) Requirements [Child Restraints] (§27-34-104)

Every driver who transports a child under 15 years of age in a passenger automobile, van, or pickup truck, other than one operated for hire, which is registered in this or any other state, shall provide while the motor vehicle is in motion and operated on a public road, street, or highway of this state for the protection of the child by properly placing, maintaining, and securing the child in a child passenger restraint system properly secured to the vehicle and meeting applicable federal motor vehicle safety standards in effect on January 1, 1995.

A child who is less than 6 years of age and who weighs less than 60 lbs. must be restrained in a child passenger safety seat properly secured to the vehicle. If a child is at least six 6 years of age or at least 60 lbs. in weight, a safety belt properly secured to the vehicle will be sufficient to meet the requirements of this section.

### *(18.27) Riding in Spaces Not For Passengers (§ 27-35-104)*

No person may ride on any vehicle upon any portion of the vehicle not designed or intended for the use of passengers. This section does not apply to any employee engaged in the necessary discharge of a duty or to persons riding within bodies of trucks in space intended for merchandise.

### *(18.28) Spilling Loads on Highways Prohibited (§27-35-110)*

No vehicle may be driven or moved on any highway unless the vehicle is so constructed or loaded as to prevent any of its load from dropping, sifting, leaking, or otherwise escaping.

Sand may be dropped for the purpose of securing traction, or water or other substance may be sprinkled on a roadway in cleaning or maintaining the roadway.

For a motor vehicle or a trailer with an open bed manufactured after September 30, 2001, no sand, gravel, or rock shall be transported on the paved public streets and highways of this state in a motor vehicle or trailer with an open bed unless the open bed is securely covered with a material which will prevent the load from dropping, sifting, leaking, or otherwise escaping therefrom. The cover must be securely fastened to prevent the covering from becoming loose, detached, or in any manner a hazard to other users of the highway.

For a motor vehicle or a trailer with an open bed manufactured on or before September 30, 2001, a vehicle with an open bed transporting sand, gravel, or rock is required to be covered as described above unless six inches (6") of freeboard is maintained at the perimeter of the load within the open bed of the vehicle or trailer carrying the load. Measurements are to be taken at the perimeter of the vehicle's or trailer's bed and measured from the top edge of the bed down to the sand, gravel, or rock being transported.

### *(18.29) When Lighted Lamps Required (§27-36-204)*

Every vehicle, except motorcycles and motor-driven cycles, upon a highway within this state at any time from one-half hour after sunset to one-half hour before sunrise *and at any other time when there is not sufficient light to render clearly discernible persons and vehicles on the highway at a distance of 500'* ahead must display lighted lamps and illuminating devices as respectively required for different classes of vehicles.

Every vehicle, except motorcycles and motor-driven cycles, upon a street or highway within this state must display lighted lamps and illuminating devices, as respectively required for different classes of vehicles, during any period in which the vehicle's windshield wipers are being used for clearing or cleaning rain, snow, or other precipitation from the windshield because of inclement weather[172].

Every motorcycle and every motor-driven cycle upon a street or highway within this state at any time shall display lighted lamps and illuminating devices as respectively required for different classes of vehicles, subject to exceptions with respect to parked vehicles as stated. During the period between sunrise and ending at sunset, the headlamp displayed by a motorcycle or motor-driven cycle may use either a continuous beam or a pulsating beam.

### *(18.30) Use of Multiple-Beam Road Lighting Equipment (§27-36-211)*

Vehicle lighting must conform to the following requirements and limitations:

---

[172] No vehicle or the operator of the vehicle shall be stopped, inspected, or detained solely for violations of the requirements of this subdivision.

- Whenever a driver of a vehicle approaches an oncoming vehicle within 500', the driver shall use a distribution of light, or composite beam, so aimed that the glaring rays are not projected into the eyes of the oncoming driver[173] (i.e., low beams)
- Whenever the driver of a vehicle follows another vehicle within 200' to the rear, except when engaged in the act of overtaking and passing, the driver must use a distribution of light other than the uppermost distribution of light (i.e., low beams)

### (18.31) Violations (§27-36-301)

It is unlawful for any person, firm, or corporation to exhibit a red or amber rotating or flashing light on any vehicle except as otherwise provided by the statutes of the State of Arkansas or to activate a flashing, rotating, or oscillating purple light except during a funeral procession.

If any person affixes or has affixed any red or amber light on any vehicle, this fact is prima facie proof that this person did exhibit the light.

Except as otherwise provided by the statutes of the State of Arkansas, it is unlawful for any person to install or activate or operate a blue light in or on any vehicle in this state or to possess in or on any vehicle in this state a blue light that is not sealed in the manufacturer's original package. A violation of the blue light prohibition is a Class A misdemeanor.

### (18.32) Windshields, Etc., To Be Unobstructed (§27-37-302)

No person may drive any motor vehicle with any sign, poster, or other nontransparent material[174] upon the front windshield, sidewings, side, or rear windows of the vehicle other than a certificate or other paper required to be so displayed by law if it obstructs the operator's view or the safe operation of the vehicle.

### (18.33) Obstruction of Interior Prohibited (§27-37-304)

It is unlawful for any person to operate a motor vehicle which has any substance or material except rearview mirrors and decals required by law attached to the windshield at any point more than four and one-half inches (4 1/2") above the bottom of the windshield *if the substance or material obstructs the operator's view or the safe operation of the vehicle.*

It is unlawful for any person to operate a motor vehicle which has any substance or material attached to the window of either front door except substances or materials attached by the manufacturer *if the substance or material obstructs the operator's view or the safe operation of the vehicle.*

*The provisions of this section do not apply to motorists driving motor vehicles registered in other states that have enacted legislation regulating the shading of windshields or windows of motor vehicles and who are driving on Arkansas roads and highways.*

A violation of this section is a Class C misdemeanor.

### (18.34) Light Levels for Tinting Of Vehicle Windows (§27-37-306)

It is unlawful to operate a vehicle on the public highways if after-market tinting material, together with striping material, has been applied to any windows of the vehicle or if letters or logos larger than one-quarter inch (1/4") have been applied to the windows of the vehicle.

---

[173] The lowermost distribution of light, or composite beam shall be deemed to avoid glare at all times, regardless of road contour and loading.

[174] Frost and moisture don't count.  See *Wood v. Combs*, 237 Ark. 738, 375 S.W.2d 800 (1964)

After-market tinting of vehicle windows are lawful only as follows:

- The glass immediately in front of the operator may have a strip of tinting material applied to the top edge, known in the industry as an "eyebrow", but it may not extend downward more than five inches (5") from the top center of the windshield
- On all 1994 model vehicles and later model vehicles, the side windows and side wings located on the immediate right or left of the driver or to the right or left immediately behind the driver may be covered with an after-market tinting material which results in at least twenty-five percent (25%) net light transmission, except that the side windows immediately behind the driver on any truck, bus, trailer, motor home, or multiple purpose passenger vehicle may be covered with an after-market tinting material which results in at least ten percent (10%) net light transmission.
- On all 1994 model vehicles and later model vehicles, the rearmost window may be covered with an after-market tinting material which results in at least ten percent (10%) net light transmission.

Any vehicle that is operated on Arkansas roads with after-market tinting material on any glass shall have attached to the front glass immediately to the operator's left a label containing the name and phone number of the company installing the tinting material and affirming that all tinting on the vehicle conforms to the requirements of this section.

*The provisions of this section do not apply to motorists operating vehicles registered in other states that have enacted legislation regulating the shading of windshields or windows of motor vehicles who are driving on Arkansas roads and highways.*

A motorist shall be exempt from this section if the motorist is diagnosed by a physician as having a disease or disorder, including, but not limited to, albinism or lupus, for which the physician determines it is in the best interest of the motorist to be exempt from the requirements of this section. The motorist must carry in his or her motor vehicle a physician's certification.

The provisions of this section are not applicable to vehicles or operators of vehicles used exclusively or primarily for the transportation of dead human bodies.

Any installer of motor vehicle glass tinting material who installs any glass tinting in violation of this section or otherwise violates the provisions of this section or any person operating any motor vehicle with glass tinting or other after-market alteration of the glass in the vehicle which is contrary to the provisions of this section shall be guilty of a Class B misdemeanor.

Notwithstanding any other provision of this section or any other law to the contrary, windshields of law enforcement vehicles may be tinted to the extent that the windshield permits at least fifty percent (50%) net light transmission.

### (18.35) Obedience to Police Officers Required (§27-49-107)

No person may willfully fail or refuse to comply with any lawful order or direction of any police officer invested by law with authority to direct, control, or regulate traffic.

### (18.36) Drivers of Authorized Emergency Vehicles (§27-49-109)

The driver of any authorized emergency vehicle *when responding to an emergency call* upon approaching a red or stop signal or any stop sign must slow down as necessary for safety but may proceed cautiously past the red or stop sign or signal. At other times, drivers of authorized emergency vehicles must stop in obedience to a stop sign or signal.

No driver of any authorized emergency vehicle will assume any special privilege under this act except when the vehicle is operated in response to an emergency call or in the immediate pursuit of an actual or suspected violator of the law.

### (18.37)  Reckless Driving (§27-50-308)

Any person who drives any vehicle in such a manner as to indicate a wanton disregard for the safety of persons or property is guilty of reckless driving.

If physical injury to a person results, every person convicted of reckless driving will be punished upon a first conviction by imprisonment for a period of not less than 30 days and not more than 90 days or by a fine of not less than $100 and not more than $1,000, or by both fine and imprisonment.

Otherwise, every person convicted of reckless driving shall be punished upon a first conviction by imprisonment for a period of not less than 5 days and not more than 90 days or a fine of not less than $25.00 and not more than $500, or by both fine and imprisonment.

For a second or subsequent offense occurring within 3 years of the first offense, every person convicted of reckless driving will be punished by imprisonment for not less than 30 days and not more than 6 months or by a fine of not less than $500 and not more than $1,000, or by both fine and imprisonment.

However, if the second or subsequent offense involves physical injury to a person, the person convicted will be punished by imprisonment for not less than 60 days and not more than 1 year or by a fine of not less than $500 and not more than $1,000, or by both fine and imprisonment.

### (18.38)  Racing On Public Highways (§27-50-309)

This section prohibits any person driving a motor vehicle or motor bicycle upon a public highway in this state in a race.

### (18.39)  Careless and Prohibited Driving (§27-51-104)

It is unlawful for any person to drive or operate any vehicle in such a careless manner as to evidence a failure to keep a proper lookout for other traffic, vehicular or otherwise, or in such a manner as to evidence a failure to maintain proper control on the public thoroughfares or private property in the State of Arkansas.

It is unlawful for any person to operate or drive any vehicle on the public thoroughfares or private property in the State of Arkansas in violation of the following prohibited acts:

- Improper or unsafe lane changes on public roadways
- Driving onto or across private property to avoid intersections, stop signs, traffic control devices, or traffic lights
- Driving in such a manner, or at such a speed, so as to cause a skidding, spinning, or sliding of tires or a sliding of the vehicle
- Driving too close to, or colliding with, parked or stopped vehicles, fixtures, persons, or objects adjacent to the public thoroughfares
- Driving a vehicle which has any part thereof, or any object, extended in such fashion as to endanger persons or property
- To operate any vehicle in such a manner which would cause a failure to maintain control
- To operate or drive a vehicle wherein or whereon passengers are located in such a manner as to be dangerous to the welfare of such passengers
- To operate a vehicle in any manner, when the driver is inattentive, and such inattention is not reasonable and prudent in maintaining vehicular control.

A person who violates this section shall be subject to a fine not to exceed o$100.

### (18.40) Limitations Generally (§27-51-201)

No person may drive a vehicle on a highway at a speed greater than is reasonable and prudent under the conditions and having regard to the actual and potential hazards then existing.

In every event, speed must be so controlled as may be necessary to avoid colliding with any person, vehicle, or other conveyance on or entering the highway in compliance with legal requirements and the duty of all persons to use due care.

On all facilities other than controlled-access highways, except when a special hazard exists, the limits specified in this section or established as authorized shall be maximum lawful speeds, and no person shall drive a vehicle on a highway at a speed in excess of the following limits:

- 30 miles per hour in any urban district
- 50 miles per hour for trucks of one and one-half (1 1/2) ton capacity or more in other locations
- 60 miles per hour for other vehicles in other locations
- No vehicle which is over width, over length, or over height or the gross load of which is in excess of 64,000 lbs, excluding the front axle, even if operated under a special permit, shall be operated in excess of 30 miles per hour
- The driver of every vehicle shall drive at an appropriate reduced speed when
  - approaching and crossing an intersection or railway grade crossing
  - when approaching and going around a curve
  - when approaching the crest of a hill
  - when traveling upon any narrow or winding roadway
  - when special hazard exists with respect to pedestrians or other traffic
  - weather or highway conditions dictate

*In every charge of violation of this section, the complaint and the summons or notice to appear shall specify the speed at which the defendant is alleged to have driven and the prima facie speed applicable within the district or location.*

### (18.41) Restrictions Not Applicable To Emergency Vehicles (§27-51-202)

The prima facie speed limitations set forth in this subchapter shall not apply to authorized emergency vehicles *when responding to emergency calls* when the driver thereof is operating the vehicle's emergency lights and is also operating an audible signal by bell, siren, or exhaust whistle if other vehicles are present.

This section shall not relieve the driver of an authorized emergency vehicle from the duty to drive with due regard for the safety of all persons using the street, nor shall it protect the driver of any emergency vehicle from the consequence of a reckless disregard of the safety of others.

For purposes of this section, **emergency call** means legitimate emergency situations which call for the operation of an emergency vehicle, including a police vehicle.

### (18.42) Speed Limit near Schools – Exceptions (§27-51-212)

No person may operate a motor vehicle in excess of 25 miles per hour when passing a school building or school zone during school hours when children are present and outside the building.

This speed limit shall not be applicable upon the freeways and interstate highways of this state or to school zones adequately protected by a steel fence limiting access to and egress from safety crossings.

### (18.43) Vehicles to Be Driven On Right – Exceptions (§27-51-301)

Upon all roadways of sufficient width, a vehicle shall be driven upon the right half of the roadway, except as follows:

- When overtaking and passing another vehicle proceeding in the same direction under the rules governing that movement.
- When the right half of a roadway is closed to traffic while under construction or repair.
- Upon a roadway divided into 3 marked lanes for traffic under the rules applicable thereon.
- Upon a roadway designated and signposted for one-way traffic.

*Motor vehicles may not be operated continuously in the left lane of a multilane roadway whenever it impedes the flow of other traffic*

### (18.44) One-Way Roadways and Rotary Traffic Islands (§27-51-304)

Upon a roadway designated and signposted for one-way traffic, a vehicle must be driven only in the direction designated.

A vehicle passing around a rotary traffic island must be driven only to the right of such island.

### (18.45) Following Too Closely (§27-51-305)

The driver of a motor vehicle must not follow another vehicle more closely than is reasonable and prudent, having due regard for the speed of vehicles and the traffic upon and the condition of the highway.

The driver of any motor truck or any motor vehicle drawing another vehicle when traveling upon a roadway outside of a business or residence district shall not follow within 200' of another motor vehicle.

The provisions of this subsection shall not be construed to prevent overtaking and passing.

### (18.46) Restrictions on Passing on Left (§27-51-307)

No vehicle shall be driven to the left side of the center of the roadway in overtaking and passing another vehicle proceeding in the same direction unless the left side is clearly visible and is free of oncoming traffic for a sufficient distance ahead to permit overtaking and passing to be completely made without interfering with the safe operation of any vehicle approaching from the opposite direction or any vehicle overtaken.

In every event, the overtaking vehicle must return to the right-hand side of the roadway before coming within 100' of any vehicle approaching from the opposite direction.

No vehicle may, in overtaking and passing another vehicle or at any other time, except upon a one-way roadway, be driven to the left side of the roadway, under the following conditions:

- When approaching the crest of a grade or upon a curve in the highway where the driver's view along the highway is obstructed.
- When approaching within 100' of or traversing any intersection or railroad grade crossing.
- When the view is obstructed upon approaching within 100' of any bridge, viaduct, or tunnel.
- Where official signs are in place directing that traffic keep to the right, or a distinctive center line is marked.

### (18.47) Conditions When Overtaking On Right (§27-51-308)

The driver of a vehicle may overtake and pass upon the right of another vehicle only under the following conditions:

- When the vehicle overtaken is making or about to make a left turn.
- Upon a street or highway with unobstructed pavement not occupied by parked vehicles of sufficient width for 2 or more lines of moving vehicles in each direction.
- Upon a one-way street or upon any roadway on which traffic is restricted to 1 direction of movement where the roadway is free from obstructions and of sufficient width for 2 or more lines of moving vehicles.
- The driver of a vehicle may overtake and pass another vehicle upon the right only under conditions permitting this movement in safety.

*In no event shall this movement be made by driving off the pavement or main-traveled portion of the roadway.*

### (18.48) Turning at Intersections (§27-51-401)

The driver of a vehicle intending to turn at an intersection must do so as follows:

- Both the approach for a right turn and a right turn must be made as close as practical to the right-hand curb or edge of the roadway
- The approach for a left turn must be made in that portion of the right half of the roadway nearest the center line of the road. After entering the intersection, the left turn shall be made so as to leave the intersection to the right of the center line of the roadway being entered
- The approach for a left turn from a two-way street into a one-way street shall be made in that portion of the right one-half (1/2) of the roadway nearest the center line and by passing to the right of the center line where it enters the intersection
- A left turn from a one-way street into a two-way street shall be made by passing to the right of the center line of the street being entered upon leaving the intersection

### (18.49) Stop Signs and Yield Signs (§27-51-601)

Preferential right-of-way at an intersection may be indicated by stop signs or yield signs as authorized by law.

Except when directed to proceed by a police officer or traffic-control signal, every driver of a vehicle and every motorman of a streetcar approaching a stop intersection indicated by a stop sign must stop *before entering the crosswalk* on the near side of the intersection. In the event there is no crosswalk, the driver or motorman must stop at a clearly marked stop line, but if none, then at the point nearest the intersecting roadway where the driver has a view of approaching traffic on the intersecting roadway before entering the intersection.

The driver of a vehicle approaching a yield sign, if required for safety to stop, must stop before entering the crosswalk on the near side of the intersection. In the event there is no crosswalk, the driver must stop at a clearly marked stop line, but if none, then at the point nearest the intersecting roadway where the driver has a view of approaching traffic on the intersecting roadway.

### (18.50) Yield on Entering Highway from Private Road (§27-51-603)

The driver of a vehicle about to enter or cross a highway from a private road or driveway shall yield the right-of-way to all vehicles approaching on the highway.

### (18.51) Obedience to Signals at Crossings Required (§27-51-702)

Whenever any person driving a vehicle approaches a railroad grade crossing under any of the circumstances stated in this section, then the driver of the vehicle must stop within 50' but not less than 15' from the nearest rail of such railroad and must not proceed until he can do so safely. These requirements shall apply when:

- A clearly visible electric or mechanical signal device gives warning of the immediate approach of a railroad train.

- A crossing gate is lowered or a human flagman gives or continues to give a signal of the approach or passage of a railroad train.
- A railroad train approaching within approximately 1500' of the highway crossing emits a signal audible from such distance and the railroad train, by reason of its speed or nearness to the crossing, is an immediate hazard.
- An approaching railroad train is plainly visible and is in hazardous proximity to the crossing.

No person may drive any vehicle through, around, or under any crossing gate or barrier at a railroad crossing while the gate or barrier is closed or is being opened or closed.

### (18.52) Approach of Emergency Vehicles (§27-51-901)

Upon the immediate approach of an authorized emergency vehicle, when the driver is giving audible signal by siren, exhaust whistle, or bell, the driver of every other vehicle must yield the right-of-way and must immediately drive to a position parallel to, and as close as possible to, the right-hand edge or curb of the highway clear of any intersection and *must stop* and remain in such position until the authorized emergency vehicle has passed, except when otherwise directed by a police officer.

*This section shall not operate to relieve the driver of an authorized emergency vehicle from the duty to drive with due regard for the safety of all persons using the highway.*

### (18.53) Passing When Stopped School Bus Prohibited (§27-51-1004)

When a school bus vehicle stops and displays its flashing red lights, every operator of a motor vehicle or motorcycle approaching it from any direction must bring the motor vehicle or motorcycle to a full stop before proceeding in any direction.

In the event the school bus vehicle is receiving or discharging passengers, the operator of the motor vehicle or motorcycle shall not start up or attempt to pass in any direction until the school bus vehicle has finished receiving or discharging its passengers and is in motion again.

### (18.54) Obedience to Official Devices Required (§27-52-103)

No driver of a vehicle or motorman of a streetcar shall disobey the instructions of any official traffic-control device, unless at the time otherwise directed by a police officer.

# PART THREE

# EVIDENCE AND PROCEDURE

# Chapter 19: Evidence Law

## (19.1) Evidence Law in General

In previous sections, we discussed the elements of crimes and how they must be proven beyond a reasonable doubt to secure a conviction. To prove these elements in court, we must resort to evidence. The chapter deals with how that evidence can be used in court. Many LEOs ignore this area of law, thinking that such concerns are for the district attorney. This is unfortunate. The case the DA can build is only as good as the evidence supplied by the police. The more officers know about the selection, collection, preservation of evidence, the better the chances that an investigation will result in a conviction.

## (19.2) Hearsay

### a. Defining Hearsay

Hearsay is second hand information. Hearsay occurs when someone testifies about what someone else told him or her, not what he or she personally saw or heard. Hearsay evidence is generally prohibited in criminal trials. The reason for this is that it violates the defendant's due process rights because it does not allow the defendant to confront the real witness—the person who actually heard or saw something of evidentiary value.

A **Statement** is either (1) an oral or written assertion, or (2) a nonverbal conduct of a person, if he intends it as an assertion[175]. A *declarant* is a person who makes a statement.

The official definition of **hearsay** in Arkansas is "*a statement, other than one made by the declarant while testifying at the trial or hearing, offered in evidence to prove the truth of the matter asserted.*"[176]

### b. Hearsay Exceptions

The **Arkansas Rules of Evidence** differentiate between hearsay exceptions that require the witness to be unavailable before they are invoked and exceptions where the availability of the witness is immaterial. The following are not excluded by the hearsay rule, even though the declarant is available as a witness:

- *Present Sense Impression.* A statement describing or explaining an event or condition made while the declarant was perceiving the event or condition, or immediately thereafter. Arkansas courts require that two criteria be met before a statement can be considered a present sense impression:

  o It must describe or explain the event the declarant is perceiving
  o The statement must be made while the event or condition is being perceived or very near the time that it was perceived[177].

---

[175] Ark. R. Evid., Rule 801(a)
[176] Ark. R. Evid., Rule 801(c)
[177] *Brown v. State*, 320 Ark. 201

- ***Excited Utterance***. A statement relating to a startling event or condition made while the declarant was under the stress of excitement caused by the event or condition[178]. *Police officers wishing to use such statements in evidence should make notes as to the declarant's excited condition.*

- ***Then Existing Mental, Emotional, or Physical Condition***. A statement of the declarant's then existing state of mind, emotion, sensation, or physical condition, such as intent, plan, motive, design, mental feeling, pain, and bodily health, but not including a statement of memory or belief to prove the fact remembered or believed unless it relates to the execution, revocation, identification, or terms of declarant's will[179].

- ***Statements for Purposes of Medical Diagnosis or Treatment***. Statements made for purposes of medical diagnosis or treatment and describing medical history, or past or present symptoms, pain, or sensation, or the inception or general character of the cause or external source thereof insofar as reasonably pertinent to diagnosis or treatment[180].

- ***Recorded Recollection***. A memorandum or record concerning a matter about which a witness once had knowledge but now has insufficient recollection to enable him to testify fully and accurately, shown to have been made or adopted by the witness when the matter was fresh in his memory and to reflect that knowledge correctly. If admitted, the memorandum or record may be read into evidence but may not itself be received as an exhibit unless offered by an adverse party[181].

- ***Records of Regularly Conducted Business Activity***. A memorandum, report, record, or data compilation, in any form, of acts, events, conditions, opinions, or disagnoses [sic], made at or near the time by, or from information transmitted by, a person with knowledge, if kept in the course of a regularly conducted business activity, and if it was the regular practice of that business activity to make the memorandum, report, record, or data compilation, all as shown by the testimony of the custodian or other qualified witness, unless the source of information or the method or circumstances of preparation indicate lack of trustworthiness. The term "business" as used in this paragraph includes business, institution, association, profession, occupation, and calling of every kind, whether or not conducted for profit[182].

- ***Absence of Entry in Records Kept in Accordance With the Provisions of Paragraph 6***. Evidence that a matter is not included in the memoranda, reports, records, or data compilations, in any form, kept in accordance with the provisions of paragraph (6), to prove the nonoccurrence or nonexistence of the matter, if the matter was of a kind of which a memorandum, report, record, or data compilation was regularly made and preserved, unless the sources of information or other circumstances indicate lack of trustworthiness[183].

- ***Public Records and Reports***. To the extent not otherwise provided in this paragraph, records, reports, statements, or data compilations in any form of a public office or agency setting forth its regularly conducted and regularly recorded activities, or matters observed pursuant to duty imposed by law and as to which there was a duty to report, or factual findings resulting from an investigation made pursuant to authority granted by law. The following are not within this exception to the hearsay rule:

  o investigative reports by police and other law enforcement personnel
  o investigative reports prepared by or for a government, a public office, or an agency when offered by it in a case in which it is a party

---

[178] Ark. R. Evid., Rule 803(2)
[179] Ark. R. Evid., Rule 803(3)
[180] Ark. R. Evid., Rule 803(4)
[181] Ark. R. Evid., Rule 803(5)
[182] Ark. R. Evid., Rule 803(6)
[183] Ark. R. Evid., Rule 803(7)

- o   factual findings offered by the government in criminal cases
- o   factual findings resulting from special investigation of a particular complaint, case, or incident
- o   any matter as to which the sources of information or other circumstances indicate lack of trustworthiness[184].

- ***Records of Vital Statistics.***  Records or data compilations, in any form, of birth, fetal deaths, deaths, or marriages, if the report thereof was made to a public office pursuant to requirements of law[185].

- ***Absence of Public Record or Entry.***  To prove the absence of a record, report, statement, or data compilation, in any form, or the nonoccurrence or nonexistence of a matter of which a record, report, statement, or data compilation, in any form, was regularly made and preserved by a public office or agency, evidence in the form of a certification in accordance with Rule 902, or testimony, that diligent search failed to disclose the record, report, statement, or data compilation, or entry[186].

- ***Records of Religious Organizations.***  Statements of births, marriages, divorces, death, legitimacy, ancestry, relationship by blood or marriage, or other similar facts of personal or family history, contained in a regularly kept record of a religious organization[187].

- ***Marriage, Baptismal, and Similar Certificates.***  Statements of fact contained in a certificate that the maker performed a marriage or other ceremony or administered a sacrament, made by a clergyman, public official, or other person authorized by the rules or practices of a religious organization or by law to perform the act certified, and purporting to have been issued at the time of the act or within a reasonable time thereafter[188].

- ***Family Records.***  Statements of fact concerning personal or family history contained in family Bibles, genealogies, charts, engravings on rings, inscriptions on family portraits, engravings on urns, crypts, or tombstones, or the like[189].

- ***Records of Documents Affecting an Interest in Property.***  The record of a document purporting to establish or affect an interest in property, as proof of the content of the original recorded document and its execution and delivery by each person by whom it purports to have been executed, if the record is a record of a public office and applicable statute authorizes the recording of documents of that kind in that office[190].

- ***Statements in Documents Affecting an Interest in Property.***  A statement contained in a document purporting to establish or affect an interest in property if the matter stated was relevant to the purpose of the document, unless dealings with the property since the document was made have been inconsistent with the truth of the statement or the purport of the document[191].

- ***Statements in Ancient Documents.***  Statements in a document in existence twenty (20) years or more the authenticity of which is established[192].

---

[184] Ark. R. Evid., Rule 803(8)
[185] Ark. R. Evid., Rule 803(9)
[186] Ark. R. Evid., Rule 803(10)
[187] Ark. R. Evid., Rule 803(11)
[188] Ark. R. Evid., Rule 803(12)
[189] Ark. R. Evid., Rule 803(13)
[190] Ark. R. Evid., Rule 803(14)
[191] Ark. R. Evid., Rule 803(15)
[192] Ark. R. Evid., Rule 803(16)

- ***Market Reports, Commercial Publications****.*  Market quotations, tabulations, lists, directories, or other published compilations, generally used and relied upon by the public or by persons in particular occupations[193].

- ***Learned Treatises****.*  To the extent called to the attention of an expert witness upon cross-examination or relied upon by him in direct examination, statements contained in published treatises, periodicals, or pamphlets on a subject of history, medicine, or other science or art, established as a reliable authority by testimony or admission of the witness or by other expert testimony or by judicial notice.  If admitted, the statements may be read into evidence but may not be received as exhibits[194].

- ***Reputation Concerning Personal or Family History****.*  Reputation among members of his family by blood, adoption, or marriage, or among his associates, or in the community, concerning a person's birth, adoption, marriage, divorce, death, legitimacy, relationship by blood, adoption, or marriage, ancestry, or other similar fact of his personal or family history[195].

- ***Reputation Concerning Boundaries or General History****.*  Reputation in a community, arising before the controversy, as to boundaries of or customs affecting lands in the community, and reputation as to events of general history important to the community or state or nation in which located[196].

- ***Reputation as to Character****.*  Reputation of a person's character among his associates or in the community[197].

- ***Judgment of Previous Conviction****.*  Evidence of a final judgment, (entered after a trial or upon a plea of guilty,) adjudging a person guilty of a crime punishable by death or imprisonment in excess of 1 year, to prove any fact essential to sustain the judgment, but not including, when offered by the state in a criminal prosecution for purposes other than impeachment, judgments against persons other than the accused.  The pendency of an appeal may be shown but does not affect admissibility[198].

- ***Judgment as to Personal, Family or General History, or Boundaries****.*  Judgments as proof of matters of personal, family or general history, or boundaries, essential to the judgment, if the same would be provable by evidence of reputation[199].

- ***Other Exceptions****.*  A statement not specifically covered by any of the foregoing exceptions but having equivalent circumstantial guarantees of trustworthiness, if the court determines that

    o   the statement is offered as evidence of a material fact
    o   the statement is more probative on the point for which it is offered than any other evidence which the proponent can procure through reasonable efforts
    o   the general purposes of these rules and the interests of justice will best be served by admission of the statement into evidence.

    However, a statement may not be admitted under this exception unless the proponent of it makes known to the adverse party sufficiently in advance to provide the adverse party with a fair opportunity to prepare to meet it,

---

[193] Ark. R. Evid., Rule 803(17)
[194] Ark. R. Evid., Rule 803(18)
[195] Ark. R. Evid., Rule 803(19)
[196] Ark. R. Evid., Rule 803(20)
[197] Ark. R. Evid., Rule 803(21)
[198] Ark. R. Evid., Rule 803(22)
[199] Ark. R. Evid., Rule 803(23)

his intention to offer the statement and the particulars of it, including the name and address of the declarant[200].

- ***Child Hearsay When Declarant is Available at Trial and subject to Cross-examination***.  A statement made by a child under the age of ten (10) years concerning any type of sexual offense, or attempted sexual offense, with, on, or against that child, which is inconsistent with the child's testimony and offered in a criminal proceeding, provided:

  o The trial court conducts a hearing outside the presence of the jury and finds that the statement offered possesses a reasonable guarantee of trustworthiness considering the competency of the child both at the time of the out of court statement and at the time of the testimony.
  o The proponent of the statement gives the adverse party reasonable notice of his intention to offer the statement and the particulars of the statement.
  o This section shall not be construed to limit the admission of an offered statement under any other hearsay exception or applicable rule of evidence[201].

Arkansas Rules of Evidence Rule 804 governs hearsay exceptions that deal with situations where the declarant is unavailable.  According to the rule, **unavailability** includes situations where the declarant:

- Is exempted on the ground of *privilege* from testifying concerning the subject matter of his statement.
- Persists in refusing to testify concerning the subject matter of his statement despite an order of the court to do so.
- Testifies to a lack of memory of the subject matter of his statement.
- Is unable to be present or to testify at the hearing because of death, then existing physical or mental illness, or infirmity.
- Is absent from the hearing and the proponent of his statement has been unable to procure his attendance .

A declarant is *not* unavailable as a witness if his exemption, refusal, claim of lack of memory, inability, or absence is due to the procurement or wrongdoing of the proponent of his statement for the purpose of preventing the witness from attending or testifying[202].

The following are not excluded by the hearsay rule if the declarant is unavailable as a witness:

- ***Former testimony***.  Testimony given as a witness at another hearing of the same or a different proceeding, or in a deposition taken in compliance with law in the course of the same or another proceeding, if the party against whom the testimony is now offered, or, in a civil action or proceeding a predecessor in interest, had an opportunity and similar motive to develop the testimony by direct, cross, or redirect examination[203].

- ***Statement under belief of impending death***.  A statement made by a declarant while believing that his death was imminent, concerning the cause or circumstances of what he believed to be his impending death[204].

- ***Statement against interest***.  A statement which was at the time of its making so far contrary to the declarant's pecuniary or proprietary interest, or so far tended to subject him to civil or criminal liability or to render invalid a claim by him against another or to make him an object of hatred, ridicule, or disgrace, that a reasonable man in his position would not have made the statement unless he believed it to be true. A statement tending to expose the declarant to criminal liability and offering to exculpate the accused is not admissible

---

[200] Ark. R. Evid., Rule 803(24)
[201] Ark. R. Evid., Rule 803(25)
[202] Ark. R. Evid., Rule 804(a)
[203] Ark. R. Evid., Rule 804(b)(1)
[204] Ark. R. Evid., Rule 804(b)(2)

unless corroborating circumstances clearly indicate the trustworthiness of the statement. A statement or confession offered against the accused in a criminal case, made by a codefendant or other person implicating both himself and the accused, is not within this exception[205].

- ***Statement of personal or family history.***  A statement concerning the declarant's own birth, adoption, marriage, divorce, legitimacy, relationship by blood, adoption, marriage, anecestry [ancestry], or other similar fact of personal or family history, even though declarant had no means of acquiring personal knowledge of the matter stated.  In addition, a statement concerning the foregoing matters and death also, of another person, if the declarant was related to the other by blood, adoption, or marriage or was so intimately associated with the other's family as to be likely to have accurate information concerning the matter declared[206].

- ***Other exceptions.***  A statement not specifically covered by any of the foregoing exceptions but having equivalent circumstantial guarantees of trustworthiness, if the court determines that

    o   The statement is offered as evidence of a material fact
    o   The statement is more probative on the point for which it is offered than any other evidence which the proponent can procure through reasonable efforts
    o   The general purposes of these rules and the interests of justice will best be served by admission of the statements into evidence.

    However, a statement may not be admitted under this exception unless the proponent of it makes known to the adverse party sufficiently in advance to provide the adverse party with a fair opportunity to prepare to meet it, his intention to offer the statement and the particulars of it, including the name and address of the declarant[207].

***Child hearsay in criminal cases.***  A statement made by a child under the age of 10 years concerning any type of sexual offense against that child, where the Confrontation Clause of the Sixth Amendment of the United States is applicable, provided:  The trial court conducts a hearing outside the presence of the jury, and, with the evidentiary presumption that the statement is unreliable and inadmissible, finds that the statement offered possesses sufficient guarantees of trustworthiness that the truthfulness of the child's statement is so clear from the surrounding circumstances that the test of cross-examination would be of marginal utility. The trial court may employ any factor it deems appropriate including, but not limited to those listed below, in deciding whether the statement is sufficiently trustworthy.

- The spontaneity of the statement.
- The lack of time to fabricate.
- The consistency and repetition of the statement and whether the child has recanted the statement.
- The mental state of the child.
- The competency of the child to testify.
- The child's use of terminology unexpected of a child of similar age.
- The lack of a motive by the child to fabricate the statement.
- The lack of bias by the child.
- Whether it is an embarrassing event the child would not normally relate.
- The credibility of the person testifying to the statement.
- Suggestiveness created by leading questions.

---

[205] Ark. R. Evid., Rule 804(b)(3)
[206] Ark. R. Evid., Rule 804(b)(4)
[207] Ark. R. Evid., Rule 804(b)(5)

- Whether an adult with custody or control of the child may bear a grudge against the accused offender, and may attempt to coach the child into making false charges.
- The proponent of the statement gives the adverse party reasonable notice of his intention to offer the statement and the particulars of the statement.

This section shall not be construed to limit the admission of an offered statement under any other hearsay exception or applicable rule of evidence[208].

### (19.3) Judicial Notice

Under the Arkansas Rules of Evidence, Rule 201 governs judicial notice of *adjudicative facts*[209].

A judicially noticed fact must be one *not* subject to reasonable dispute. According the rule, this means that it must be either generally known within the territorial jurisdiction of the trial court, or capable of accurate and ready determination by resort to sources whose accuracy cannot reasonably be questioned[210]. Judicial notice may be taken at any stage of the proceeding[211]. Once the court has taken judicial notice of a fact, it will instruct the jury to treat that fact as conclusive[212].

### (19.4) Relevancy

#### a. Defining Relevancy

Because *evidence that is not relevant is not admissible*[213], it is important to understand the legal idea of relevancy.

**Relevant evidence** means evidence having any tendency to make the existence of any fact that is of consequence to the determination of the action more probable or less probable than it would be without the evidence[214].

All relevant evidence is admissible, unless some statute, rule of evidence, or other rule excludes it[215].

#### b. Exclusion of Relevant Evidence

Although relevant, evidence may be excluded if its probative value is substantially outweighed by the danger of unfair prejudice, confusion of the issues, or misleading the jury, or by considerations of undue delay, waste of time, or needless presentation of cumulative evidence[216].

#### c. Character and Habit Evidence

Generally, evidence of a person's character is not admissible for proving that he acted in conformity with his or her character *on a particular occasion*. There are three major exceptions to the general rule:

1. Evidence of a pertinent trait of his character offered by an accused, or by the prosecution to rebut the same.
2. Evidence of a pertinent trait of character of the victim of the crime offered by an accused, or by the prosecution to rebut the same, or evidence of a character trait of peacefulness of the victim offered by the prosecution in a homicide case to rebut evidence that the victim was the first aggressor
3. Evidence of the character of a witness, as provided in Rules 607, 608, and 609[217].

---

[208] Ark. R. Evid., Rule 804(b)(7)
[209] Ark. R. Evid., Rule 201(a)
[210] Ark. R. Evid., Rule 201(b)
[211] Ark. R. Evid., Rule 201(f)
[212] Ark. R. Evid., Rule 201(g)
[213] Ark. R. Evid., Rule 402
[214] Ark. R. Evid., Rule 401
[215] Ark. R. Evid., Rule 402
[216] Ark. R. Evid., Rule 403

Evidence of other crimes, wrongs, or acts is not admissible to prove the character of a person in order to show that he acted in conformity to that character. It may, however, be admissible for other purposes, such as proof of motive, opportunity, intent, preparation, plan, knowledge, identity, or absence of mistake or accident[218].

Rule 405 stipulates two methods used to prove character. In all cases in which evidence of character is admissible, proof may be made by testimony as to reputation or by testimony in the form of an opinion. On cross-examination, inquiry is allowable into relevant specific instances of conduct[219]. In cases in which character or a trait of character of a person is an essential element of a charge, claim, or defense, proof may also be made of specific instances of his conduct[220].

Rule 406 deals with the admissibility and proof of evidence tending to show habit or routine practice. Evidence of the habit of a person or of the routine practice of an organization, whether corroborated or not and regardless of the presence of eyewitnesses, is relevant to prove that the conduct of the person or organization on a particular occasion was in conformity with the habit or routine practice[221]. Habit or routine practice may be proved by testimony in the form of an opinion or by specific instances of conduct sufficient in number to warrant a finding that the habit existed or that the practice was routine[222].

### d. Pleas and Offers

Evidence of a plea of nolo contendere, whether or not later withdrawn, and of a plea, later withdrawn, of guilty or admission to the charge, or of an offer to plead to the crime charged or any other crime, or of statements made in connection with any of the foregoing pleas or offers, is not admissible in any civil or criminal action, case, or proceeding against the person who made the plea or offer[223].

## (19.5) Privileges

### a. Privilege In General

Except as otherwise provided by constitution or statute or by these or other rules promulgated by the Supreme Court of this State, no person has a privilege to:

1. refuse to be a witness
2. refuse to disclose any matter
3. refuse to produce any object or writing
4. prevent another from being a witness or disclosing any matter or producing any object or writing

### b. Lawyer-client privilege

A client has a privilege to refuse to disclose and to prevent any other person from disclosing confidential communications made for facilitating the rendition of professional legal services to the client under five circumstances:

1. between himself or his representative and his lawyer or his lawyer's representative
2. between his lawyer and the lawyer's representative

---

[217] Ark. R. Evid., Rule 404(a)
[218] Ark. R. Evid., Rule 404(b)
[219] Ark. R. Evid., Rule 405(a)
[220] Ark. R. Evid., Rule 405(b)
[221] Ark. R. Evid., Rule 406(a)
[222] Ark. R. Evid., Rule 406(b)
[223] Ark. R. Evid., Rule 410

3. by him or his representative or his lawyer or a representative of the lawyer to a lawyer or a representative of a lawyer representing another party in a pending action and concerning a matter of common interest therein
4. between representatives of the client or between the client and a representative of the client, or
5. among lawyers and their representatives representing the same client[224]

There are several exceptions to the lawyer-client privilege. Only those relevant to criminal cases are provided here. The privilege does not exist of the following is true:

1. If the services of the lawyer were sought or obtained to enable or aid anyone to commit or plan to commit what the client knew or reasonably should have known to be a crime or fraud[225]
2. As to a communication between a public officer or agency and its lawyers unless the communication concerns a pending investigation, claim, or action and the court determines that disclosure will seriously impair the ability of the public officer or agency to process the claim or conduct a pending investigation, litigation, or proceeding in the public interest

### c. Physician and psychotherapist-patient privilege

A patient has a privilege to refuse to disclose and to prevent any other person from disclosing his medical records or confidential communications made for the purpose of diagnosis or treatment of his physical, mental or emotional condition, including alcohol or drug addiction, among himself, physician or psychotherapist, and persons who are participating in the diagnosis or treatment under the direction of the physician or psychotherapist, including members of the patient's family[226].

There are three major exceptions to the patient privilege:

1. There is no privilege under this rule for communications relevant to an issue in proceedings to hospitalize the patient for mental illness, if the psychotherapist in the course of diagnosis or treatment has determined that the patient is in need of hospitalization[227].
2. If the court orders an examination of the physical, mental, or emotional condition of a patient, whether a party or a witness, communications made in the course thereof are not privileged under this rule with respect to the particular purpose for which the examination is ordered unless the court orders otherwise[228].
3. There is no privilege under this rule as to medical records or communications relevant to an issue of the physical, mental, or emotional condition of the patient in any proceeding in which he or she relies upon the condition as an element of his or her claim or defense, or, after the patients death, in any proceeding in which any party relies upon the condition as an element of his or her claim or defense[229].

### d. Husband-wife privilege

An accused in a criminal proceeding has a privilege to prevent his spouse from testifying as to any confidential communication between the accused and the spouse. The privilege may be claimed by the accused or by the spouse on behalf of the accused[230].

There is no privilege under this rule in a proceeding in which one spouse is charged with a crime against the person or property of *any* of the following:

---

[224] Ark. R. Evid., Rule 502(b)
[225] Ark. R. Evid., Rule 502(d)(1)
[226] Ark. R. Evid., Rule 503(b)
[227] Ark. R. Evid., Rule 503(d)(1)
[228] Ark. R. Evid., Rule 503(d)(2)
[229] Ark. R. Evid., Rule 503(d)(3)
[230] Ark. R. Evid., Rule 504(b)

1. the other
2. a child of either
3. a person residing in the household of either
4. a third person committed in the course of committing a crime against any of them[231]

### e. Religious privilege

A person has a privilege to refuse to disclose and to prevent another from disclosing a confidential communication by the person to a clergyman in his professional character as spiritual adviser[232].

### f. Political vote

Every person has a privilege to refuse to disclose the tenor of his vote at a political election conducted by secret ballot[233]. This privilege does not apply if the court finds that the vote was cast illegally or determines that the disclosure should be compelled pursuant to the election laws[234].

### g. Identity of informer

The United States or a state or subdivision thereof (i.e., local law enforcement) has a privilege to refuse to disclose the identity of a person who has furnished information relating to or assisting in an investigation of a possible violation of a law to a law enforcement officer or member of a legislative committee or its staff conducting an investigation[235]. Several exceptions do, however, exist to this rule[236].

### h. Waiver of privilege by voluntary disclosure

A person upon whom these rules confer a privilege against disclosure waives the privilege if he or his predecessor while holder of the privilege voluntarily discloses or consents to disclosure of any significant part of the privileged matter[237]. This rule does not apply if the disclosure itself is privileged.

## *(19.6) Witnesses*

### a. Witnesses in General

Every person is competent to be a witness except as otherwise provided in the Rules of Evidence[238]. A witness may not testify to a matter unless evidence is introduced sufficient to support a finding that he has personal knowledge of the matter. Evidence to prove personal knowledge may, but need not, consist of the testimony of the witness himself[239].

Before testifying, every witness shall be required to declare that he will testify truthfully, by oath or affirmation administered in a form calculated to awaken his conscience and impress his mind with his duty to do so[240].

### b. Witness Credibility

Any party, including the party calling him, may attack the credibility of a witness[241].

---

[231] Ark. R. Evid., Rule 504(d)
[232] Ark. R. Evid., Rule 505(b)
[233] Ark. R. Evid., Rule 506(a)
[234] Ark. R. Evid., Rule 506(b)
[235] Ark. R. Evid., Rule 509(a)
[236] see Ark. R. Evid., Rule 509(c)
[237] Ark. R. Evid., Rule 510
[238] Ark. R. Evid., Rule 601
[239] Ark. R. Evid., Rule 602
[240] Ark. R. Evid., Rule 603
[241] Ark. R. Evid., Rule 607

The credibility of a witness may be attacked or supported by evidence in the form of opinion or reputation, but subject to both of the following limitations:

1. the evidence may refer only to character for truthfulness or untruthfulness
2. evidence of truthful character is admissible only after the character of the witness for truthfulness has been attacked by opinion or reputation evidence or otherwise[242]

Specific instances of the conduct of a witness, for the purpose of attacking or supporting his credibility[243] may not be proved by extrinsic evidence. They may, however, in the discretion of the court, if probative of truthfulness or untruthfulness, be inquired into on cross-examination of the witness concerning his character for truthfulness or concerning the character for truthfulness or untruthfulness of another witness as to which character the witness being cross-examined has testified.

The giving of testimony, whether by an accused or by any other witness, does not operate as a waiver of his privilege against self-incrimination when examined with respect to matters which relate only to credibility.

For the purpose of attacking the credibility of a witness, evidence that he has been convicted of a crime shall be admitted under two circumstances. First, evidence can be admitted if the crime was a felony and the court determines that the probative value of admitting this evidence outweighs its prejudicial effect to a party or a witness. Second, the evidence can be admitted if the offense involved dishonesty or false statement, regardless of the punishment[244].

Evidence of the beliefs or opinions of a witness on matters of religion is not admissible for the purpose of showing that by reason of their nature his credibility is impaired or enhanced[245].

### c. Writing or object used to refresh memory

If, while testifying, a witness uses a writing or object to refresh his memory, an adverse party is entitled to have the writing or object produced at the trial, hearing, or deposition in which the witness is testifying[246].

If, before testifying, a witness uses a writing or object to refresh his memory for the purpose of testifying and the court in its discretion determines that the interests of justice so require, an adverse party is entitled to have the writing or object produced, if practicable, at the trial, hearing, or deposition in which the witness is testifying.

### *(19.7) Opinions and Expert Testimony*

### a. Lay Witness Testimony

If the witness is not testifying as an expert, his testimony in the form of opinions or inferences is limited to those opinions or inferences that are rationally based on the perception of the witness and helpful to a clear understanding of his testimony or the determination of a fact in issue[247].

### b. Expert Witness Testimony in General

If scientific, technical, or other specialized knowledge will assist the trier of fact to understand the evidence or to determine a fact in issue, a witness qualified as an expert by knowledge, skill, experience, training, or education, may testify thereto in the form of an opinion or otherwise[248].

---

[242] Ark. R. Evid., Rule 608(a)

[243] other than conviction of crime as provided in Rule 609

[244] Ark. R. Evid., Rule 609

[245] Ark. R. Evid., Rule 610

[246] Ark. R. Evid., Rule 612(a)

[247] Ark. R. Evid., Rule 701

The facts or data in the particular case upon which an expert bases an opinion or inference may be those perceived by or made known to him at or before the hearing. If of a type reasonably relied upon by experts in the particular field in forming opinions or inferences upon the subject, the facts or data need not be admissible in evidence[249].

Testimony in the form of an opinion or inference otherwise admissible is not objectionable because it embraces an ultimate issue to be decided by the trier of fact[250].

---

[248] Ark. R. Evid., Rule 702
[249] Ark. R. Evid., Rule 703
[250] Ark. R. Evid., Rule 704

# Chapter 20: The Fourth Amendment

*The right of the people to be secure in their persons, houses, papers, and effects, against unreasonable searches and seizures, shall not be violated, and no warrants shall issue, but upon probable cause, supported by oath or affirmation, and particularly describing the place to be searched, and the persons or things to be seized.*

—Fourth Amendment of the Constitution of the United States

*The right of the people of this State to be secure in their persons, houses, papers and effects against unreasonable searches and seizures shall not be violated; and no warrant shall issue except upon probable cause, supported by oath or affirmation, and particularly describing the place to be searched and the person or thing to be seized.*

—Article 1, Section 15 of the Arkansas Constitution

## (20.1) Encounters Less than Arrest

### a. Voluntary Contact

You do not need to have any evidence of a crime to approach a person and engage them in conversation. This includes asking the person's name and to see the person's identification. This type of contact with citizens must be **voluntary**. You may *not* create a situation where reasonable persons would believe that they are under official control and are not free to leave[251].

Such contact may include a request for permission to search the person and the person's belongings. You do not have to tell the person that they are not required to cooperate[252].

In general, you do not have the authority to detain a person for investigation. Unless there is a special reason for the detention (**investigative detention**), an officer must rely on voluntary cooperation.

You may, however, ask people to cooperate in investigation or prevention of crime. You may ask them to respond to questions, to appear at a police station, or to comply with any other reasonable request[253].

A citizen has not been "detained" within the meaning of the law if you simply ask them a question concerning his or her identity.

For a citizen encounter ***not*** to be considered a "detention," two things must be present:

1.  No physical control or official authority can be exerted over the person.

---

[251] *Florida v. Royer*, 460 U.S. 491 (1983)
[252] *Florida v. Bostick*, 501 U.S. 429 (1991)
[253] *Ark. R. Crim. P.* Rule 2.2(a)

2.  A reasonable person in the citizen's situation would believe that he or she is free to end the encounter at any time.

You may *not* indicate that a person is legally obligated to furnish information or other cooperation if no such obligation exists. Compliance with the request for cooperation will not be considered involuntary or coerced by the courts merely because the request came from a law enforcement officer[254].

When a citizen encounter takes place in a confined space such as a bus or a room with only one door, you should take care not to block the exits in such a way that a reasonable person would believe that he or she is not free to go[255].

If you ask a person to voluntarily come or remain at a police station, prosecuting attorney's office, or other similar place, you must take reasonable steps to make clear that there is no legal obligation to comply with the request[256].

### b. K-9 Contact

A trained police dog may sniff a person or the person's property, so long as the encounter is reasonably conducted and the person's freedom of movement and control of their property is not interfered with[257].

The result of a dog sniff may create evidence for a subsequent **investigative detention** or probable cause for an arrest.

Likewise, having a dog sniff a vehicle in a public place does not constitute a search. However, the ARSC has determined that once a routine traffic stop is completed, independent reasonable suspicion is required to conduct a sniff[258].

### c. Investigative Detention (a.k.a. Terry Stop)

If you have specific facts that amount to **reasonable suspicion** that a person is committing, has committed, or is about to commit a crime, you may detain the person briefly to ask for identification and question them about the suspected crime[259].

In Arkansas, reasonable suspicion is defined as "a suspicion based on facts or circumstances which of themselves do not give rise to the probable cause required to justify a lawful arrest, but which give rise to more than bare suspicion; that is, a suspicion that is reasonable as opposed to an imaginary or purely conjectural suspicion."[260]

You may use reasonable, non-deadly force to exercise control, but only if the force is obviously necessary[261].

The existence of a **reasonable suspicion** depends on the **totality of the circumstances**. The USSC has said that this evidence must be evaluated in the light of the officer's training and experience[262].

---

[254] *Ark. R. Crim. P.* Rule 2.2(b)

[255] Arkansas Attorney General's Office. (2004). *Arkansas Law Enforcement Pocket Manual.* Little Rock: Arkansas Attorney General's Office. (p. 1).

[256] *Ark. R. Crim. P.* Rule 2.3

[257] *United States v. Place*, 462 U.S. 696 (1983)

[258] *Sims v. Sate*, CR03-63 (2004)

[259] *Terry v. Ohio*, 392 U.S. 1 (1968)

[260] *Ark. R. Crim. P.* Rule 2.1

[261] *Ark. R. Crim. P.* Rule 3.3

[262] *United States v. Arviza*, 534 U.S. 266 (2002)

*In order to have **reasonable suspicion**, you must have reasons indicating that a suspect may be involved in criminal activity. Those reasons must be (1) **specific**, (2) **particularized**, and (3) **articulable**[263].*

The USSC has also ruled that an anonymous tip that a person is carrying a gun is not by itself enough to justify a stop[264]. If you can corroborate the tip sufficiently, then you may have reasonable suspicion to make the stop.

A person's flight from the police may be considered among the facts supporting reasonable suspicion, but generally cannot be taken alone as reasonable suspicion[265].

Once the purpose of the detention is carried out, the detainee must be released, unless enough evidence exists to establish PC for an arrest.

A prolonged detention or unnecessary control may convert the stop to an arrest (regardless of your intention), which would be unlawful without PC[266]. Under Arkansas law, you should not detain the person more than 15 minutes[267]. Such a detention may be longer than 15 minutes if you can articulate good reason, such as the suspect initially providing you with a false identity.

*Miranda* warnings are not required for this type of contact.

Arkansas law makes a special consideration for witnesses to crimes[268]. If you have reasonable cause to believe that any person found at or near the scene of a felony is a witness to the offense, you may stop that person. After having identified yourself, you must advise the person of the purpose of the stop and demand the person's name, address, and any information he or she may have regarding the offense. This type of detention must be reasonable and should not exceed 15 minutes unless the person refuses to give the requested information, in which case the person may be brought before any judicial officer or prosecuting attorney to be examined with reference to his name, address, or the information he or she has regarding the offense.

### d. Personal Property

Personal property may be detained for a short period of time for investigation following the same guidelines as the detention of persons.

Prolonged detention of property is a seizure, which is illegal without probable cause[269].

The physical manipulation of soft containers (luggage, purses, etc.) to determine the nature of the contents is a search and must be based on PC[270].

If you can articulate specific facts providing a reasonable belief that the contents of a lawfully detained container may present an *immediate* danger to yourself or others, the container may be opened.

---

[263] Arkansas Attorney General's Office. (2004). *Arkansas Law Enforcement Pocket Manual.* Little Rock: Arkansas Attorney General's Office. (p. 2).

[264] *Florida v. J.L.*, 529 U.S. 266 (2000)

[265] *Illinois v. Wardlow*, 528 U.S. 119 (2000)

[266] *Florida v. Royer*, 460 U.S. 491 (1983)

[267] *Ark. R. Crim. P.* Rule 3.1

[268] *Ark. R. Crim. P.* Rule 3.5

[269] *United States v. Place*, 462 U.S. 696 (1983)

[270] *Bond v. United States*, 529 U.S. 334 (2000)

### e. Protective Frisks

If you can articulate specific facts providing a reasonable belief (you reasonably suspect) that a person is armed and dangerous, then you may frisk that person.

The justification for a frisk may arise out of voluntary contact with a private citizen or an investigative detention.

The scope of a frisk is limited to a pat-down of the person's outer clothing. If during the pat-down you discover something that may be a weapon, you may reach into pockets, waistbands, and so forth, to remove the object for further inspection. Arkansas law also provides for a search of the person's "immediate surroundings."[271]

A frisk is permitted only for the protection of persons. It may not legally be used to search for evidence. If, however, you find evidence subject to seizure during a valid frisk, then you may lawfully seize it[272].

If during a frisk for weapons you feel something that is *immediately identifiable* as subject to seizure, you may remove it from the person's possession and seize it. Immediately identifiable means that you cannot make an intrusion or manipulate the person's clothing beyond what is necessary to search for weapons.

### f. Vehicle Stops

A *Terry* stop of a person in a vehicle is authorized under the same circumstances as a person on foot[273] by the USSC. Arkansas law is more stringent that the USSC requires. Under Arkansas law, you must "reasonably suspect that one of its [the vehicle's] occupants is committing, has committed, or is about to commit a felony or misdemeanor involving danger or forcible injury to persons or appropriation of, or damage to, property."[274]

You may stop a vehicle if you have PC to believe that an offense has been committed, including any violation of the Motor Vehicle and Traffic Laws.

Following a valid vehicle stop, you may order the occupants out of the vehicle until the stop has been completed[275].

You may frisk occupants of a stopped vehicle on the same grounds as a person on foot. The frisk may extend into the passenger compartment of the vehicle to any location where a weapon may be hidden and accessible to the occupants[276].

A *random* stop of a vehicle without reasonable suspicion or PC is *unlawful*.

An exception to this evidence requirement is at a checkpoint or roadblock. Checkpoints or roadblocks are permissible under the following circumstances:

- The basis for the stop is predetermined and does not depend on the whim of individual officers (sobriety checkpoints have been upheld).
- The intrusiveness of the stop is slight.
- The stop is reasonably related to a legitimate law enforcement function[277].

---

[271] *Ark. R. Crim. P.* Rule 3.4
[272] *Terry v. Ohio*, 392 U.S. 1 (1968)
[273] *Delaware v. Prouse*, 440 U.S. 648 (1979)
[274] *Ark. R. Crim. P.* Rule 3.1
[275] *Pennsylvania v. Mimms*, 434 U.S. 106 (1977)
[276] *Michigan v. Long*, 463 U.S. 1032 (1983)
[277] *Michigan Department of State Police v. Sitz*, 496 U.S. 444 (1990)

A roadblock conducted to detect evidence of ordinary criminal activity (such as narcotics enforcement roadblocks) is *not* permissible[278].

A stop with an ulterior motive is permissible under the Arkansas Constitution[279], but an arrest for an offense with an ulterior motive is *not* constitutional.

### (20.2) Arrest

### a. Defining Arrest

For constitutional purposes, an arrest is a seizure of a person. This means that the Fourth Amendment applies to arrests. Technically, an arrest is the seizure of a person by the use of physical force or by the display of official authority whereby the person is taken into custody[280]. Regardless of your intent, if you restrict the freedom of a person to move and they are not free to go you have arrested them[281].

In investigative detention (Terry stop) is not an arrest. A brief interference with a person's freedom to move, such as normal crowd control and public order maintenance, does not constitute an arrest.

Merely following a person is not an arrest, so long as there is no physical contact between you and the person or a show of official authority to which the person submits.

### b. Probable Cause for Arrest

Because the Fourth Amendment applies, you must have PC to make an arrest. Simply put, all arrests must be based on PC to be legal[282].

PC for an arrest is established when facts and circumstances known to you at the time of the arrest justify a reasonable belief that the person has committed or is committing a crime[283].

An arrest may be made either with or without an arrest warrant. For arrests without a warrant, certain conditions must be met. If the crime is a felony, you must have probable cause to believe that the person has committed or is committing a felony. If the crime is a misdemeanor, the offense must be committed in your presence[284].

Arkansas law further provides that you can make an arrest without a warrant when you have reasonable cause to believe that a person has committed a traffic offense involving: (A) death or physical injury to a person, (B) damage to property, or (C) driving a vehicle while under the influence of any intoxicating liquor or drug[285].

You may also make an arrest of you have reasonable cause to believe that a person has committed acts which constitute a crime under Arkansas law and which constitute domestic abuse as defined by law against a family or household member and which occurs within 4 hours preceding the arrest if no physical injury was involved or 12 hours preceding the arrest if physical injury was involved[286].

***If it is at all possible to get a warrant, do so.***

---

[278] *City of Indianapolis v. Edmond*, 531 U.S. 32 (2000)
[279] *State v. Harmon*, 353 Ark. 647 (2002).
[280] *California v. Hodari D.*, 499 U.S. 621 (1991)
[281] *Orozco v. Texas*, 394 U.S. 324 (1969)
[282] *Draper v. United States*, 358 U.S. 307 (1959)
[283] *Draper v. United States*, 358 U.S. 307 (1959)
[284] *Atwater v. City of Lago Vista*, 532 U.S. 318 (2001), § 16-81-106
[285] *Ark. R. Crim. P.* Rule 4.1(a)(ii)
[286] *Ark. R. Crim. P.* Rule 4.1(c)(iv)

While reasonable cause is generally required, it is not necessary for you to have it to make an arrest so long as knowledge sufficient to show reasonable cause is collectively held by your agency[287].

### c. Arrest Warrants

An arrest warrant is an order, issued by a magistrate, directing any law enforcement officer to take a named person into custody and bring them before the court.

An arrest warrant is usually issued on the basis of information contained in a sworn affidavit made by the officer applying for the warrant. The affidavit must contain sufficient information to establish PC to believe that the named person committed the crimes alleged.

Generally, an arrest warrant remains valid until the person has been arrested or the warrant is withdrawn.

You do not need to have a warrant in your possession to make an arrest so long as you know that a warrant exists[288]. Any law enforcement officer may arrest a person pursuant to a warrant in any county in the state[289].

### d. Arrest and Place

An arrest warrant is not required to make an arrest in a public place. An arrest warrant is required to enter the premises of the person to be arrested[290].

To make a forcible entry to execute an arrest warrant, officers must "knock and announce." This means that you must first identify yourself as a police officer and make known your reason for wanting to enter (there are exceptions).

A *search warrant* is required to enter the premises of a person other than the person to be arrested[291]. The affidavit for the warrant must contain PC to believe that the person to be arrested will be found on those premises.

A warrant is generally not required to enter private premises to make an arrest if there is consent to the entry or some emergency.

### e. Arrest and the Use of Force

When making an arrest, you may use as much force as is *reasonably* necessary to carry out the arrest and for the protection of persons.

You may use **deadly force** to make an arrest only to protect persons from immediate threat of *death* or *serious physical injury*[292]. [Deadly force is force that is reasonably likely to cause death or serious physical injury].

You may *only* use deadly force to prevent escape when you have PC to believe that the person poses a threat of death or serious physical injury to you or others[293].

If it is reasonably safe to do so, you should always issue a warning before using deadly force. *The use of unreasonable force may subject you and your agency to both civil and criminal liability.*

---

[287] *Ark. R. Crim. P.* Rule 4.1(d)

[288] *Ark. R. Crim. P.* Rule 4.3

[289] *Ark. R. Crim. P.* Rule 4.2

[290] *Payton v. New York*, 445 U.S. 573 (1980)

[291] *Steagald v. United States*, 451 U.S. 204 (1985)

[292] *Tennessee v. Garner*, 471 U.S. 1 (1985)

[293] *Tennessee v. Garner*, 471 U.S. 1 (1985)

### f. Search Incident to Arrest

After you have made a lawful arrest, you may search the arrestee without a warrant[294]. Such a search is said to be "incident to the arrest."

A search can be considered incident to an arrest if it takes place at the same time and place as the arrest. A warrantless search of the place of arrest after the arrestee has been removed is *not* incident to the arrest and is therefore not legal[295].

The USSC has limited the scope of a search incident to an arrest as follows[296]:

- The person and clothing of the arrestee
- The personal effects of the arrestee (items in pockets, wallets, purses, etc.) in the arrestee's possession at the time of the arrest
- A small area in close proximity to the arrestee where weapons or a means of escape might be "grabbed"

Large containers such as boxes and suitcases should *not* be searched. They may be taken into custody and searched later with a search warrant[297].

### g. Arrest and Jurisdiction

As a general rule, an officer may make an arrest only within the territorial jurisdiction of that officer's employing agency. This tradition is based on the logic that a community is best served by officers who know the local neighborhoods[298]. This rule is apparently satisfied when at least one officer in a multi-jurisdictional group is from the county where the arrest is made[299].

The Arkansas courts only recognize four instances where officers may arrest outside their territorial jurisdiction:

1. When the officer is in "hot" pursuit.
2. When the officer has a warrant for the arrest.
3. When an officer is requested to come to a foreign jurisdiction per a written agreement between agencies.
4. When the sheriff in a contiguous county requests an officer to come into his county for the purposes of drug interdiction .

### (20.3) Search and Seizure

### a. Probable Cause for Searches and Seizures

Note that **reasonable grounds** and *probable cause* are used interchangeably in legal materials.

The phrase Probable Cause appears in both the United States and the Arkansas constitutions in the context of searches and seizures.

PC has been defined by the USSC as follows:

---

[294] *Chimel v. California*, 395 U.S. 752 (1969)
[295] *Ark. R. Crim. P.* Rule 12.5(b)
[296] *Chimel v. California*, 395 U.S. 752 (1969)
[297] *United States v. Chadwick*, 433 U.S. 1 (1977)
[298] *Perry v. State*, 303 Ark. 100 (1990)
[299] *Logan v. State*, 264 Ark. 920 (1979)

Probable cause exists when the facts and circumstances [known to an officer] . . . are sufficient in themselves to warrant a man of reasonable caution in the belief that an offense has been or is being committed[300].

The test for probable cause to search is the same as that for arrest, but with the added requirement of a reasonable belief that the property to be seized will be found in a particular place or on a particular person.

You generally do not need PC if a search is authorized by **consent**, or the search can be considered an **administrative inspection**. Otherwise, you must have PC even if an exception to the warrant requirement is present.

### b. What May be Seized

You may seize property if you have PC to believe that:

- The property is evidence of a crime, including contraband (narcotics, etc.), fruits of the crime (stolen property, etc.), or an instrumentality of the crime (weapons, burglary tools, clothing, etc.)[301]
- The property is subject to forfeiture

*A seizure is lawful only if you are lawfully present where the seized property is found.* Thus, it is extremely important to follow correct procedure when conducting searches.

### c. Searches of Private Premises

Unless a specific exception to the search warrant requirement comes into play, a search of private premises is permissible only with a valid warrant.

*If at all possible, get a warrant.*

Private premises means a place that is not open to the public in which a person has a **reasonable expectation of privacy**. This generally includes the idea of **curtilage**, which is the area designated for private use surrounding the premises (lawns, carports, etc.)[302].

In contrast to curtilage are **open fields**. These are privately owned areas beyond the curtilage that are not considered part of the premises for Fourth Amendment purposes. A search warrant is generally not required to search open fields[303]. The Arkansas courts call this type of search "open lands[304]."

*If you have any doubt whether property is part of the curtilage, obtain a warrant.*

### d. Search Warrants

A search warrant is a court order (issued by an impartial magistrate) authorizing the search of the premises and seizure of the property specified in the warrant. Under Arkansas law, a search warrant must be issued by a "judicial officer," which is defined as "a person in whom is vested authority to preside over the trial in criminal cases."[305]

---

[300] *Draper v. United States*, 358 U.S. 307 (1959)
[301] *Ark. R. Crim. P.* Rule 10.2
[302] *Hester v. United States*, 265 U.S. 57 (1924); *United States v. Dunn*, 480 U.S. 294 (1987)
[303] *Hester v. United States*, 265 U.S. 57 (1924)
[304] *Ark. R. Crim. P.* Rule 14.2
[305] *Ark. R. Crim. P.* Rule 1.6(a)

A warrant is issued on the basis of information contained in a sworn affidavit made by the LEO applying for the warrant. The information in the affidavit (and only that information) will be used by the magistrate to determine if PC exists to believe that the property to be seized will be found on the premises to be searched[306].

The warrant must clearly indicate the premises to be searched. This must be specific. For a single family dwelling, a street address is usually sufficient. For an apartment, ample information must be provided such that the exact apartment to be searched can be identified.

It is common practice to include a physical description of the place to be searched to avert problems arising over a mistaken address.

Not only must the place to be searched be particularly described, but the things to be seized must also be described clearly and specifically. Generic phrases will not suffice. Avoid general phrases such as "instruments of crime" or "fruits of crime."

There are no clear-cut guidelines when determining how specific is specific enough to satisfy the court.

---

[306] *Illinois v. Gates*, 462 U.S. 213 (1983)

---

**Rule 13.2. Contents of search warrant.**

(a) A search warrant shall be dated, issued in duplicate, and shall be addressed to any officer.

(b) The warrant shall state, or describe with particularity:

(i) the identity of the issuing judicial officer and the date and place where application for the warrant was made;

(ii) the judicial officer's finding of reasonable cause for issuance of the warrant;

(iii) the identity of the person to be searched, and the location and designation of the places to be searched;

(iv) the persons or things constituting the object of the search and authorized to be seized; and

(v) the period of time, not to exceed five (5) days after execution of the warrant, within which the warrant is to be returned to the issuing judicial officer.

(c) Except as hereafter provided, the search warrant shall provide that it be executed between the hours of six a.m. and eight p.m., and within a reasonable time, not to exceed sixty (60) days. Upon a finding by the issuing judicial officer of reasonable cause to believe that:

(i) the place to be searched is difficult of speedy access; or

(ii) the objects to be seized are in danger of imminent removal; or

(iii) the warrant can only be safely or successfully executed at nighttime or under circumstances the occurrence of which is difficult to predict with accuracy;

the issuing judicial officer may, by appropriate provision in the warrant, authorize its execution at any time, day or night, and within a reasonable time not to exceed sixty (60) days from the date of issuance.

(d) If the warrant authorizes the seizure of documents other than lottery tickets, policy slips, and other nontestimonial documents used as instrumentalities of crime, the warrant shall require that it be executed in accordance with the provisions of Rule 13.5 and may, in the discretion of the issuing judicial officer, direct that any files or other collections of documents, among which the documents to be seized are reasonably believed to be located, shall be impounded under appropriate protection where found.

---

### e. Telephonic Warrants

If there is not time or it is not practical to apply in person for a search warrant, federal law permits officers to apply to a judicial official over a telephone. Arkansas law allows such telephonic warrants. The telephonic warrant procedure is regulated by A. C. A. § 16-82-201(e) under the heading of "Warrant upon Oral Testimony."

Under this section, any judicial officer of the state may issue a warrant based upon sworn oral testimony communicated by telephone (or other means). The person requesting the warrant must prepare a document known as a "duplicate original warrant" and must read that document verbatim to the judicial officer. The judicial officer in turn must make a verbatim copy of what is read—this is called the "original warrant." The statute authorizes the judicial officer to direct the warrant to be modified.

If the judicial officer is satisfied that the circumstances are such as to make it reasonable to dispense with a written affidavit and that PC exists, the judicial officer will order the issuance of the warrant and direct the person requesting the warrant to sign the judicial officer's name on the duplicate original warrant. The judicial officer will then immediately sign and enter the exact time on the face of the warrant.

The determination of PC by the magistrate for a telephonic warrant is the same as with a warrant based on an affidavit, and the content requirements are the same.

The statute dictates that each person making testimony must be placed under oath, and the entire conversation must be recorded on a voice-recording device, if available. If a voice-recording device is not available, then a stenographic or longhand record must be made. All records must be transcribed and entered into the records of the court. Failure to make such a record will generally cause the warrant to be a constitutional violation and lead the suppression of evidence[307].

### f. Execution of Search Warrants

You must execute a search warrant within the time specified in the warrant. Unless you obtain special authorization, you must conduct the search during daylight hours.

Under Arkansas law, any LEO may execute a search warrant. Such other officers or persons as may be reasonably necessary for the successful execution of the warrant with all practicable safety may accompany the officer charged with the execution of the warrant[308].

### g. Forcing Entry

Prior to entering a dwelling to execute a search warrant, you must make known your presence and authority for entering the dwelling. This is generally referred to as the "knock and announce" rule. You must give the occupants a reasonable time to respond before entering when the knock and announce rule applies.

If there is no response from within or there is an unreasonable delay, then you may enter forcibly. You may only use a level of force that is reasonably necessary[309].The general rule does not apply in circumstances where you reasonably suspect that making known your presence would be

- Dangerous
- Futile
- Detrimental to the effective investigation of the crime (e.g., allowing the destruction of evidence)

For warrant execution purposes, a dwelling means "a vehicle, building, or other structure (i) where any person lives (ii) which is customarily used for overnight accommodations of persons whether or not a person is actually present." Each unit if a structure divided into separately occupied units (e.g., apartments, dorm rooms, etc.) is itself a dwelling[310].

You cannot allow any person to be present that is not present to aid in the execution of the warrant, including the media[311].

### h. Notification Requirements

You must give a copy of the warrant to the person to be searched or the person in apparent control of the premises to be searched. The copy must be furnished before undertaking the search unless you have a reasonable belief that such action would endanger the safe execution of the warrant. If the copy is not furnished prior to the search, you

---

[307] *State v. Anderson*, 286 Ark. 58, 688 S.W.2d 947 (1985)
[308] *Ark. R. Crim. P.* Rule 13.3(a)
[309] *Wilson v. Arkansas*, 514 U.S. 927 (1995)
[310] *Ark. R. Crim. P.* Rule 13.3(b)
[311] *Wilson v. Layne*, 526 U.S. 603 (1999)

must provide it as soon as practicable. If the premises are unoccupied by anyone in apparent and responsible control, you must leave a copy of the warrant "suitably affixed to the premises[312]."

Upon completion of the search, you must make and deliver a receipt "fairly describing" the things seized to the person from whose possession they are taken. If practicable, the list needs to be prepared in the presence of the person. If the premises are unoccupied by anyone in apparent and responsible control, you must leave the receipt suitably affixed to the premises[313].

### i. Scope of the Search

You may only search places where the things to be seized (as described in the warrant) may reasonably be hidden. When the things listed in the warrant have been found, you must stop searching[314]. If you find items which you reasonably believe are subject to seizure (but not listed in the warrant) during the course of a lawful search, you may seize them[315].

### j. Use of Force

You (and other officers accompanying you) may use such degree of non-deadly force, against persons, or to effect an entry or to open containers as is reasonably necessary for the safe and successful execution of the warrant.

Deadly force outside of self defense is only authorized when you reasonably believe that there is a substantial risk that the persons or things to be seized will suffer, cause, or be used to cause death or serious bodily harm if their seizure is delayed. In addition, the force employed cannot create unnecessary risk of injury to other persons[316].

### k. Return of the Warrant

If you fail to execute a search warrant, you must return it to the issuing judicial official within a reasonable time (not to exceed 60 days from the time it was issued), together with a report of the reason(s) why it was not executed[317].

If you do execute a search warrant, you (or another officer) must (as soon as possible and no later than the date specified on the warrant) return the warrant to the issuing judicial officer together with a report of the facts and circumstances of execution, including a list of things seized[318].

### l. Warrants for Documents

If a warrant authorizes documentary seizure, you must identify the documents to be seized without examining the contents of documents not covered by the warrant[319].

If the documents to be seized cannot be searched for or identified without examining the contents of other documents, or if they constitute items or entries into account books, diaries, or other documents containing matter not specified in the warrant, you must not examine the documents. Rather, you must impound then under appropriate protection where found, or seal and remove them for safekeeping[320].

---

[312] *Ark. R. Crim. P.* Rule 13.3(c)

[313] *Ark. R. Crim. P.* Rule 13.3(e)

[314] *Horton v. California*, 496 U.S. 128 (1990)

[315] *Ark. R. Crim. P.* Rule 13.3(d)

[316] *Ark. R. Crim. P.* Rule 13.3(f)

[317] *Ark. R. Crim. P.* Rule 13.4(a)

[318] *Ark. R. Crim. P.* Rule 13.4(b)

[319] *Ark. R. Crim. P.* Rule 13.5(a)

[320] *Ark. R. Crim. P.* Rule 13.5(b)

If you impound such evidence, you must report the fact and circumstances of the impounding to the issuing judicial officer for further action[321] (See *Arkansas Rules of Criminal Procedure*, Rules 13, 15, and 16 for more information on the Magistrate's role).

### m. Good Faith

If you reasonably and in good faith believe that a warrant is valid, evidence seized pursuant to that warrant will not be excluded from evidence at trial if it is determined that the warrant was invalid[322].

### n. Persons on Premises to Be Searched

You may not search persons on the premises named in a search warrant unless they are specifically included in the warrant[323].

If in the course of a search you lawfully arrest a person on the premises, the law regarding a **search incident to arrest** applies.

You may exert reasonable control over persons present during the search so far as necessary to carry out the search safely. You may conduct a **protective frisk**, if appropriate. Persons on the premises may be detained until the search is complete, if they may be subject to arrest if the things named in the warrant are found, or for your safety or the safety of others[324].

### o. Protective Sweep

During the execution of a search warrant (or arrest warrant), you may conduct a "protective sweep" if you have reasonable grounds to believe that other persons may be present who pose a danger. The protective sweep is limited to a brief viewing of areas where a person may reasonably be hiding. Areas adjacent to the place of an arrest from which you may be attacked may be swept incident to the arrest without any specific grounds[325]. Property subject to seizure that is in plain view when you are making such sweeps may be seized.

### p. Search and Seizure by Consent

You may conduct searches and seizures without a search warrant (or any other authority) if consent is given to search[326].

Searches by consent are limited to the following 3 cases:

1. Search of an individual's person by that individuals consent (or a parent or guardian if under age 14)
2. Searches of vehicles by the consent of the registered owner or person in control of operation or contents of the vehicle at the time
3. Searches of premises, by a person who is apparently entitled to give or withhold consent[327]

The person giving the consent does not have to be the person whom you are seeking evidence against.

A person has authority to consent to a search of premises if he or she has regular use of the premises or property without needing to get permission from someone else[328]. Note the term *apparent authority*: this means that if you

---

[321] *Ark. R. Crim. P.* Rule 13.5(c)
[322] *United States v. Leon*, 468 U.S. 897 (1984)
[323] *Ybarra v. Illinois*, 444 U.S. 85 (1979)
[324] *Michigan v. Summers*, 452 U.S. 692 (1981)
[325] *Maryland v. Buie*, 494 U.S. 325 (1990)
[326] *Ark. R. Crim. P.* Rule 11.1
[327] *Ark. R. Crim. P.* Rule 11.2
[328] *United States v. Matlock*, 415 U.S. 164 (1974)

have a reasonable, good faith belief that a person's authority to consent is valid, then the consent is legally sufficient even if the belief turns out to be mistaken[329].

In cases where premises are shared by co-occupants, the occupants' authority to consent to a search depends on how the use of the premises is understood by the occupants. In this type of situation, some spaces may be considered private (bedrooms, closets, drawers, etc.) and other areas may be shared (living rooms, kitchens, etc.). One person cannot consent to the search of the private space of another[330].

Consent is only considered valid by the courts when it is given voluntarily and not obtained by force or threat. In determining the voluntariness of consent, the courts will look at all of the circumstances surrounding the consent. Traditionally, you did not have to advise a person of their right to refuse consent or disclose why you want to search[331]. Recently, however, the ARSC has determined that the state constitution requires police to advise a resident of the right to refuse to give consent[332]. Once you obtain valid consent and begin your search, you may *not* search beyond the time and area of the consent given[333]. Consent may be withdrawn or limited at any time prior to the completion of the search. If consent is withdrawn or limited, you must observe those new limitations for the search to remain legal. Things discovered and subject to seizure prior to such withdrawal of consent remain subject to seizure despite the change or termination of consent[334].

### q. Plain View

If you are lawfully in a public or private place, either as a member of the public or while performing official duties, and you come across property that is subject to seizure in *plain view*, you may seize that property. It does not matter whether you were looking for the property or expected to find it[335].

Property can be considered in plain view only if it can be seen and recognized as subject to seizure without further searching or being disturbed. That is, you have to see it for what it is from a place you have the right to be[336]. Generally, you may look inside of or listen to sounds coming from private premises so long as what you see or hear can reasonably be said to be exposed to the public[337].

Looking in from the outside of private premises, such as through a window, does not by itself authorize you to make a warrantless entry. In such a case, it is best to use what you have seen as PC to obtain a search warrant.

Common visual aids, such as binoculars, may be used to confirm unaided observations.

Observation of private premises from aircraft is permissible so long as the aircraft is within "navigable air space." Flying over premises is not considered a search and no warrant is required[338].

---

[329] *Illinois v. Rodriguez*, 497 U.S. 177 (1990)
[330] *United States v. Matlock*, 415 U.S. 164 (1974)
[331] This is still the USSC's opinion, see *Schnekloth v. Bustamonte*, 412 U.S. 218 (1973)
[332] *Arkansas v. Brown*, Supreme Court of Arkansas, No. CR 03-914 (2004)
[333] *Ark. R. Crim. P.* Rule 11.3
[334] *Ark. R. Crim. P.* Rule 11.5
[335] *Horton v. California*, 496 U.S. 128 (1990)
[336] *Arizona v. Hicks*, 480 U.S. 321 (1987)
[337] *Katz v. United States*, 389 U.S. 347 (1967)
[338] *California v. Ciraolo*, 475 U.S. 207 (1986)

### r. Exigent Circumstances (Emergency)

You do not need a warrant to enter private premises so long as you have PC to believe that such entry is necessary to respond to some emergency[339]. Such an emergency does not exist if it is reasonably possible to get a warrant or the emergency situation was caused by the action of the police.

Appropriate emergency situations include:

- Danger to life or property (fire, bomb, sniper, cries for help, etc.)
- Hot pursuit
- Destruction of evidence

A lawful entry and search in response to exigent circumstances is limited to the emergency and must end when the emergency is over. After the emergency is over, you need to obtain a search warrant or other authorization before conducting further searches.

### s. Hot Pursuit

If you are pursing a person whom you have PC to believe is committing or has just committed a crime, you may follow that person into private premises without a warrant in order to make an arrest. You generally may use force to make the entry of reasonably necessary[340].

### t. Administrative Inspections

Statutes and ordinances often authorize officers or other public officials (fire marshals, health inspectors, etc.) to enter private premises for the purpose of duties other than criminal investigations. In such cases, those statutes and ordinances may provide for entry into those places without a warrant.

If, while making a lawful administrative inspection, you find property that is subject to seizure in plain view, you may seize it.

*An administrative inspection cannot be used as a pretext for unauthorized criminal investigation.*

### (20.4) Searches of People

### a. Searches of People in General

You may lawfully conduct a thorough (beyond a weapons search) search a person:

- By authorization of a search warrant naming the specific person
- As a search incident to an arrest
- As part of the booking procedure following arrest

You may also search a person (according to the same rules governing searches of premises) with **consent,** or in **exigent circumstances**.

In addition, a person can be compelled to produce non-testimonial evidence (fingerprints, handwriting samples, blood, etc.) or to appear for an identification procedure (lineup, showup, photo array, etc.) pursuant to a court order[341].

---

[339] *Warden v. Hayden*, 387 U.S. 294 (1967)
[340] *Warden v. Hayden*, 387 U.S. 294 (1967)
[341] *Schmerber v. California*, 384 U.S. 757 (1966)

### b. Booking Searches

A person who has been lawfully arrested and is going to be detained may be subjected to a full search of his or her person. This includes clothing and articles carried on the arrestee's person, such as a wallet. Under these circumstances a warrant is not required[342].

Blood samples may be taken from a person who is arrested for driving under the influence of drugs or alcohol, but only under specific conditions[343].

### c. Bodily Samples

Modern forensic science necessitates the collection of bodily substances (such as blood, hairs, saliva, and so forth) by LEOs. In addition, foreign substances concealed inside a person's body must sometimes be removed.

You may remove substances from a person's body without a warrant if you have reasonable grounds to believe that the substance may be evidence of a crime and the substance can be obtained safely and with minimal discomfort[344]. If the person physically resists the removal of the substance, force should not be used without a court order.

A blood sample may be taken from a person who is arrested for driving under the influence, provided that there is clear evidence that the blood sample will provide evidence of intoxication. In such cases, the sample must be taken in a medically approved way[345].

*It is unadvisable to make any other type of intrusion into a person's body without a court order.*

### (20.5) Search of Vehicles

### a. Searches of Vehicles in General

The laws regulating vehicle searches apply to motor vehicles in general, including boats and aircraft. It even applies to recreational vehicles (RVs) so long as they are subject to quickly be moved.

Warrants for the search of a vehicle are obtained in the same way as warrants for the search of premises.

The general exceptions to the warrant requirement apply to vehicle searches—consent, search incident to arrest, exigent circumstances, and so forth.

Special rules apply to the search of a vehicle without a warrant. The scope of a vehicle search is dictated by the type of authorization.

### b. Vehicle Exception

The USSC has carved out an exception to the search warrant requirement for vehicles, citing the mobility inherent in vehicles as a reason. You may search a vehicle without a warrant if two conditions are met:

1. There is PC to believe that the vehicle or property contained in the vehicle is subject to seizure
2. The vehicle is mobile[346]

---

[342] *United States v. Edwards*, 415 U.S. 800 (1974)
[343] *Schmerber v. California*, 384 U.S. 757 (1966)
[344] *Cupp v. Murphy*, 412 U.S. 291 (1979)
[345] *Schmerber v. California*, 384 U.S. 757 (1966)
[346] *Chambers v. Maroney*, 399 U.S. 42 (1970)

Mobility means that the vehicle is capable of being moved. This does not mean that the vehicle must be in motion or recently have been in motion. A vehicle that cannot be readily moved, such as one on blocks or an RV that is connected to utility lines, is not considered mobile.

You may search a vehicle where and when it comes under police control or at a reasonable time afterwards if still legally under police control[347].

The scope of a search under the vehicle exception includes any part of the vehicle where objects of the search may be hidden, including passengers' personal belongings[348]. If, however, probable cause is limited to a specific container, then only that container may be searched[349].

If you have any doubt about whether the vehicle exception is applicable, it is best to get a search warrant. If there is PC, you generally have the authority to impound the vehicle in order to obtain a search warrant. If you choose to get a warrant, you must do so as promptly as possible.

### c. Search Incident to Arrest of Vehicle Occupants

If you lawfully arrest the occupants of a vehicle, the passenger compartment (only) may be searched without a warrant as a search incident to the arrest[350].

The scope of such a search is limited to the passenger compartment and containers (fixed or movable) within the vehicle, such as glove compartments, suitcases, and purses. The scope of the search may *not* extend under to hood or to the trunk[351].

You have the same authority to conduct a protective frisk of vehicle occupants as you do people on foot.

Mere authority to make an arrest does not alone give authority to conduct a search. If you merely issue a citation, then you may not conduct a search incident to arrest. You must make the arrest for a search incident to arrest to be valid[352].

### d. Vehicle Inventory

If you lawfully impound a vehicle and retain it in custody, you may enter the vehicle and inventory its contents without a warrant[353].

You must carry out such an inventory according to standard departmental policy. You do not get to choose whether to inventory a vehicle.

You may conduct the inventory when and where the vehicle comes under police control, or you may wait until it is taken to a storage location. After you have completed the inventory you may not conduct further searches for evidence. If you have PC at this point, get a warrant.

While conducting the inventory, you may inspect both the exterior and interior of the vehicle, as well as the truck and other compartments and containers.

---

[347] *Chambers v. Maroney*, 399 U.S. 42 (1970)
[348] *Wyoming v. Houghton*, 526 U.S. 295 (1999); *United States v. Ross*, 456 U.S. 798 (1982)
[349] *California v. Acevedo*, 500 U.S. 565 (1991)
[350] *New York v. Belton*, 453 U.S. 454 (1981); *Ark. R. Crim. P*. Rule 12.4
[351] *New York v. Belton*, 453 U.S. 454 (1981)
[352] *Knowles v. Iowa*, 525 U.S. 113 (1998)
[353] *South Dakota v. Oppermam*, 428 U.S. 364 (1976); *Ark. R. Crim. P*. Rule 12.6

If while conducting the inventory you find property that is subject to seizure in **plain view**, you may seize it.

---

**Rule 14.1.  Vehicular searches.**

(a) An officer who has reasonable cause to believe that a moving or readily movable vehicle is or contains things subject to seizure may, without a search warrant, stop, detain, and search the vehicle and may seize things subject to seizure discovered in the course of the search where the vehicle is:

(i) on a public way or waters or other area open to the public;

(ii) in a private area unlawfully entered by the vehicle; or

(iii) in a private area lawfully entered by the vehicle, provided that exigent circumstances require immediate detention, search, and seizure to prevent destruction or removal of the things subject to seizure.

(b) If the officer does not find the things subject to seizure by his search of the vehicle, and if:

(i) the things subject to seizure are of such a size and nature that they could be concealed on the person; and

(ii) the officer has reason to suspect that one (1) or more of the occupants of the vehicle may have the things subject to seizure so concealed;

the officer may search the suspected occupants; provided that this subsection shall not apply to individuals traveling as passengers in a vehicle operating as a common carrier.

(c) This rule shall not be construed to limit the authority of an officer under Rules 2 and 3 hereof.

---

*(20.6) Miscellaneous Search Procedures*

### e. Container Searches

Ordinarily, you may search containers such as suitcases, briefcases, and purses under the authority of a valid search warrant[354].

If you have PC to search a container that you lawfully found in a vehicle, then the vehicle exception will apply and you may search the container without a warrant.

Containers that come under your control by the arrest or detention of the possessor may be detained for a reasonable time in order for you to obtain a warrant.

If a container is found within a larger area that you have authority to search, you may open the container *only* if you reasonably believe that the object of the search could be found inside.

### f. Abandoned Property and Trash

You may search abandoned property without a warrant[355].

Property can be considered abandoned if the possessor leaves it in a public or private place under circumstances that indicate that he or she no longer intents to retain any interest in the property.

---

[354] *United States v. Chadwick*, 433 U.S. 1 (1977)
[355] *Abel v. United States*, 362 U.S. 217 (1960)

Generally you must obtain a warrant or other lawful authority to enter private premises in order to seize property abandoned there.

Trash left in a public place, such as the curb in front of a house, is considered abandoned property and may be searched without a warrant. You may *not*, however, go onto private property to seize trash without a warrant or other lawful authority.

### g. Narcotic Field Tests

You may perform a chemical field test on a substance that you have lawfully seized without a warrant. You must reasonable believe that the substance is a controlled substance[356].

### (20.7) Computer Searches

The requirements of a lawful search apply to digital data and information. That is, the search warrant requirement is in force for computer related items, including hardware, software, and data. The search warrant exceptions may also be applicable.

A warrant to search computer files must satisfy the specificity requirement by clearly stating the files to be searched and the information to be seized. Computer files are usually considered documentary in nature and enjoy some special protections. The idea of plain view does not really apply. Specifically, while you may review files to determine whether they are covered by the warrant, you may *not* further examine a file once you have determined it is beyond the scope of the warrant. For example, if you are searching for files that contain evidence of gambling transactions and discover images of child pornography, you may not begin to search for further evidence of child pornography without obtaining another warrant that specifies child pornography as the evidence sought.

### (20.8) Electronic Surveillance

### a. Electronic Surveillance in General

The constitutional (both the US and Arkansas constitutions) requirements for a lawful search apply to the use of electronic devices for wiretapping and surveillance. Special rules apply due to federal and state legislation.

### b. Intercepting Communications

Generally, the use of an electronic device to intercept any nonpublic communication (wire, oral, or electronic) is a violation of federal law, unless you have a court order or the consent of at least one of the parties to the communication. Under exigent circumstances, an interception may be started without a court order, but an application for such an order must be made promptly[357].

The consent of one party to a conversation is sufficient to authorize the use of a concealed device to listen to or record a conversation[358].

An undercover officer or an informant may carry a hidden recording device and intercept a conversation to which he or she is a party. However, a concealed device should never be used to record a conversation between an attorney and a client.

---

[356] *United States v. Jacobsen*, 466 U.S. 109 (1984)
[357] 18 U.S.C. §§ 2510-3521
[358] *United States v. White*, 401 U.S. 745 (1971)

### c. Pen Registers and Trap and Trace Devices

A *pen register* is a device that records telephone numbers of outgoing calls made from a telephone. A *trap and trace device* records incoming telephone numbers. Both devices generally require a court order to use absent exigent circumstances.

### d. Closed Circuit Television (CCTV)

Surveillance by CCTV or other video device is permissible without a court order so long as the device is installed without an unlawful entry and you do not monitor the object when it is not in public view.

Otherwise, consent of one of the parties being surveilled is sufficient. In the absence of consent or exigent circumstances, a warrant or court order is required.

### d. Tracking Devices

You may install and use a tracking device to monitor the location of a vehicle or other property without a warrant so long as the device can be installed without an unlawful entry (attaching it to the property in a public place) and monitoring is stopped when the property is not in public view. To monitor property while on private premises, a court order is required[359].

### e. Thermal Imaging

You may use a thermal imager to detect and record head patterns originating from within a private premises where there is a reasonable expectation of privacy *only* with a search warrant[360].

---

[359] *United States v. Knotts*, 460 U.S. 276 (1983)
[360] *Kyllo v. United States*, 533 U.S. 27 (2001)

# Chapter 21: Undercover Investigations & Informants

## (21.1) Informants

### a. Informants in General

Private individuals who cooperate with or act at the direction of a law enforcement officer are legally regarded as *agents* of the police. As agents of the police, they are generally subject to the same rules. For this reason you should not encourage others to take steps that you may not lawfully take to further an investigation.

A private person who acts independently of the police to obtain evidence of a crime generally is not subject to the rules that regulate police conduct[361].

In the case of a private person who is not acting as an agent of the state, that person is considered an ordinary witness—the exclusionary rule does not apply to evidence obtained by such a person.

**Caveat**: Evidence that is obtained illegally by a private person may subject that person to civil and/or criminal penalties even if it can be used in court against another person.

### b. Informer's Privilege

The phrase "informer's privilege" refers to the idea that you are not ordinarily required to reveal the identity of a CI. This privilege does, however, give way if the identity of the informant may be significantly helpful to the defendant's case[362].

## (21.2) Concealing LEO Identity

### a. Undercover Procedure in General

It is generally permissible for an officer to act undercover in the course of a criminal investigation. You may get the voluntary consent or assistance of a person who would not ordinarily provide it if they knew you were an officer[363].

### b. Obtaining Evidence

As an undercover officer, you may pose as a friend or acquaintance of a person under investigation. If the person voluntarily reveals evidence of a crime, it is admissible even though it would not have been revealed if your LE affiliation was known[364].

---

[361] *Burdeau v. McDowell*, 256 U.S. 465 (1921)
[362] *Roviaro v. United States*, 364 U.S. 53 (1957)
[363] *Lewis v. United States*, 385 U.S. 206 (1966)
[364] *Lewis v. United States*, 385 U.S. 206 (1966); *United States v. White*, 401 U.S. 745 (1971)

### c. Private Premises

As an undercover officer, you may enter private premises by invitation. Your conduct on those premises is limited to the purpose of the invitation[365].

### d. Right to Counsel

Even after the right to counsel has attached, you may still listen *passively* to a defendant's voluntary statements. You may *not*, however, solicit information. In such a case, *Miranda* warnings are not required[366].

### e. Meetings with Attorneys

As an undercover officer, you should avoid meetings between a defendant and his or her lawyer. Charges may be dismissed if you overhear defense tactics and relate that information to the prosecutor[367].

An exception to the above guideline is that you are not prohibited from attending a meeting between a defendant and an attorney if it is necessary not to "blow your cover" or for protection from danger[368]. Even under such circumstances, evidence will be dismissed if the case of the defense is prejudiced. You should take careful steps to ensure that information revealed in such a meeting is not given to the prosecutor, and you should make a record of those steps.

---

[365] *Lewis v. United States*, 385 U.S. 206 (1966)
[366] *Kuhlman v. Wilson*, 477 U.S. 436 (1986)
[367] *Weatherford v. Bursey*, 429 U.S. 545 (1977)
[368] *Weatherford v. Bursey*, 429 U.S. 545 (1977)

# Chapter 22: Interrogations and Confessions

## (22.1) Interrogation Generally

You may ask a person for information about criminal activity, whether or not you consider the person asked a suspect, under the following conditions[369].

1. You do not restrict the liberty of the person
2. The person is free not to answer questions
3. You do not cause the person to believe that they may not leave or that he or she is required to answer

Special considerations arise under the following specific circumstances:

1. The person is not competent to make voluntary choices
2. The person is in police custody
3. Formal proceedings have begin against the person

## (22.2) Voluntariness

Generally, a person's incriminating statements are admissible in court only of the statements are made voluntarily.

Statements are considered voluntary if they are freely given (without coercive conduct by police)[370].

The court will determine the voluntariness of statements by considering *all* the circumstances under which the statements were given[371].

When asking questions, you *may not* threaten or humiliate the person being questioned.

You *may not* indicate that you will protect the person from harm or do them favors if they answer questions.

In addition, you *may not* question people so intensively that they believe that they have no choice other than to answer your questions.

You should not ask questions of a person who cannot be considered to be in a condition to make a voluntary choice of whether or not to answer. This includes (but is not limited to) persons weakened by injury, illness, fatigue, intoxication, or mental disease.

---

[369] *Florida v. Royer*, 460 U.S. 491 (1983); *California v. Hodari D.*, 499 U.S. 621 (1991)
[370] *Spano v. New York*, 360 U.S. 315 (1959); *Colorado v. Connelly*, 479 U.S. 157 (1986)
[371] *Colombe v. Connecticut*, 367 U.S. 568 (1961)

## (22.3) Custodial Interrogations

You may interrogate a suspect in custody only when the following conditions have been met:

1. *Miranda* warnings have been given
2. Suspect has waived rights
3. The waive remains effective

Interrogation includes both direct questioning of the suspect and what the courts have called its "functional equivalent." The *functional equivalent* of an interrogation is activity by an officer (both words and conduct) intended to or likely to elicit a response from the suspect[372].

Miranda warning are not generally required to ask booking questions, such as the suspects name, address, height, weight, age, date of birth, and so forth[373].

You can reach a level of detention that the courts will consider custodial without making an arrest. For purposes of determining whether an interrogation is custodial, the courts will examine whether or not you *significantly restricted the person's freedom of movement*[374]. This is an *objective test*: it does not depend on your subjective opinion or that of the suspect[375].

Custody, then, is not limited to jails or police stations. Depending on the circumstances, *Miranda* warnings can be required on in police cars, on private premises, or even on public streets.

An investigative detention is not generally considered custody for *Miranda* purposes, so the warnings do not have to be given. Likewise, a traffic stop is generally not considered custody[376].

### b. *Miranda* Warnings

Before you can interrogate any suspects in custody, you must first advise them:

1. That they have the right to remain silent
2. That anything they say may be used as evidence against them
3. That they have the right to speak to an attorney before and during questioning
4. That if they cannot afford an attorney, one will be provided[377]

The courts have determined that you must issue these warnings in a way that conveys their complete substance. Most departments require that the warnings be read verbatim from an officially issued form so that nothing is accidentally changed or left out by officers.

If a suspect does not understand English, you must issue the warnings in the language that the suspect understands.

### c. Miranda Waivers

After suspects have been given the *Miranda* warnings, they may not be questioned without an attorney present only of they waive their rights.

---

[372] *Rhode Island v. Innis*, 446 U.S. 291 (1980)
[373] *Pennsylvania v. Muniz*, 496 U.S. 582 (1990)
[374] *Orozco v. Texas*, 394 U.S. 324 (1969)
[375] *Stansbury v. California*, 511 U.S. 318 (1994)
[376] *Berkemer v. McCarty*, 468 U.S. 420 (1984)
[377] *Miranda v. Arizona*, 384 U.S. 436 (1966)

For Miranda purposes, waiver means that suspects freely and voluntarily decide to answer the questions. Suspects must indicate clearly that they are willing to be questioned. Suspects' silence after the warnings are given cannot be taken by itself to be a waiver.

If suspects indicate that they are willing to be questioned only under certain specified conditions, those conditions must be honored.

If a suspect remains silent after being given the Miranda warnings and does not request a lawyer or to have an attorney present, then you should not ask questions.

If there is a substantial break between the beginning and subsequent questions, you should reissue the *Miranda* warnings.

If after waiving rights a suspect indicates that they are no longer willing to answer questions, then questioning must stop. If a suspect clearly asks to speak to a lawyer, questioning must stop[378].

### d. Further Contact

If suspects do not specifically waive their right to remain silent, you may inquire again whether they are willing to answer questions after a substantial amount of time has passed (two hours minimum). You must still obtain a waiver before any questions can be asked[379].

If suspects do not waive their rights to speak with an attorney, you cannot question them further unless counsel is present or unless the suspect expresses a willingness to answer questions. Even if the suspect initiates such a conversation with you, you should still repeat the warnings and obtain a waiver.

### e. Undercover Interrogations

As an undercover officer, you may ask a suspect in custody about any crime. However, you may only do so if *formal proceedings* to prosecute the suspect have not begun. Such statements will be admissible so long as the suspect is *not* aware of your law enforcement capacity and engages in the conversation *voluntarily*, as with a friend or fellow inmate[380].

### f. Exigent Circumstances Exception

If you reasonably believe that a danger to the public safety exists and that the danger requires immediate action, you may ask a person questions relating to that danger without *Miranda* warnings[381].

### *(22.4) Right to Counsel*

### a. Right to Counsel in General

After formal proceedings against a suspect have begun, the Sixth Amendment right to counsel attaches. This amendment prohibits all questioning of the defendant (about the crime for which they are being prosecuted—it does not apply to other crimes[382]) without the defendant's attorney being present.

This prohibition applies to police and anyone cooperating with the police, whether or not the questioning is custodial[383].

---

[378] *Davis v. United States*, 512 U.S. 452 (1994)
[379] *Michigan v. Mosley*, 423 U.S. 96 (1975)
[380] *Illinois v. Perkins*, 496 U.S. 292 (1990)
[381] *New York v. Quarles*, 467 U.S. 649 (1984)
[382] *McNeil v. Wisconsin*, 501 U.S. 171 (1991)
[383] *Massiah v. United States*, 377 U.S. 201 (1964)

**Caveat**: The *Miranda* rights of a defendant are independent of the constitutional right to counsel. Be sure to keep the requirements of each in mind.

The right to counsel does not prohibit you from listening passively to a defendant's voluntary statements about a crime. You may not, however, solicit information from the defendant[384].

### b. Waiver of Right to Counsel

A criminal defendant may waive his or her constitutional right to counsel[385].

The requirements of a valid waiver are applied strictly.

---

[384] *Kuhlman v. Wilson*, 477 U.S. 436 (1986)
[385] *Patterson v. Illinois*, 487 U.S. 285 (1988)

# Chapter 23:  Remedies

*(23.1) Constitutional Rights Violations*

### a. Remedies in General

In the general legal context, a *remedy* provides a method for rectifying some wrongdoing.  This chapter covers remedies for constitutional violations.  This is critically important because constitutional rights violations by the police can have an incredible negative impact: evidence can be lost, cases can be dismissed, and you, your agency, and your political unit can be sued for money.

### b. Civil Remedy Terminology

When a person's constitutional rights are violated, they can sue.  Such a suit is referred to as *civil litigation*.  Lawsuits where people seek money compensation are called *damage suits*.

*(23.2) 1983 Suits*

### a. 1983 Suits in General

42 U.S.C. § 1983 provides a remedy in federal court for the "deprivation of any rights. . . secured by the constitution and laws" of the United States.  The law makes several provisions detailing who may be sued by whom.

### b. Color of Law

One of the requirements for bringing a 1983 suit to court is that the person being sued acted "under color of law." According to the USSC, someone is acting under color of law when they are acting in an official capacity[386].

In addition, plaintiffs can sue *private parties* under Section 1983 if they conspire with officers acting under color of office.

### c. Constitutional Violation

The second major requirement for bringing a successful 1983 suit to court is that a constitutional rights violation must have taken place.  This means that the plaintiff must establish that a specific provision of the constitution was violated by police conduct.  This makes violations of the Fourth Amendment especially problematic for police: First, you have evidence excluded in court, and, second, you can be sued for the violation.

The recent trend is for the courts to require plaintiffs to demonstrate that police have violated constitutional rights with a certain level of **culpability**.  That is, they generally must prove that the officers intended the violation to occur.  The level of culpability required varies depending on the type of unconstitutional conduct.

---

[386] *Lugar v. Edmondson Oil Co.*, 457 U.S. 922, 937 (1982)

### d. Theories of Liability

The phrase *theory of liability* boils down to who the defendant is.

*Individual liability* requires that a plaintiff show that someone acting under color of law violated his or her constitutional rights.

Allegations of Fourth Amendment violations are evaluated by the courts using a "reasonable officer" test.

Supervisors can be sued under Section 1983, but only if it can be shown that there is a clear link between the supervisor and the constitutional violation committed by a subordinate. This type of liability is commonly referred to as *supervisory liability*.

Cities and counties can also be sued under Section 1983, but only if they implement policies that become responsible for constitutional rights violations[387]. This is known as *municipal liability*.

The USSC has also held that cities and counties can be liable for inadequately training their LEOs.

### (23.3) Defenses to 1983 Suits

### a. Sovereign Immunity

The Eleventh Amendment provides protection to state officials acting in their official capacity from being sued in federal court. However, lawsuits against other government employees as well as lower levels of government (cities and counties) can still be sued.

### b. Qualified Immunity

Qualified immunity is a type of defense that was created by judges and not a part of the language of Section 1983.

A defendant is said to have acted in an *objectively reasonable* fashion is he or she does not violate clearly established rights which a reasonable person would have known[388].

In essence, qualified immunity provides LEOs protection from suites based on constitutional violations which are the result of reasonably mistaken beliefs. That is, it is a defense for ignorance, so long as that ignorance is reasonable.

### (23.4) Exclusionary Rule

### a. Exclusionary Rule in General

The *exclusionary rule* provides that evidence obtained in violation of the Constitution cannot be used in a criminal trial to prove the defendant's guilt. The purpose of the rule is to punish LE for violating citizens' constitutional rights.

The rule was created by the courts because the Constitution contains no provision for enforcing the protections contained in the Bill of Rights[389]. The rule developed over a relatively long period of time. It began with the USSC decision in *Weeks v. United States*[390], where the court established the rule for Federal Courts. It was not until 1961 that the USSC applied the exclusionary rule to the states in Mapp v. Ohio[391].

---

[387] see *Monell v. Department of Social Services*, 436 U.S. 658 (1978)
[388] *Harlow v. Fitzgerald*, 457 U.S. 800 (1982)
[389] The phrase *Bill of Rights* refers to the first ten Amendments to the Constitution of the United States.
[390] *Weeks v. United States*, 232 U.S. 383 (1914)
[391] *Mapp v. Ohio*, 367 U.S. 643 (1961)

## b. Exceptions to the Exclusionary Rule

There are two exceptions to the rule: (1) the *good faith exception* and (2) the *impeachment exception*.

Generally, when an honest and "good faith" mistake is made during the course of a search and seizure by LE, any subsequently obtained evidence will be considered admissible[392].

The good faith exception does not apply if you act in good faith on a statute that is later found to be unconstitutional[393].

In addition, the rule does not apply if you act in good faith on a computer record that turns out to be inaccurate.

If the prosecution seeks to use illegally obtained evidence for the purpose of attacking the credibility of (impeaching) a witness, then the evidence will be admissible, but only for that purpose[394].

### (23.5) Fruit of the Poisonous Tree Doctrine

#### a. Fruit of the Poisonous Tree Doctrine in General

The *fruit of the poisonous tree doctrine* provides that the exclusionary rule applies not only to evidence obtained as a direct result of a constitutional rights violation, but also to evidence indirectly derived from the constitutional rights violation[395].

b. Exceptions the Fruit of the Poisonous Tree Doctrine

The *purged taint exception* stipulates that if the "chain" of evidence stemming from the unconstitutional act is sufficiently removed from the evidence in question, then the evidence can be admitted. The USSC has established a four-part test to determine if the taint has been purged:

1. Whether Miranda warnings were given prior to a voluntary confession
2. The closeness in time of the illegal police conduct and verbal statements made by the suspect
3. The presence of intervening events and circumstances
4. The "purpose and flagrancy" of the police misconduct[396]

The *independent source exception* says that if the evidence is obtained by or through an independent source, such as a disconnected third party, it will be admissible[397].

The *inevitable discovery exception* says that if the evidence would be found regardless of unconstitutional police conduct, then it is admissible[398].

---

[392] *United States v. Leon*, 468 U.S. 897 (1984); *Massachusetts v. Sheppard*, 468 U.S. 981 (1984)
[393] *Michigan v. DeFillippo*, 443 U.S. 31 (1979)
[394] *Walder v. United States*, 347 U.S. 62 (1954)
[395] *Silverthorne Lumber Co. v. United States*, 251 U.S. 385 (1920)
[396] *Wong Sun v. United States*, 371 U.S. 47 (1963)
[397] *Segura v. United States*, 468 U.S. 796 (1984)
[398] *Nix v. Williams*, 467 U.S. 431 (1984)

# Chapter 24: Identification

## (24.1) Identification Generally

Identification includes any procedure whereby a witness identifies someone connected to a crime. The most common form of identification is *visual identification* by an eyewitness. There may also be identifications utilizing the other senses.

No matter which type of identification procedure is used, it is critical that the witnesses rely solely on their own observations and are not led to identify a particular individual by police conduct. In the eyes of the law, it makes no difference whether the police conduct was deliberate or accidental. You cannot pressure witnesses to make an identification when they are not sure[399].

If you cannot avoid singling out a particular suspect for a witness, you should emphasize that the identification is uncertain. You should ask the witness not to verify your suspicion unless it is in agreement with the witness's own judgment[400].

Before a witness is asked to make an identification by lineup or other means, you should have them describe the suspect and record the description.

## (24.2) Field Identification

If you respond to the scene of a crime and have a basis for investigative detention, you may detain a person for a short period in order to allow an eyewitness to see the detained person for identification purposes.

The witness should be brought to the place where the person is detained if possible. It is generally inappropriate to move the detainee from the crime scene (such as to a hospital or a witness's home) without making an arrest. Such movement is permissible, however, if delay may lead to loss of the identification, such as when the witness is grievously injured and may die.

## (24.3) Lineup

A lineup is a procedure where a witness views a number of people, including the suspect, that have the same general description and asked to identify the person who committed the crime.
A person who has been lawfully arrested may be required to participate in a lineup[401].

A person who is not in police custody can be compelled to participate in a lineup by court order[402].

Force may not be used to compel an unwilling person to participate in a lineup procedure.

---

[399] *United States v. Wade*, 388 U.S. 218 (1967); *Neil v. Biggers*, 409 U.S. 188 (1972)
[400] *Stovall v. Denno*, 388 U.S. 293 (1967)
[401] *United States v. Wade*, 388 U.S. 218 (1967)
[402] *United States v. Dionisio*, 410 U.S. 1 (1973)

Identification obtained through a lineup procedure will not be admissible in court unless it is reasonably designed to avoid unreliable identification. When you conduct a lineup, be sure to follow established procedures and record the procedures used in each particular case[403].

Generally, a lineup should consist of at least six persons that resemble the witness's description of the person.

If you have more than one witness, have each view the lineup separately, and do not allow the witnesses to communicate with each other until the lineup is complete.

If you ask any person in the lineup to wear special clothing, make certain gestures, or say certain phrases, you must make each person in the lineup do the same.

If a lineup is conducted *before* formal proceedings against the suspect have begun, the presence of defense council is not required and the suspect's lawyer does not have to be notified[404]. While not necessary, it is generally a good idea to allow the suspect's attorney to attend the lineup as this increases the chances of having the identification admitted into evidence.

The persons in the lineup should be photographed or videotaped.

After *formal proceedings* against he suspect have begun, the defendant has the right to have a lawyer present at a lineup[405]. Formal proceedings can be regarded as beginning when a person is brought before a judicial officer and advised of the charges against him, or the person is formally accused by indictment or information. This right to counsel means that a lineup must be conducted at a reasonable time and that the defense attorney must be notified in advance and given an opportunity to attend.

The role of the defense attorney at a lineup is strictly as an observer. If, however, the attorney makes recommendations, they should be considered and followed if reasonable. If the attorney makes suggestions that are not followed, it is prudent to make a record of the recommendations and your reasons for not following them.

### (24.4) Photographic Array (Photo Spread)

You may ask a witness to make an identification by viewing photographs. Similar to the requirements of a lineup, the witness should be shown an array of about 6 similar photographs where one of the photographs is of the suspect.

Generally, there is no right to have an attorney present at a photographic array, no matter whether formal proceedings have begun or not[406].

---

[403] *United States v. Wade*, 388 U.S. 218 (1967)
[404] *Kirby v. Illinois*, 406 U.S. 682 (1972)
[405] *United States v. Wade*, 388 U.S. 218 (1967)
[406] *Simmons v. United States*, 390 U.S. 377 (1968)

# Appendix 1: Offense Keyword Table

| Keyword Description | Statutory Name | Code Section | Text Section |
|---|---|---|---|
| Prosecutions, Malicious | Frivolous...or malicious prosecutions | 5-53-131 | NA |
| Abortion, Unlawful | Unlawful abortion | 5-61-102 | NA |
| Absconding | Absconding | 5-54-131 | 15.27 |
| Abuse of an Impaired Person | ...abuse of an endangered or impaired person | 5-28-103 | 11.34 |
| Abuse of athletic contest officials | Abuse of athletic contest officials | 5-13-209 | 11.13 |
| Adult Abuse | ...abuse of an endangered or impaired person | 5-28-103 | 11.34 |
| Advocating Overthrow of Government | Advocating personal injury, destruction of... | 5-51-205 | NA |
| Aiding an Unauthorized Departure | Aiding an unauthorized departure | 5-54-116 | 15.17 |
| Aiding, Consummation of an Offense | Aiding consummation of offense | 5-54-106 | 15.13 |
| AIDS, Exposing Another Person To | Exposing another person to human... | 5-14-123 | 10.7 |
| Aircraft, Operating While Intoxicated | Unlawful acts. | 5-75-102 | NA |
| Animals (Impounded), Food and Water | Impounded animals - Food and water | 5-62-118 | NA |
| Animals, Allowing Into Enclosures | Allowing animals into enclosures... | 5-38-210 | NA |
| Animals, Bear Exploitation | Unlawful bear exploitation | 5-62-124 | NA |
| Animals, Cruelty in Transportation | Cruelty in transportation | 5-62-119 | NA |
| Animals, Cruelty To | Cruelty to animals | 5-62-101 | 15.36 |
| Animals, Diseased | Diseased animals - Sale - Destruction | 5-62-116 | NA |
| Animals, Dog Fighting | Unlawful dog fighting | 5-62-120 | 15.39 |
| Animals, Larceny Of | Larceny of animals including carcasses... | 5-62-123 | NA |
| Animals, Permitting to Run at Large | Permitting livestock to run at large | 5-62-122 | 15.40 |
| Animals, Seed Horse, Mule, or Jack at Large | Seed horse...mule, or jack running at large | 5-38-211 | NA |
| Animals, Transfer of Chicks, Ducks, Rabbits | Transfer of certain chicks, ducklings, or rabbits | 5-62-121 | NA |
| Animals, Use of Decompression Chambers | Decompression chambers | 5-62-117 | NA |
| Arrest, Resisting | Resisting arrest - Refusal to submit to arrest | 5-54-103 | 15.10 |
| Assassination or Overthrow of Government | Advocating assassination or overthrow... | 5-51-202 | NA |
| Assault on a Family Member, Agg. | Aggravated assault on a family... | 5-26-306 | 11.18 |
| Assault on Family, First Degree | First degree assault on family or household... | 5-26-307 | 11.18 |
| Assault on Family, Second Degree | Second degree assault on family... | 5-26-308 | 11.18 |
| Assault on Family, Third Degree | Third degree assault on a family... | 5-26-309 | 11.18 |
| Assault, Aggravated | Aggravated Assault | 5-13-204 | 11.11 |
| Assault, Aggravated on a CO | Aggravated assault... | 5-13-211 | NA |
| Assault, First Degree | Assault in the first degree | 5-13-205 | 11.11 |
| Assault, Second Degree | Assault in the second degree | 5-13-206 | 11.11 |

| Keyword Description | Statutory Name | Code Section | Text Section |
|---|---|---|---|
| Assault, Third Degree | Assault in the third degree | 5-13-207 | 11.11 |
| Assembly, Unlawful | Unlawful assembly | 5-71-205 | 15.64 |
| Battery, First Degree | Battery in the first degree | 5-13-201 | 11.10 |
| Battery, Second Degree | Battery in the second degree | 5-13-202 | 11.10 |
| Battery, Third Degree | Battery in the third degree | 5-13-203 | 11.10 |
| Bestiality | Bestiality | 5-14-122 | 10.6 |
| Bigamy | Bigamy | 5-26-201 | NA |
| Birth, Concealing | Concealing birth | 5-26-203 | NA |
| Blue Lights, Sale Of | Blue light or blue lens cap sales | 5-77-201 | 15.104 |
| Body Armor, Criminal Possession | Criminal possession of body armor | 5-79-101 | 15.107 |
| Booby Traps | Booby traps | 5-73-126 | 15.93 |
| Breaking and Entering | Breaking and entering | 5-39-202 | 12.9 |
| Bribery, Public Servant | Abuse of public trust | 5-52-101 | 15.5 |
| Bribery, Witness | Witness Bribery | 5-53-108 | NA |
| Bridges, Destroying and Injuring | Injuring or destroying bridges, dams... | 5-72-108 | NA |
| Burglary | Residential burglary - Commercial burglary | 5-39-201 | 12.8 |
| Campus, Disruption of Activities | Disruption of campus activities | 5-71-226 | 15.77 |
| Capital Murder | Capital Murder | 5-10-101 | 9.2 |
| Catastrophe, Causing or Threatening | Causing a catastrophe - Threatening to cause... | 5-38-202 | 13.23 |
| Cemeteries, Access and Disturbances | Cemeteries - Access - Debris - Disturbance | 5-39-212 | 12.12 |
| Cemeteries, Unlawful Entries | Cemeteries - Mining and other unlawful entries | 5-39-211 | 12.12 |
| Child, Sexual Indecency with | Sexual indecency with a child | 5-14-110 | 10.3 |
| Children, Exposing to Chemicals or Meth | Exposing a child to a chemical substance... | 5-27-230 | 11.30 |
| Children, Interference with Custody | Interference with court-ordered custody | 5-26-502 | NA |
| Children, Interference with Visitation | Interference with visitation | 5-26-501 | NA |
| Children, Nonsupport | Nonsupport | 5-26-401 | NA |
| Coercion | Coercion | 5-13-208 | 11.12 |
| Coin Operated Machine, Slugs | Unlawfully using a slug | 5-37-212 | 13.17 |
| Communications, Unlawful Computerized | Unlawful computerized communications | 5-41-108 | 14.6 |
| Compensation, Soliciting Unlawful | Soliciting unlawful compensation | 5-52-104 | 15.7 |
| Compounding | Compounding | 5-54-107 | 15.14 |
| Computer Fraud | Computer fraud | 5-41-103 | 14.7 |
| Computer trespass | Computer trespass | 5-41-104 | 14.8 |
| Computer, Unlawful Communications | Unlawful computerized communications | 5-41-108 | 14.6 |
| Confidential Information, Misuse Of | Misuse of confidential information | 5-52-106 | NA |
| Contributing to Delinquency of a Juvenile | Contributing to the delinquency of a juvenile | 5-27-220 | 11.23 |
| Contributing to the Delinquency of a Minor | Contributing to the delinquency of a minor | 5-27-209 | 11.21 |
| Correctional Officer, Agg. Assault on | Aggravated assault... | 5-13-211 | NA |
| Criminal Mischief, 1st Degree | Criminal mischief in the first degree | 5-38-203 | 13.28 |
| Criminal Mischief, 2nd Degree | Criminal mischief in the second degree | 5-38-204 | 13.29 |
| Dead Beat Dad | Nonsupport | 5-26-401 | NA |
| Death Threat, Student or Teacher | Communicating a death threat... | 5-17-101 | 11.35 |
| Defacing Objects of Public Respect | Defacing objects of public respect | 5-71-215 | 15.74 |
| Defrauding a Judgment Creditor | Defrauding a judgment creditor | 5-37-211 | NA |

| Keyword Description | Statutory Name | Code Section | Text Section |
|---|---|---|---|
| Defrauding a Secured Creditor | Defrauding a secured creditor | 5-37-203 | NA |
| Departure, Furnishing Implements | Furnishing implement for...departure | 5-54-118 | 15.19 |
| Disorderly Conduct | Disorderly conduct | 5-71-207 | 15.66 |
| Domestic Battering, First Degree | Domestic battering in the first degree | 5-26-303 | 11.17 |
| Domestic Battering, Second Degree | Domestic battering in the second degree | 5-26-304 | 11.17 |
| Domestic Battering, Third Degree | Domestic battering in the third degree | 5-26-305 | 11.17 |
| Drains (natural), Obstruction | Obstructing natural drains | 5-72-106 | NA |
| Drains, Obstruction by Timber | Obstruction of drains by timber or material... | 5-72-105 | NA |
| Drinking in Public | Public intoxication - Drinking in public | 5-71-212 | 15.71 |
| Drive by | Unlawful discharge of a firearm from a vehicle | 5-74-107 | 15.100 |
| Driving While Intoxicated | Driving While Intoxicated | 5-64-103 | 17.3 |
| Driving with a DWI Suspension | Operation...during period of license suspension... | 5-65-105 | 17.5 |
| Drugs, Continuing Criminal Enterprise | Continuing criminal enterprise | 5-64-405 | 16.4 |
| Drugs, Fraud and Paraphernalia | Fraud - Criminal penalties - Drug paraphernalia | 5-64-403 | 16.2 |
| Drugs, Manufacturing and Delivery | Criminal penalties (drug offenses) | 5-64-401 | 16.2 |
| Drugs, Precursors | Drug precursors | 5-64-415 | 16.4 |
| Drugs, Use of a Communications Device | Use of a communication device | 5-64-404 | NA |
| Enclosures, Allowing Animals Into | Allowing animals into enclosures... | 5-38-210 | NA |
| Endangering a Minor, 1st Degree | Endangering the welfare of a minor... | 5-27-205 | 11.20 |
| Endangering a Minor, 2nd Degree | Endangering the welfare of a minor... | 5-27-206 | 11.20 |
| Endangering a Minor, 3rd Degree | Endangering the welfare of a minor... | 5-27-207 | 11.20 |
| Endangering an Incompetent, 1st Degree | Endangering the welfare of an... | 5-27-201 | 11.19 |
| Endangering an Incompetent, 2nd Degree | Endangering the welfare of an... | 5-27-202 | 11.19 |
| Endangering an Incompetent, 3rd Degree | Endangering the welfare of an... | 5-27-203 | 11.19 |
| Escape, 1st Degree | First degree escape | 5-54-110 | 15.15 |
| Escape, 2nd Degree | Second degree escape | 5-54-111 | 15.15 |
| Escape, 3rd Degree | Third degree escape | 5-54-112 | 15.15 |
| Escape, Furnishing Implements | Furnishing implement for escape | 5-54-117 | 15.18 |
| Escape, Permitting in the First Degree | Permitting escape in the first degree | 5-54-113 | 15.16 |
| Escape, Permitting in the Second Degree | Permitting escape...in the second degree | 5-54-115 | 15.16 |
| Evidence, Tampering | Tampering with physical evidence | 5-53-111 | NA |
| Explosives, Criminal Acts | Criminal acts involving explosives | 5-73-108 | 15.84 |
| Exposing a child to a chemical substance... | Exposing a child to a chemical substance... | 5-27-230 | 11.30 |
| Failure to Appear | Failure to appear | 5-54-120 | 15.21 |
| Fake, College Diploma or Transcripts | Use of false transcript, diploma, or grade... | 5-37-225 | NA |
| Fake, Object of Art, Antique, etc. | Criminal simulation | 5-37-213 | 13.18 |
| False Alarm, Communicating | Communicating a false alarm | 5-71-210 | 15.69 |
| False Swearing | False Swearing | 5-53-103 | NA |
| Falsifying Business Records | Falsifying a business record | 5-37-202 | NA |
| Family Member, Agg. Assault On | Aggravated assault on a family... | 5-26-306 | 11.18 |
| Family Member, Second Degree Assault | Second degree assault on family... | 5-26-308 | 11.18 |
| Family Member, Third Degree Assault | Third degree assault on a family... | 5-26-309 | 11.18 |

| Keyword Description | Statutory Name | Code Section | Text Section |
|---|---|---|---|
| Fencing | Aiding consummation of offense | 5-54-106 | 15.13 |
| Filing False Report with Law Enforcement | Filing false report with law enforcement agency | 5-54-122 | 15.23 |
| Financial Identity Fraud | Financial identity fraud | 5-37-227 | 13.19 |
| Fire or Bombing, Threatening | Threatening a fire or bombing | 5-71-211 | 15.70 |
| Firearm, Student's | Parental responsibility for student's firearm... | 5-27-210 | 11.22 |
| Firearms (Handgun), On School Property | Handguns - Possession by minor... | 5-73-119 | 15.87 |
| Firearms (Handgun), Possession by Minor | Handguns - Possession by minor... | 5-73-119 | 15.87 |
| Firearms, Carrying in Public Buildings | Carrying a firearm in publicly owned buildings... | 5-73-122 | 15.90 |
| Firearms, Defacing | Defacing a firearm | 5-73-106 | 15.83 |
| Firearms, Discharge from a Vehicle | Unlawful discharge of a firearm from a vehicle | 5-74-107 | 15.100 |
| Firearms, Furnishing to a Minor | Furnishing a deadly weapon to a minor | 5-73-109 | 15.85 |
| Firearms, Possession of a Defaced | Possession of a defaced firearm | 5-73-107 | 15.83 |
| Firearms, Possession of By Certain Persons | Possession of firearms by certain persons | 5-73-103 | 15.81 |
| Firearms, Possession with Drugs | Simultaneous possession of drugs and firearms | 5-74-106 | 15.99 |
| Firearms, Sale to Prohibited Persons | Sale...to person prohibited from possessing... | 5-73-132 | 15.97 |
| Fishing, Disruption Of | Obstruction of shooting, hunting, fishing... | 5-71-228 | 15.78 |
| Flag (Arkansas), Desecration Of | ...desecration of the Arkansas flag | 5-51-208 | NA |
| Flag (U.S.), Desecration Of | ...desecration of the United States flag | 5-51-207 | NA |
| Fleeing | Fleeing | 5-54-125 | 15.24 |
| Forgery | Forgery | 5-37-201 | 13.13 |
| Forgery Device, Criminal Possession | Criminal possession of a forgery device | 5-37-209 | 13.16 |
| Fraud, Computer | Computer fraud | 5-41-103 | 14.7 |
| Fraud, Credit or Debit Card | Fraudulent use of a credit card or debit card | 5-37-207 | 13.14 |
| Fraud, Defrauding a Judgment Creditor | Defrauding a judgment creditor | 5-37-211 | NA |
| Fraud, Defrauding a Secured Creditor | Defrauding a secured creditor | 5-37-203 | NA |
| Fraud, False College Diploma or Transcripts | Use of false transcript, diploma, or grade... | 5-37-225 | NA |
| Fraud, In Insolvency | Fraud in insolvency | 5-37-204 | NA |
| Fraud, Issuing False Financial Statement | Issuing a false financial statement | 5-37-205 | NA |
| Fraud, Real Property Instruments | Filing instruments affecting title...real property | 5-37-226 | NA |
| Fraud, Receiving Deposits | Receiving a deposit in a failing...institution | 5-37-206 | NA |
| Furnishing Prohibited Articles | Furnishing prohibited articles | 5-54-119 | 15.20 |
| Gambling Houses | Gambling houses | 5-66-103 | NA |
| Gambling, Bribery of Participants | Sports or games - Bribery of participants | 5-66-115 | NA |
| Gambling, Card Game Betting | Card games - Betting | 5-66-112 | NA |
| Gambling, Games of Skill Betting | Games of hazard or skill - Betting | 5-66-113 | NA |
| Gambling, Horse Race Betting | Horseracing - Betting | 5-66-116 | NA |
| Gambling, Lottery | Lottery, etc. - Tickets | 5-66-118 | 15.42 |
| Gambling, Lottery Promotion | Lottery - Promotion through sales | 5-66-119 | NA |
| Gambling, Transmitting Information | Sports or games - Transmission of information | 5-66-114 | NA |
| Gaming Devices | Gaming devices - Prohibition | 5-66-104 | NA |
| Gaming Devices, Betting | Gaming devices - Betting | 5-66-106 | NA |
| Gaming Devices, Financial Interest | Gaming devices - Financial interest | 5-66-105 | NA |
| Gaming Devices, In Buildings | Gaming devices - In buildings or on vessels | 5-66-107 | NA |

| Keyword Description | Statutory Name | Code Section | Text Section |
|---|---|---|---|
| Gaming, Keno | Keno, etc. | 5-66-110 | NA |
| Gaming, Pinball Machines | Pinball machines, etc. | 5-66-111 | NA |
| Gangs, Engaging in Criminal Enterprises | Engaging in a continuing criminal gang... | 5-74-104 | 15.98 |
| Gas Pipe, Extension Without Permission | Extension of gas pipe without permission | 5-69-101 | NA |
| Gas, Production of Carbon Black | Carbon black | 5-69-102 | NA |
| Gasoline, Theft Of | Theft of motor fuel | 5-36-120 | 13.10 |
| Governmental Operations, Obstructing | Obstructing governmental operations | 5-54-102 | 15.9 |
| Harassing Communications | Harassing communications | 5-71-209 | 15.68 |
| Harassment | Harassment | 5-71-208 | 15.67 |
| Hindering Apprehension or Prosecution | Hindering apprehension or prosecution | 5-54-105 | 15.12 |
| HIV, Exposing Another Person To | Exposing another person to human... | 5-14-123 | 10.7 |
| Homicide, Negligent | Negligent homicide | 5-10-105 | 9.6 |
| Hunting, Disruption Of | Obstruction of shooting, hunting, fishing... | 5-71-228 | 15.78 |
| ID Theft | Financial identity fraud | 5-37-227 | 13.19 |
| Impersonation, Criminal | Criminal impersonation | 5-37-208 | 13.15 |
| Incest | Incest | 5-26-202 | NA |
| Incompetents, Soliciting Money or Property | Soliciting money...from incompetents | 5-27-229 | 11.29 |
| Indecent exposure | Indecent exposure | 5-14-112 | 10.5 |
| Instruments of Crime, Possessing | Possessing instrument of crime | 5-73-102 | 15.80 |
| Interference with Court-ordered Custody | Interference with court-ordered custody | 5-26-502 | NA |
| Interference with Visitation | Interference with visitation | 5-26-501 | NA |
| Intimidating a Witness | Intimidating a witness | 5-53-109 | NA |
| Introduction of controlled substance... | Introduction of controlled substance... | 5-13-210 | 11.14 |
| Issuing a False Financial Statement | Issuing a false financial statement | 5-37-205 | NA |
| Joy Riding | Unauthorized use of a vehicle | 5-38-108 | NA |
| Juror, Approaching Commissioners | Approaching...jury commissioners to influence... | 5-53-133 | NA |
| Juror, Misconduct in Selecting | Misconduct in selecting or summoning jurors | 5-53-132 | NA |
| Juror, Retaliation Against | Retaliation against a witness, informant, or juror | 5-53-112 | NA |
| Jury Tampering | Jury tampering | 5-53-115 | NA |
| Juvenile, Contributing the Delinquency | Contributing to the delinquency of a juvenile | 5-27-220 | 11.23 |
| Kidnapping | Kidnapping | 5-11-102 | 11.2 |
| Knife, Carrying as a Weapon | Carrying a knife as a weapon | 5-73-121 | 15.89 |
| Land (State), Removal of Improvements | Removal of improvements...after forfeiture... | 5-40-103 | NA |
| Land, Forcible Possession Of | Forcible possession of land | 5-39-210 | 12.11 |
| Laser Light, Projecting On Law Enforcement | Projecting a laser light on a law enforcement... | 5-54-132 | 15.28 |
| Law Enforcement Animals, Killing or Injuring | Killing...animals used by law enforcement | 5-54-126 | 15.25 |
| Law Enforcement Insignia, Sale Of | Law enforcement insignia sales | 5-77-202 | 15.105 |
| Law Enforcement, Filing False Report With | Filing false report with law enforcement agency | 5-54-122 | 15.23 |
| Law Enforcement, Fleeing | Fleeing | 5-54-125 | 15.24 |
| Law Enforcement, Interference With | Interference with a law enforcement officer | 5-54-104 | 15.11 |
| Law Enforcement, Projecting Laser Light On | Projecting a laser light on a law enforcement... | 5-54-132 | 15.28 |

| Keyword Description | Statutory Name | Code Section | Text Section |
|---|---|---|---|
| Law Enforcement, Radio Privacy Adapters | Radio voice privacy adapters | 5-54-130 | NA |
| Law Enforcement, Refusal to Assist | Refusing to assist law enforcement officer | 5-54-109 | NA |
| Levees, Driving On | Driving on levees - Destruction of barricades | 5-72-110 | NA |
| Levees, Injuring | Injuring levees | 5-72-109 | NA |
| Loitering | Loitering | 5-71-213 | 15.72 |
| Manslaughter | Manslaughter | 5-10-104 | 9.5 |
| Medicaid Fraud Act | Medicaid Fraud Act | 5-55-101 | NA |
| Meth, Exposing Children | Exposing a child to a chemical substance... | 5-27-230 | 11.30 |
| Minor, Contributing to the Delinquency Of | Contributing to the delinquency of a minor | 5-27-209 | 11.21 |
| Minor, Endangering 1st Degree | Endangering the welfare of a minor... | 5-27-205 | 11.20 |
| Minor, Endangering 2nd Degree | Endangering the welfare of a minor... | 5-27-206 | 11.20 |
| Minor, Endangering 3rd Degree | Endangering the welfare of a minor... | 5-27-207 | 11.20 |
| Minor, Neglect Resulting in Delinquency | Neglect of minor resulting in delinquency | 5-27-222 | 11.25 |
| Minor, Permitting Abuse Of | Permitting abuse of a minor | 5-27-221 | 11.24 |
| Minor, Tobacco Use | Providing minors with tobacco products... | 5-27-227 | 11.28 |
| Mischief, 1st Degree | Criminal mischief in the first degree | 5-38-203 | 13.28 |
| Mischief, 2nd Degree | Criminal mischief in the second degree | 5-38-204 | 13.28 |
| Money Laundering | Criminal use of property or laundering criminal.. | 5-42-204 | NA |
| Motion Picture Piracy | Motion picture piracy | 5-36-122 | NA |
| Motorboats, Operating While Intoxicated | Unlawful acts | 5-76-102 | 15.103 |
| Murder, Capital | Capital Murder | 5-10-101 | 9.2 |
| Murder, First Degree | Murder in the first degree | 5-10-102 | 9.3 |
| Murder, Second Degree | Murder in the second degree | 5-10-103 | 9.4 |
| Native Growth, Destruction Of | Destruction of native growth | 5-38-212 | NA |
| Neglect of Minor Resulting in Delinquency | Neglect of minor resulting in delinquency | 5-27-222 | 11.25 |
| Negligent Homicide | Negligent homicide | 5-10-105 | 9.6 |
| Nonsupport | Nonsupport | 5-26-401 | NA |
| Nudism | Nudism | 5-68-204 | 15.51 |
| Obscenity, Exhibition of Figures | Exhibition of obscene figures | 5-68-201 | 15.48 |
| Obscenity, Films | Obscene films | 5-68-203 | 15.50 |
| Obscenity, Literature Rejected by US Mail | Sale...of literature rejected by U.S. mail | 5-68-202 | 15.49 |
| Obscenity, Nudism | Nudism | 5-68-204 | 15.51 |
| Obscenity, Public Display Of | Public display of obscenity | 5-68-205 | 15.52 |
| Obstructing Governmental Operations | Obstructing governmental operations | 5-54-102 | 15.9 |
| Order of Protection, Violation | Violation of an order of protection | 5-53-134 | NA |
| Parental Responsibility for Student's Firearm... | Parental responsibility for student's firearm... | 5-27-210 | 11.22 |
| Peeping Tom | Voyeurism | 5-16-102 | NA |
| Pepper Spray | Tear gas - Pepper spray | 5-73-124 | 15.92 |
| Perjury | Perjury | 5-53-102 | NA |
| Permitting Abuse of a Minor | Permitting abuse of a minor | 5-27-221 | 11.24 |
| Physician-assisted suicide | Physician-assisted suicide | 5-10-106 | 9.7 |
| Piracy, Movie | Motion picture piracy | 5-36-122 | NA |
| Polygamy | Bigamy | 5-26-201 | NA |
| Pornography | Obscene films | 5-68-203 | 15.50 |

| Keyword Description | Statutory Name | Code Section | Text Section |
|---|---|---|---|
| Prisoners, Furnishing Prohibited Articles To | Furnishing prohibited articles | 5-54-119 | 15.20 |
| Process, Simulating | Simulating legal process | 5-53-116 | NA |
| Property of Another Used to Facilitate Crime | ...use of another person's property to facilitate... | 5-74-105 | NA |
| Property, Advertising Without Permission | Advertising on property...owner's...permission | 5-39-213 | NA |
| Property, Conversion | Theft of...rented, or entrusted...property | 5-36-115 | 13.8 |
| Prostitution | Prostitution | 5-70-102 | 15.59 |
| Prostitution, Patronizing | Patronizing a prostitute | 5-70-103 | 15.60 |
| Prostitution, Promotion in the 1st Degree | Promoting prostitution in the first degree | 5-70-104 | 15.61 |
| Prostitution, Promotion in the 2nd Degree | Promoting prostitution in the second degree | 5-70-105 | 15.61 |
| Prostitution, Promotion in the 3rd Degree | Promoting prostitution in the third degree | 5-70-106 | 15.61 |
| Public Buildings, Defacing | Defacing public buildings | 5-71-216 | 15.75 |
| Public Drunk | Public intoxication - Drinking in public | 5-71-212 | 15.71 |
| Public Facility, Impairing Operation Of | Impairing the operation of a vital public facility... | 5-38-205 | NA |
| Public Intoxication | Public intoxication - Drinking in public | 5-71-212 | 15.71 |
| Public Record, Tampering With | Tampering with a public record | 5-54-121 | 15.22 |
| Public Roads, Advertising Signs | Advertising signs generally | 5-67-101 | 15.43 |
| Public Roads, Bridge Prohibitions | Violation of posted bridge prohibitions | 5-67-104 | 15.45 |
| Public Roads, False or Misleading Signs | False or misleading signs | 5-67-102 | 15.44 |
| Public Roads, Obstructing | Obstructing a highway or other public passage | 5-71-214 | 15.73 |
| Public Roads, Signs on Utility Poles | Attaching signs to utility poles or living plants | 5-67-103 | NA |
| Public Roads, Solicitation Near Highway | Solicitation on or near a highway | 5-67-107 | 15.47 |
| Public Roads, Use of Spotlight | Use of spotlight | 5-67-106 | 15.46 |
| Public Roads, Wreckage Near Highway | Wreckage near memorial highway | 5-67-105 | NA |
| Public Servant, Abuse of Office | Abuse of Office | 5-52-107 | 15.6 |
| Public Servant, Attempting to Influence | Attempt to influence a public servant | 5-52-105 | 15.8 |
| Public sexual indecency | Public sexual indecency | 5-14-111 | 10.4 |
| Public Trust, Abuse Of | Abuse of public trust | 5-52-101 | 15.5 |
| Radio Privacy Adapters | Radio voice privacy adapters | 5-54-130 | NA |
| Rape, Forcible | Rape | 5-14-103 | 10.2 |
| Rape, Incest | Rape | 5-14-103 | 10.2 |
| Rape, Statutory | Rape | 5-14-103 | 10.2 |
| Real Property, Instruments Affecting | Filing instruments affecting title...real property | 5-37-226 | NA |
| Receiving a Deposit in a Failing Institution | Receiving a deposit in a failing...institution | 5-37-206 | NA |
| Receiving Stolen Property | Theft by receiving | 5-36-106 | 13.6 |
| Referee, Abuse of | Abuse of athletic contest officials | 5-13-209 | 11.13 |
| Riot | Riot | 5-71-201 | 15.62 |
| Riot, Aggravated | Aggravated riot | 5-71-202 | 15.63 |
| Riot, Arming Rioters | Arming rioters | 5-71-204 | NA |
| Riot, Failure to Disperse | Failure to disperse | 5-71-206 | 15.65 |
| Riot, Inciting | Inciting riot | 5-71-203 | NA |
| Rivers, Keeping Dams Sufficiently Open | Keeping dams sufficiently open | 5-72-107 | NA |
| Rivers, Leaving Timber | Leaving timber in navigable stream... | 5-72-104 | NA |

| Keyword Description | Statutory Name | Code Section | Text Section |
|---|---|---|---|
| Rivers, Removal of Trees | Removal of trees...navigable rivers or streams | 5-72-102 | NA |
| Robbery | Robbery | 5-12-102 | 11.8 |
| Robbery, Aggravated | Aggravated Robbery | 5-12-103 | 11.9 |
| Scalping | Tickets to...Sale in excess of regular price | 5-63-201 | NA |
| School Bus, Unauthorized Entry | Unauthorized entry of a school bus | 5-39-214 | NA |
| Sex Offender, Living Near School | Registered offender living near school... | 5-14-128 | 10.9 |
| Sex Offender, Working With Children | Registered offender working with children... | 5-14-129 | 10.10 |
| Sex, in Public | Public sexual indecency | 5-14-111 | 10.4 |
| Sex, with Animals | Bestiality | 5-14-122 | 10.6 |
| Sexual Assault, First Degree | Sexual assault in the first degree | 5-14-124 | 10.8 |
| Sexual Assault, Fourth Degree | Sexual assault in the fourth degree | 5-14-127 | 10.8 |
| Sexual Assault, Second Degree | Sexual assault in the second degree | 5-14-125 | 10.8 |
| Sexual Assault, Third Degree | Sexual assault in the third degree | 5-14-126 | 10.8 |
| Sexual Indecency with a Child | Sexual indecency with a child | 5-14-110 | 10.3 |
| Shoplifting | Shoplifting | 5-36-116 | 13.9 |
| Signature, Obtained by Deception | Obtaining a signature by deception | 5-37-210 | NA |
| Simulating Legal Process | Simulating legal process | 5-53-116 | NA |
| Simulation, Criminal | Criminal simulation | 5-37-213 | 13.18 |
| Slugs, Unlawful Use | Unlawfully using a slug | 5-37-212 | 13.17 |
| Soliciting money...from incompetents | Soliciting money...from incompetents | 5-27-229 | 11.29 |
| Spotlight, Use on Public Roads | Use of spotlight | 5-67-106 | 15.46 |
| Stalking | Stalking | 5-71-229 | 15.79 |
| Suicide, Physician-assisted | Physician-assisted suicide | 5-10-106 | 9.7 |
| Survey, Destruction of Landmarks | ...destruction of landmarks...survey | 5-38-214 | NA |
| Swamps, Cutting Timber | Cutting timber on swamp and overflowed lands | 5-72-103 | NA |
| Tampering | Tampering | 5-53-110 | NA |
| Tampering, Evidence | Tampering with physical evidence | 5-53-111 | NA |
| Tampering, Jury | Jury tampering | 5-53-115 | NA |
| Tampering, Public Record | Tampering with a public record | 5-54-121 | 15.22 |
| Taser, Possession Of | Possession of a Taser stun gun | 5-73-133 | NA |
| Telephone Solicitation, Automated | Automated telephone solicitation | 5-63-204 | NA |
| Theft,  Property | Theft of property | 5-36-103 | 13.3 |
| Theft, Motor Fuel | Theft of motor fuel | 5-36-120 | 13.10 |
| Theft, Property Lost or Delivered by Mistake | Theft of property lost, mislaid, or delivered... | 5-36-105 | 13.5 |
| Theft, Receiving | Theft by receiving | 5-36-106 | 13.6 |
| Theft, Recyclable Materials | Theft of recyclable materials | 5-36-121 | NA |
| Theft, Rented or Entrusted Property | Theft of...rented, or entrusted...property | 5-36-115 | 13.8 |
| Theft, Services | Theft of services | 5-36-104 | 13.4 |
| Theft, Trade Secret | Theft of a trade secret | 5-36-107 | 13.7 |
| Tobacco, Minors | Providing minors with tobacco products... | 5-27-227 | 11.28 |
| Treason | Treason | 5-51-201 | NA |
| Trespass, Computer | Computer trespass | 5-41-104 | 14.8 |
| Trespass, Criminal | Criminal trespass | 5-39-203 | 12.10 |
| Usurping Office | Usurping office | 5-51-203 | NA |
| Usurping, Overturning, Seizing Government | Usurping, overturning, or seizing government | 5-51-204 | NA |
| Vehicle, Unauthorized Use | Unauthorized use of a vehicle | 5-38-108 | NA |

| Keyword Description | Statutory Name | Code Section | Text Section |
|---|---|---|---|
| Video Voyeurism | Crime of video voyeurism | 5-16-101 | 15.4 |
| Violent Group Activity, Engaging In | Engaging in violent criminal group activity | 5-74-108 | 15.101 |
| Vital Public Facility, Impairing Operation | Impairing the operation of a vital public facility... | 5-38-205 | NA |
| Voyeurism | Voyeurism | 5-16-102 | NA |
| Voyeurism, Video | Crime of video voyeurism | 5-16-101 | 15.4 |
| Weapons, Carrying | Carrying a weapon | 5-73-120 | 15.88 |
| Weapons, Carrying a Knife | Carrying a knife as a weapon | 5-73-121 | 15.89 |
| Weapons, Criminal Use | Criminal use of prohibited weapons | 5-73-104 | 15.82 |
| Weapons, Furnishing to Felons | Furnishing...a prohibited weapon to a felon | 5-73-129 | 15.96 |
| Weapons, Possession by Incarcerated | Possession...weapons by incarcerated persons | 5-73-131 | NA |
| Witness, Bribery | Witness Bribery | 5-53-108 | NA |
| Witness, Intimidating | Intimidating a witness | 5-53-109 | NA |
| Witness, Retaliation Against | Retaliation against a witness, informant, or juror | 5-53-112 | NA |

# Appendix 2: United States Constitution[407]

We the People of the United States, in Order to form a more perfect Union, establish Justice, insure domestic Tranquility, provide for the common defence, promote the general Welfare, and secure the Blessings of Liberty to ourselves and our Posterity, do ordain and establish this Constitution for the United States of America.

*Article. I.*

## Section. 1.

All legislative Powers herein granted shall be vested in a Congress of the United States, which shall consist of a Senate and House of Representatives.

## Section. 2.

The House of Representatives shall be composed of Members chosen every second Year by the People of the several States, and the Electors in each State shall have the Qualifications requisite for Electors of the most numerous Branch of the State Legislature.

No Person shall be a Representative who shall not have attained to the Age of twenty five Years, and been seven Years a Citizen of the United States, and who shall not, when elected, be an Inhabitant of that State in which he shall be chosen.

Representatives and direct Taxes shall be apportioned among the several States which may be included within this Union, according to their respective Numbers, which shall be determined by adding to the whole Number of free Persons, including those bound to Service for a Term of Years, and excluding Indians not taxed, three fifths of all other Persons. The actual Enumeration shall be made within three Years after the first Meeting of the Congress of the United States, and within every subsequent Term of ten Years, in such Manner as they shall by Law direct. The Number of Representatives shall not exceed one for every thirty Thousand, but each State shall have at Least one Representative; and until such enumeration shall be made, the State of New Hampshire shall be entitled to chuse three, Massachusetts eight, Rhode-Island and Providence Plantations one, Connecticut five, New-York six, New Jersey four, Pennsylvania eight, Delaware one, Maryland six, Virginia ten, North Carolina five, South Carolina five, and Georgia three.

When vacancies happen in the Representation from any State, the Executive Authority thereof shall issue Writs of Election to fill such Vacancies.

The House of Representatives shall chuse their Speaker and other Officers; and shall have the sole Power of Impeachment.

---

[407] Adapted from the website of the *National Archive*.
http://www.archives.gov/national-archives-experience/

### Section. 3.

The Senate of the United States shall be composed of two Senators from each State, chosen by the Legislature thereof for six Years; and each Senator shall have one Vote.

Immediately after they shall be assembled in Consequence of the first Election, they shall be divided as equally as may be into three Classes. The Seats of the Senators of the first Class shall be vacated at the Expiration of the second Year, of the second Class at the Expiration of the fourth Year, and of the third Class at the Expiration of the sixth Year, so that one third may be chosen every second Year; and if Vacancies happen by Resignation, or otherwise, during the Recess of the Legislature of any State, the Executive thereof may make temporary Appointments until the next Meeting of the Legislature, which shall then fill such Vacancies.

No Person shall be a Senator who shall not have attained to the Age of thirty Years, and been nine Years a Citizen of the United States, and who shall not, when elected, be an Inhabitant of that State for which he shall be chosen.

The Vice President of the United States shall be President of the Senate, but shall have no Vote, unless they be equally divided.

The Senate shall chuse their other Officers, and also a President pro tempore, in the Absence of the Vice President, or when he shall exercise the Office of President of the United States.

The Senate shall have the sole Power to try all Impeachments. When sitting for that Purpose, they shall be on Oath or Affirmation. When the President of the United States is tried, the Chief Justice shall preside: And no Person shall be convicted without the Concurrence of two thirds of the Members present.

Judgment in Cases of Impeachment shall not extend further than to removal from Office, and disqualification to hold and enjoy any Office of honor, Trust or Profit under the United States: but the Party convicted shall nevertheless be liable and subject to Indictment, Trial, Judgment and Punishment, according to Law.

### Section. 4.

The Times, Places and Manner of holding Elections for Senators and Representatives, shall be prescribed in each State by the Legislature thereof; but the Congress may at any time by Law make or alter such Regulations, except as to the Places of chusing Senators.

The Congress shall assemble at least once in every Year, and such Meeting shall be on the first Monday in December, unless they shall by Law appoint a different Day.

### Section. 5.

Each House shall be the Judge of the Elections, Returns and Qualifications of its own Members, and a Majority of each shall constitute a Quorum to do Business; but a smaller Number may adjourn from day to day, and may be authorized to compel the Attendance of absent Members, in such Manner, and under such Penalties as each House may provide.

Each House may determine the Rules of its Proceedings, punish its Members for disorderly Behaviour, and, with the Concurrence of two thirds, expel a Member.

Each House shall keep a Journal of its Proceedings, and from time to time publish the same, excepting such Parts as may in their Judgment require Secrecy; and the Yeas and Nays of the Members of either House on any question shall, at the Desire of one fifth of those Present, be entered on the Journal.

Neither House, during the Session of Congress, shall, without the Consent of the other, adjourn for more than three days, nor to any other Place than that in which the two Houses shall be sitting.

## Section. 6.

The Senators and Representatives shall receive a Compensation for their Services, to be ascertained by Law, and paid out of the Treasury of the United States. They shall in all Cases, except Treason, Felony and Breach of the Peace, be privileged from Arrest during their Attendance at the Session of their respective Houses, and in going to and returning from the same; and for any Speech or Debate in either House, they shall not be questioned in any other Place.

No Senator or Representative shall, during the Time for which he was elected, be appointed to any civil Office under the Authority of the United States, which shall have been created, or the Emoluments whereof shall have been encreased during such time; and no Person holding any Office under the United States, shall be a Member of either House during his Continuance in Office.

## Section. 7.

All Bills for raising Revenue shall originate in the House of Representatives; but the Senate may propose or concur with Amendments as on other Bills.

Every Bill which shall have passed the House of Representatives and the Senate, shall, before it become a Law, be presented to the President of the United States: If he approve he shall sign it, but if not he shall return it, with his Objections to that House in which it shall have originated, who shall enter the Objections at large on their Journal, and proceed to reconsider it. If after such Reconsideration two thirds of that House shall agree to pass the Bill, it shall be sent, together with the Objections, to the other House, by which it shall likewise be reconsidered, and if approved by two thirds of that House, it shall become a Law. But in all such Cases the Votes of both Houses shall be determined by yeas and Nays, and the Names of the Persons voting for and against the Bill shall be entered on the Journal of each House respectively. If any Bill shall not be returned by the President within ten Days (Sundays excepted) after it shall have been presented to him, the Same shall be a Law, in like Manner as if he had signed it, unless the Congress by their Adjournment prevent its Return, in which Case it shall not be a Law.

Every Order, Resolution, or Vote to which the Concurrence of the Senate and House of Representatives may be necessary (except on a question of Adjournment) shall be presented to the President of the United States; and before the Same shall take Effect, shall be approved by him, or being disapproved by him, shall be repassed by two thirds of the Senate and House of Representatives, according to the Rules and Limitations prescribed in the Case of a Bill.

## Section. 8.

The Congress shall have Power To lay and collect Taxes, Duties, Imposts and Excises, to pay the Debts and provide for the common Defence and general Welfare of the United States; but all Duties, Imposts and Excises shall be uniform throughout the United States;

To borrow Money on the credit of the United States;

To regulate Commerce with foreign Nations, and among the several States, and with the Indian Tribes;

To establish an uniform Rule of Naturalization, and uniform Laws on the subject of Bankruptcies throughout the United States;

To coin Money, regulate the Value thereof, and of foreign Coin, and fix the Standard of Weights and Measures;

To provide for the Punishment of counterfeiting the Securities and current Coin of the United States;

To establish Post Offices and post Roads;

To promote the Progress of Science and useful Arts, by securing for limited Times to Authors and Inventors the exclusive Right to their respective Writings and Discoveries;

To constitute Tribunals inferior to the supreme Court;

To define and punish Piracies and Felonies committed on the high Seas, and Offences against the Law of Nations;

To declare War, grant Letters of Marque and Reprisal, and make Rules concerning Captures on Land and Water;

To raise and support Armies, but no Appropriation of Money to that Use shall be for a longer Term than two Years;

To provide and maintain a Navy;

To make Rules for the Government and Regulation of the land and naval Forces;

To provide for calling forth the Militia to execute the Laws of the Union, suppress Insurrections and repel Invasions;

To provide for organizing, arming, and disciplining, the Militia, and for governing such Part of them as may be employed in the Service of the United States, reserving to the States respectively, the Appointment of the Officers, and the Authority of training the Militia according to the discipline prescribed by Congress;

To exercise exclusive Legislation in all Cases whatsoever, over such District (not exceeding ten Miles square) as may, by Cession of particular States, and the Acceptance of Congress, become the Seat of the Government of the United States, and to exercise like Authority over all Places purchased by the Consent of the Legislature of the State in which the Same shall be, for the Erection of Forts, Magazines, Arsenals, dock-Yards, and other needful Buildings;--And

To make all Laws which shall be necessary and proper for carrying into Execution the foregoing Powers, and all other Powers vested by this Constitution in the Government of the United States, or in any Department or Officer thereof.

### Section. 9.

The Migration or Importation of such Persons as any of the States now existing shall think proper to admit, shall not be prohibited by the Congress prior to the Year one thousand eight hundred and eight, but a Tax or duty may be imposed on such Importation, not exceeding ten dollars for each Person.

The Privilege of the Writ of Habeas Corpus shall not be suspended, unless when in Cases of Rebellion or Invasion the public Safety may require it.

No Bill of Attainder or ex post facto Law shall be passed.

No Capitation, or other direct, Tax shall be laid, unless in Proportion to the Census or enumeration herein before directed to be taken.

No Tax or Duty shall be laid on Articles exported from any State.

No Preference shall be given by any Regulation of Commerce or Revenue to the Ports of one State over those of another; nor shall Vessels bound to, or from, one State, be obliged to enter, clear, or pay Duties in another.

No Money shall be drawn from the Treasury, but in Consequence of Appropriations made by Law; and a regular Statement and Account of the Receipts and Expenditures of all public Money shall be published from time to time.

No Title of Nobility shall be granted by the United States: And no Person holding any Office of Profit or Trust under them, shall, without the Consent of the Congress, accept of any present, Emolument, Office, or Title, of any kind whatever, from any King, Prince, or foreign State.

### Section. 10.

No State shall enter into any Treaty, Alliance, or Confederation; grant Letters of Marque and Reprisal; coin Money; emit Bills of Credit; make any Thing but gold and silver Coin a Tender in Payment of Debts; pass any Bill of Attainder, ex post facto Law, or Law impairing the Obligation of Contracts, or grant any Title of Nobility.

No State shall, without the Consent of the Congress, lay any Imposts or Duties on Imports or Exports, except what may be absolutely necessary for executing it's inspection Laws: and the net Produce of all Duties and Imposts, laid by any State on Imports or Exports, shall be for the Use of the Treasury of the United States; and all such Laws shall be subject to the Revision and Controul of the Congress.

No State shall, without the Consent of Congress, lay any Duty of Tonnage, keep Troops, or Ships of War in time of Peace, enter into any Agreement or Compact with another State, or with a foreign Power, or engage in War, unless actually invaded, or in such imminent Danger as will not admit of delay.

### *Article. II.*

### Section. 1.

The executive Power shall be vested in a President of the United States of America. He shall hold his Office during the Term of four Years, and, together with the Vice President, chosen for the same Term, be elected, as follows:

Each State shall appoint, in such Manner as the Legislature thereof may direct, a Number of Electors, equal to the whole Number of Senators and Representatives to which the State may be entitled in the Congress: but no Senator or Representative, or Person holding an Office of Trust or Profit under the United States, shall be appointed an Elector.

The Electors shall meet in their respective States, and vote by Ballot for two Persons, of whom one at least shall not be an Inhabitant of the same State with themselves. And they shall make a List of all the Persons voted for, and of the Number of Votes for each; which List they shall sign and certify, and transmit sealed to the Seat of the Government of the United States, directed to the President of the Senate. The President of the Senate shall, in the Presence of the Senate and House of Representatives, open all the Certificates, and the Votes shall then be counted. The Person having the greatest Number of Votes shall be the President, if such Number be a Majority of the whole Number of Electors appointed; and if there be more than one who have such Majority, and have an equal Number of Votes, then the House of Representatives shall immediately chuse by Ballot one of them for President; and if no Person have a Majority, then from the five highest on the List the said House shall in like Manner chuse the President. But in chusing the President, the Votes shall be taken by States, the Representation from each State having one Vote; A quorum for this purpose shall consist of a Member or Members from two thirds of the States, and a Majority of all the States shall be necessary to a Choice. In every Case, after the Choice of the President, the Person having the greatest Number of Votes of the Electors shall be the Vice President. But if there should remain two or more who have equal Votes, the Senate shall chuse from them by Ballot the Vice President.

The Congress may determine the Time of chusing the Electors, and the Day on which they shall give their Votes; which Day shall be the same throughout the United States.

No Person except a natural born Citizen, or a Citizen of the United States, at the time of the Adoption of this Constitution, shall be eligible to the Office of President; neither shall any Person be eligible to that Office who shall not have attained to the Age of thirty five Years, and been fourteen Years a Resident within the United States.

In Case of the Removal of the President from Office, or of his Death, Resignation, or Inability to discharge the Powers and Duties of the said Office, the Same shall devolve on the Vice President, and the Congress may by Law provide for the Case of Removal, Death, Resignation or Inability, both of the President and Vice President, declaring what Officer shall then act as President, and such Officer shall act accordingly, until the Disability be removed, or a President shall be elected.

The President shall, at stated Times, receive for his Services, a Compensation, which shall neither be increased nor diminished during the Period for which he shall have been elected, and he shall not receive within that Period any other Emolument from the United States, or any of them.

Before he enter on the Execution of his Office, he shall take the following Oath or Affirmation:--"I do solemnly swear (or affirm) that I will faithfully execute the Office of President of the United States, and will to the best of my Ability, preserve, protect and defend the Constitution of the United States."

### Section. 2.

The President shall be Commander in Chief of the Army and Navy of the United States, and of the Militia of the several States, when called into the actual Service of the United States; he may require the Opinion, in writing, of the principal Officer in each of the executive Departments, upon any Subject relating to the Duties of their respective Offices, and he shall have Power to grant Reprieves and Pardons for Offences against the United States, except in Cases of Impeachment.

He shall have Power, by and with the Advice and Consent of the Senate, to make Treaties, provided two thirds of the Senators present concur; and he shall nominate, and by and with the Advice and Consent of the Senate, shall appoint Ambassadors, other public Ministers and Consuls, Judges of the supreme Court, and all other Officers of the United States, whose Appointments are not herein otherwise provided for, and which shall be established by Law: but the Congress may by Law vest the Appointment of such inferior Officers, as they think proper, in the President alone, in the Courts of Law, or in the Heads of Departments.

The President shall have Power to fill up all Vacancies that may happen during the Recess of the Senate, by granting Commissions which shall expire at the End of their next Session.

### Section. 3.

He shall from time to time give to the Congress Information of the State of the Union, and recommend to their Consideration such Measures as he shall judge necessary and expedient; he may, on extraordinary Occasions, convene both Houses, or either of them, and in Case of Disagreement between them, with Respect to the Time of Adjournment, he may adjourn them to such Time as he shall think proper; he shall receive Ambassadors and other public Ministers; he shall take Care that the Laws be faithfully executed, and shall Commission all the Officers of the United States.

### Section. 4.

The President, Vice President and all civil Officers of the United States, shall be removed from Office on Impeachment for, and Conviction of, Treason, Bribery, or other high Crimes and Misdemeanors.

*Article III.*

### Section. 1.

The judicial Power of the United States shall be vested in one supreme Court, and in such inferior Courts as the Congress may from time to time ordain and establish. The Judges, both of the supreme and inferior Courts, shall hold their Offices during good Behaviour, and shall, at stated Times, receive for their Services a Compensation, which shall not be diminished during their Continuance in Office.

### Section. 2.

The judicial Power shall extend to all Cases, in Law and Equity, arising under this Constitution, the Laws of the United States, and Treaties made, or which shall be made, under their Authority;--to all Cases affecting Ambassadors, other public Ministers and Consuls;--to all Cases of admiralty and maritime Jurisdiction;--to Controversies to which the United States shall be a Party;--to Controversies between two or more States;--between a State and Citizens of another State;--between Citizens of different States;--between Citizens of the same State claiming Lands under Grants of different States, and between a State, or the Citizens thereof, and foreign States, Citizens or Subjects.

In all Cases affecting Ambassadors, other public Ministers and Consuls, and those in which a State shall be Party, the supreme Court shall have original Jurisdiction. In all the other Cases before mentioned, the supreme Court shall have appellate Jurisdiction, both as to Law and Fact, with such Exceptions, and under such Regulations as the Congress shall make.

The Trial of all Crimes, except in Cases of Impeachment, shall be by Jury; and such Trial shall be held in the State where the said Crimes shall have been committed; but when not committed within any State, the Trial shall be at such Place or Places as the Congress may by Law have directed.

### Section. 3.

Treason against the United States, shall consist only in levying War against them, or in adhering to their Enemies, giving them Aid and Comfort. No Person shall be convicted of Treason unless on the Testimony of two Witnesses to the same overt Act, or on Confession in open Court.

The Congress shall have Power to declare the Punishment of Treason, but no Attainder of Treason shall work Corruption of Blood, or Forfeiture except during the Life of the Person attainted.

*Article. IV.*

### Section. 1.

Full Faith and Credit shall be given in each State to the public Acts, Records, and judicial Proceedings of every other State. And the Congress may by general Laws prescribe the Manner in which such Acts, Records and Proceedings shall be proved, and the Effect thereof.

### Section. 2.

The Citizens of each State shall be entitled to all Privileges and Immunities of Citizens in the several States.

A Person charged in any State with Treason, Felony, or other Crime, who shall flee from Justice, and be found in another State, shall on Demand of the executive Authority of the State from which he fled, be delivered up, to be removed to the State having Jurisdiction of the Crime.

No Person held to Service or Labour in one State, under the Laws thereof, escaping into another, shall, in Consequence of any Law or Regulation therein, be discharged from such Service or Labour, but shall be delivered up on Claim of the Party to whom such Service or Labour may be due.

### Section. 3.

New States may be admitted by the Congress into this Union; but no new State shall be formed or erected within the Jurisdiction of any other State; nor any State be formed by the Junction of two or more States, or Parts of States, without the Consent of the Legislatures of the States concerned as well as of the Congress.

The Congress shall have Power to dispose of and make all needful Rules and Regulations respecting the Territory or other Property belonging to the United States; and nothing in this Constitution shall be so construed as to Prejudice any Claims of the United States, or of any particular State.

### Section. 4.

The United States shall guarantee to every State in this Union a Republican Form of Government, and shall protect each of them against Invasion; and on Application of the Legislature, or of the Executive (when the Legislature cannot be convened), against domestic Violence.

### Article. V.

The Congress, whenever two thirds of both Houses shall deem it necessary, shall propose Amendments to this Constitution, or, on the Application of the Legislatures of two thirds of the several States, shall call a Convention for proposing Amendments, which, in either Case, shall be valid to all Intents and Purposes, as Part of this Constitution, when ratified by the Legislatures of three fourths of the several States, or by Conventions in three fourths thereof, as the one or the other Mode of Ratification may be proposed by the Congress; Provided that no Amendment which may be made prior to the Year One thousand eight hundred and eight shall in any Manner affect the first and fourth Clauses in the Ninth Section of the first Article; and that no State, without its Consent, shall be deprived of its equal Suffrage in the Senate.

### Article. VI.

All Debts contracted and Engagements entered into, before the Adoption of this Constitution, shall be as valid against the United States under this Constitution, as under the Confederation.

This Constitution, and the Laws of the United States which shall be made in Pursuance thereof; and all Treaties made, or which shall be made, under the Authority of the United States, shall be the supreme Law of the Land; and the Judges in every State shall be bound thereby, any Thing in the Constitution or Laws of any State to the Contrary notwithstanding.

The Senators and Representatives before mentioned, and the Members of the several State Legislatures, and all executive and judicial Officers, both of the United States and of the several States, shall be bound by Oath or Affirmation, to support this Constitution; but no religious Test shall ever be required as a Qualification to any Office or public Trust under the United States.

### Article. VII.

The Ratification of the Conventions of nine States, shall be sufficient for the Establishment of this Constitution between the States so ratifying the Same.

The Word, "the," being interlined between the seventh and eighth Lines of the first Page, the Word "Thirty" being partly written on an Erazure in the fifteenth Line of the first Page, The Words "is tried" being interlined between the thirty second and thirty third Lines of the first Page and the Word "the" being interlined between the forty third and forty fourth Lines of the second Page.

Attest William Jackson Secretary

Done in Convention by the Unanimous Consent of the States present the Seventeenth Day of September in the Year of our Lord one thousand seven hundred and Eighty seven and of the Independence of the United States of America the Twelfth In witness whereof We have hereunto subscribed our Names. . . .

# Appendix 3: The Bill of Rights

*The Appendix provides the text of the Bill of Rights, which are the first ten Amendments to the United States Constitution. In addition, the text of the Fourteenth Amendment is provided, which applied many of these rights to state government.*

***Bill of Rights***

## Amendment I

Congress shall make no law respecting an establishment of religion, or prohibiting the free exercise thereof; or abridging the freedom of speech, or of the press; or the right of the people peaceably to assemble, and to petition the government for a redress of grievances.

## Amendment II

A well regulated militia, being necessary to the security of a free state, the right of the people to keep and bear arms, shall not be infringed.

## Amendment III

No soldier shall, in time of peace be quartered in any house, without the consent of the owner, nor in time of war, but in a manner to be prescribed by law.

## Amendment IV

The right of the people to be secure in their persons, houses, papers, and effects, against unreasonable searches and seizures, shall not be violated, and no warrants shall issue, but upon probable cause, supported by oath or affirmation, and particularly describing the place to be searched, and the persons or things to be seized.

## Amendment V

No person shall be held to answer for a capital, or otherwise infamous crime, unless on a presentment or indictment of a grand jury, except in cases arising in the land or naval forces, or in the militia, when in actual service in time of war or public danger; nor shall any person be subject for the same offense to be twice put in jeopardy of life or limb; nor shall be compelled in any criminal case to be a witness against himself, nor be deprived of life, liberty, or property, without due process of law; nor shall private property be taken for public use, without just compensation.

## Amendment VI

In all criminal prosecutions, the accused shall enjoy the right to a speedy and public trial, by an impartial jury of the state and district wherein the crime shall have been committed, which district shall have been previously ascertained by law, and to be informed of the nature and cause of the accusation; to be confronted with the witnesses against him; to have compulsory process for obtaining witnesses in his favor, and to have the assistance of counsel for his defense.

## Amendment VII

In suits at common law, where the value in controversy shall exceed twenty dollars, the right of trial by jury shall be preserved, and no fact tried by a jury, shall be otherwise reexamined in any court of the United States, than according to the rules of the common law.

## Amendment VIII

Excessive bail shall not be required, nor excessive fines imposed, nor cruel and unusual punishments inflicted.

## Amendment IX

The enumeration in the Constitution, of certain rights, shall not be construed to deny or disparage others retained by the people.

## Amendment X

The powers not delegated to the United States by the Constitution, nor prohibited by it to the states, are reserved to the states respectively, or to the people.

## *Amendment XIV*

### Section. 1.

All persons born or naturalized in the United States and subject to the jurisdiction thereof, are citizens of the United States and of the State wherein they reside. No State shall make or enforce any law which shall abridge the privileges or immunities of citizens of the United States; nor shall any State deprive any person of life, liberty, or property, without due process of law; nor deny to any person within its jurisdiction the equal protection of the laws.

### Section. 2.

Representatives shall be apportioned among the several States according to their respective numbers, counting the whole number of persons in each State, excluding Indians not taxed. But when the right to vote at any election for the choice of electors for President and Vice President of the United States, Representatives in Congress, the Executive and Judicial officers of a State, or the members of the Legislature thereof, is denied to any of the male inhabitants of such State, being twenty-one years of age, and citizens of the United States, or in any way abridged, except for participation in rebellion, or other crime, the basis of representation therein shall be reduced in the proportion which the number of such male citizens shall bear to the whole number of male citizens twenty-one years of age in such State.

### Section. 3.

No person shall be a Senator or Representative in Congress, or elector of President and Vice President, or hold any office, civil or military, under the United States, or under any State, who, having previously taken an oath, as a member of Congress, or as an officer of the United States, or as a member of any State legislature, or as an executive or judicial officer of any State, to support the Constitution of the United States, shall have engaged in insurrection or rebellion against the same, or given aid or comfort to the enemies thereof. But Congress may by a vote of two-thirds of each House, remove such disability.

### Section. 4.

The validity of the public debt of the United States, authorized by law, including debts incurred for payment of pensions and bounties for services in suppressing insurrection or rebellion, shall not be questioned. But neither the United States nor any State shall assume or pay any debt or obligation incurred in aid of insurrection or rebellion against the United States, or any claim for the loss or emancipation of any slave; but all such debts, obligations and claims shall be held illegal and void.

## Section. 5.

The Congress shall have power to enforce, by appropriate legislation, the provisions of this article.

# Appendix 4: Constitution of the State of Arkansas

*This Appendix provides excerpts from the Constitution of the State of Arkansas. These sections were included because they impact the making of law and the administration of the criminal justice system.*

### Preamble.

We, the People of the State of Arkansas, grateful to Almighty God for the privilege of choosing our own form of government; for our civil and religious liberty; and desiring to perpetuate its blessings, and secure the same to our selves and posterity; do ordain and establish this Constitution.

### Article 1. Boundaries.

We do declare and establish, ratify and confirm, the following as the permanent boundaries of the State of Arkansas, that is to say: Beginning at the middle of the main channel of the Mississippi River, on the parallel of thirty-six degrees of north latitude, running thence west with said parallel of latitude to the middle of the main channel of the St. Francis River; thence up the main channel of said last-named river to the parallel of thirty-six degrees thirty minutes of north latitude; thence west with the southern boundary line of the State of Missouri to the southwest corner of said last-named state; thence to be bounded on the west to the north bank of Red River, as by act of Congress and treaties existing January 1, 1837, defining the western limits of the Territory of Arkansas, and to be bounded across and south of Red River by the boundary line of the State of Texas as far as to the northwest corner of the State of Louisiana; thence easterly with the northern boundary line of said last-named State to the middle of the main channel of the Mississippi River; thence up the middle of the main channel of said last-named river, including an island in said river known as "Belle Point Island," and all other land originally surveyed and included as a part of the Territory or State of Arkansas, to the thirty-sixth degree of north latitude, the place of beginning.

## Seat of Government

The seat of government of the state of Arkansas shall be and remain at Little Rock, where it is now established.

### Article 2. Declaration of Rights.

## § 1. Source of power.

All political power is inherent in the people and government is instituted for their protection, security and benefit; and they have the right to alter, reform or abolish the same, in such manner as they may think proper.

## § 2. Freedom and independence.

All men are created equally free and independent, and have certain inherent and inalienable rights; amongst which are those of enjoying and defending life and liberty; of acquiring, possessing and protecting property, and reputation; and of pursuing their own happiness. To secure these rights governments are instituted among men, deriving their just powers from the consent of the governed.

### § 3. Equality before the law.

The equality of all persons before the law is recognized, and shall ever remain inviolate; nor shall any citizen ever be deprived of any right, privilege or immunity; nor exempted from any burden or duty, on account of race, color or previous condition.

### § 4. Right of assembly and of petition.

The right of the people peaceably to assemble, to consult for the common good; and to petition, by address or remonstrance, the government, or any department thereof, shall never be abridged.

### 5. Right to bear arms.

The citizens of this State shall have the right to keep and bear arms, for their common defense.

### § 6. Liberty of the press and of speech - Libel.

The liberty of the press shall forever remain inviolate. The free communication of thoughts and opinions, is one of the invaluable rights of man; and all persons may freely write and publish their sentiments on all subjects, being responsible for the abuse of such right. In all criminal prosecutions for libel, the truth may be given in evidence to the jury; and, if it shall appear to the jury that the matter charged as libelous is true, and was published with good motives and for justifiable ends, the party charged shall be acquitted.

### 7. Jury trial - Right to - Waiver - Civil cases - Nine jurors agreeing[408].

The right of trial by jury shall remain inviolate, and shall extend to all cases at law, without regard to the amount in controversy; but a jury trial may be waived by the parties in all cases in the manner prescribed by law; and in all jury trials in civil cases, where as many as nine of the jurors agree upon a verdict, the verdict so agreed upon shall be returned as the verdict of such jury, provided, however, that where a verdict is returned by less than twelve jurors all the jurors consenting to such verdict shall sign the same.

### § 8. Criminal charges - Self-incrimination - Due process - Double jeopardy - Bail.

No person shall be held to answer a criminal charge unless on the presentment or indictment of a grand jury, except in cases of impeachment or cases such as the General Assembly shall make cognizable by justices of the peace, and courts of similar jurisdiction; or cases arising in the army and navy of the United States; or in the militia, when in actual service in time of war or public danger; and no person, for the same offense, shall be twice put in jeopardy of life or liberty; but if, in any criminal prosecution, the jury be divided in opinion, the court before which the trial shall be had, may, in its discretion, discharge the jury, and commit or bail the accused for trial, at the same or the next term of said court; nor shall any person be compelled, in any criminal case, to be a witness against himself; nor be deprived of life, liberty or property, without due process of law. All persons shall, before conviction, be bailable by sufficient sureties, except for capital offenses, when the proof is evident or the presumption great.

### § 9. Excessive bail or punishment prohibited - Witnesses - Detention.

Excessive bail shall not be required; nor shall excessive fines be imposed; nor shall cruel or unusual punishment be inflicted; nor witnesses be unreasonably detained.

### § 10. Right of accused enumerated - Change of venue.

In all criminal prosecutions the accused shall enjoy the right to a speedy and public trial by impartial jury of the county in which the crime shall have been committed; provided that the venue may be changed to any other county of the judicial district in which the indictment is found, upon the application of the accused, in such manner as now is, or may be, prescribed by law; and to be informed of the nature and cause of the accusation against him,

---

[408] This is the text as amended by Amendment Sixteen.

and to have a copy thereof; and to be confronted with the witnesses against him; to have compulsory process for obtaining witness in his favor, and to be heard by himself and his counsel.

### § 11. Habeas corpus.

The privilege of the writ of habeas corpus shall not be suspended; except by the General Assembly, in case of rebellion, insurrection or invasion, when the public safety may require it.

### § 12. Suspension of laws.

No power of suspending or setting aside the law or laws of the State, shall ever be exercised, except by the General Assembly.

### § 13. Redress of wrongs.

Every person is entitled to a certain remedy in the laws for all injuries or wrongs he may receive in his person, property or character; he ought to obtain justice freely, and without purchase; completely, and without denial; promptly and without delay; conformably to the laws.

### § 14. Treason.

Treason against the State shall only consist in levying and making war against the same, or in adhering to its enemies, giving them aid and comfort. No person shall be convicted of treason unless on the testimony of two witnesses to the same overt act, or on confession in open court.

### § 15. Unreasonable searches and seizures.

The right of the people of this State to be secure in their persons, houses, papers, and effects, against unreasonable searches and seizures, shall not be violated; and no warrant shall issue, except upon probable cause, supported by oath or affirmation, and particularly describing the place to be searched, and the person or thing to be seized.

### § 16. Imprisonment for debt.

No person shall be imprisoned for debt in any civil action, on mesne or final process, unless in cases of fraud.

### § 17. Attainder - Ex post facto laws.

No bill of attainder, ex post facto law, or law impairing the obligation of contracts shall ever be passed; and no conviction shall work corruption of blood or forfeiture of estate.

### § 18. Privileges and immunities - Equality.

The General Assembly shall not grant to any citizen, or class of citizens, privileges or immunities which, upon the same terms, shall not equally belong to all citizens.

### § 19. Perpetuities and monopolies.

Perpetuities and monopolies are contrary to the genius of a republic, and shall not be allowed; nor shall any hereditary emoluments, privileges or honors ever be granted or conferred in this State.

### § 20. Resident aliens - Descent of property.

No distinction shall ever be made by law, between resident aliens and citizens, in regard to the possession, enjoyment or descent of property.

### § 21. Life, liberty and property - Banishment prohibited.

No person shall be taken, or imprisoned, or disseized of his estate, freehold, liberties or privileges; or outlawed, or in any manner destroyed, or deprived of his life, liberty or property; except by the judgment of his peers, or the law of the land; nor shall any person, under any circumstances, be exiled from the State.

### § 22. Property rights - Taking without just compensation prohibited.

The right of property is before and higher than any constitutional sanction; and private property shall not be taken, appropriated or damaged for public use, without just compensation therefor.

### § 23. Eminent domain and taxation.

The State's ancient right of eminent domain and of taxation, is herein fully and expressly conceded; and the General Assembly may delegate the taxing power, with the necessary restriction, to the State's subordinate political and municipal corporations, to the extent of providing for their existence, maintenance and well being, but no further.

### § 24. Religious liberty.

All men have a natural and indefeasible right to worship Almighty God according to the dictates of their own consciences; no man can, of right, be compelled to attend, erect, or support any place of worship; or to maintain any ministry against his consent. No human authority can, in any case or manner whatsoever, control or interfere with the right of conscience; and no preference shall ever be given, by law, to any religious establishment, denomination or mode of worship, above any other.

### § 25. Protection of religion.

Religion, morality and knowledge being essential to good government, the General Assembly shall enact suitable laws to protect every religious denomination in the peaceable enjoyment of its own mode of public worship.

### § 26. Religious tests.

No religious test shall ever be required of any person as a qualification to vote or hold office; nor shall any person be rendered incompetent to be a witness on account of his religious belief; but nothing herein shall be construed to dispense with oaths or affirmations.

### § 27. Slavery - Standing armies - Military subordinate to civil power.

There shall be no slavery in this State, nor involuntary servitude, except as a punishment for crime. No standing army shall be kept in time of peace; the military shall, at all times, be in strict subordination to the civil power; and no soldier shall be quartered in any house, or on any premises, without the consent of the owner, in time of peace; nor in time of war, except in a manner prescribed by law.

### § 28. Tenure of lands.

All lands in this State are declared to be allodial; and feudal tenures of every description, with all their incidents, are prohibited.

### § 29. Enumeration of rights of people not exclusive of other rights - Protection against encroachment.

This enumeration of rights shall not be construed to deny or disparage others retained by the people; and to guard against any encroachments on the rights herein retained, or any transgression of any of the higher powers herein delegated, we declare that everything in this article is excepted out of the general powers of the government; and shall forever remain inviolate; and that all laws contrary thereto, or to the other provisions herein contained, shall be void.

*Article 4. Departments.*

### § 1. Departments of government.

The powers of the government of the State of Arkansas shall be divided into three distinct departments, each of them to be confided to a separate body of magistracy, to-wit: Those which are legislative, to one, those which are executive, to another, and those which are judicial, to another.

## § 2. Separation of departments.

No person or collection of persons, being of one of these departments, shall exercise any power belonging to either of the others, except in the instances hereinafter expressly directed or permitted.

*Article 5. Legislative Department.*

### § 1. Initiative and Referendum.

The legislative power of the people of this State shall be vested in a General Assembly, which shall consist of the Senate and House of Representatives, but the people reserve to themselves the power to propose legislative measures, laws and amendments to the Constitution, and to enact or reject the same at the polls independent of the General Assembly; and also reserve the power, at their own option to approve or reject at the polls any entire act or any item of an appropriation bill.

### Initiative.

The first power reserved by the people is the initiative. Eight per cent of the legal voters may propose any law and ten per cent may propose a constitutional amendment by initiative petition and every such petition shall include the full text of the measure so proposed. Initiative petitions for state-wide measures shall be filed with the Secretary of State not less than four months before the election at which they are to be voted upon; provided, that at least thirty days before the aforementioned filing, the proposed measure shall have been published once, at the expense of the petitioners, in some paper of general circulation.

### Referendum.

The second power reserved by the people is the referendum, and any number not less than six per cent of the legal voters may, by petition, order the referendum against any general Act, or any item of an appropriation bill, or measure passed by the General Assembly, but the filing of a referendum petition against one or more items, sections or parts of any such act or measure shall not delay the remainder from becoming operative. Such petition shall be filed with the Secretary of State not later than ninety days after the final adjournment of the session at which such Act was passed, except when a recess or adjournment shall be taken temporarily for a longer period than ninety days, in which case such petition shall be filed not later than ninety days after such recess or temporary adjournment. Any measure referred to the people by referendum petition shall remain in abeyance until such vote is taken. The total number of votes cast for the office of Governor in the last preceding general election shall be the basis upon which the number of signatures of legal voters upon state-wide initiative and referendum petitions shall be computed.

Upon all initiative or referendum petitions provided for in any of the sections of this article, it shall be necessary to file from at least fifteen of the counties of the State, petitions bearing the signature of not less than one-half of the designated percentage of the electors of such county.

### Emergency.

If it shall be necessary for the preservation of the public peace, health and safety that a measure shall become effective without delay, such necessity shall be stated in one section, and if upon a yea and nay vote two-thirds of all the members elected to each house, or two-thirds of all the members elected to city or town councils, shall vote upon separate roll call in favor of the measure going into immediate operation, such emergency measure shall become effective without delay. It shall be necessary, however, to state the fact which constitutes such emergency. Provided, however, that an emergency shall not be declared on any franchise or special privilege or act creating any vested right or interest or alienating any property of the State. If a referendum is filed against any emergency measure such measure shall be a law until it is voted upon by the people, and if it is then rejected by a majority of the electors voting thereon, it shall be thereby repealed. The provision of this sub-section shall apply to city or town councils.

## Local for Municipalities and Counties.

The initiative and referendum powers of the people are hereby further reserved to the legal voters of each municipality and county as to all local, special and municipal legislation of every character in and for their respective municipalities and counties, but no local legislation shall be enacted contrary to the Constitution or any general law of the State, and any general law shall have the effect of repealing any local legislation which is in conflict therewith.

Municipalities may provide for the exercise of the initiative and referendum as to their local legislation. General laws shall be enacted providing for the exercise of the initiative and referendum as to counties. Fifteen per cent of the legal voters of any municipality or county may order the referendum, or invoke the initiative upon any local measure. In municipalities the number of signatures required upon any petition shall be computed upon the total vote cast for the office of mayor at the last preceding general election; in counties upon the office of circuit clerk. In municipalities and counties the time for filing an initiative petition shall not be fixed at less than sixty days nor more than ninety days before the election at which it is to be voted upon; for a referendum petition at not less than thirty days nor more than ninety days after the passage of such measure by a municipal council; nor less than ninety days when filed against a local or special measure passed by the General Assembly.

Every extension, enlargement, grant, or conveyance of a franchise or any rights, property, easement, lease, or occupation of or in any road, street, alley or any part thereof in real property or interest in real property owned by municipalities, exceeding in value three hundred dollars, whether the same be by statute, ordinance, resolution, or otherwise, shall be subject to referendum and shall not be subject to emergency legislation.

*General Provisions*

## Definition.

The word "measure" as used herein includes any bill, law, resolution, ordinance, charter, constitutional amendment or legislative proposal or enactment of any character.

## No Veto.

The veto power of the Governor or mayor shall not extend to measures initiated by or referred to the people.

## Amendment and Repeal.

No measure approved by a vote of the people shall be amended or repealed by the General Assembly or by any city council, except upon a yea and nay vote on roll call of two-thirds of all the members elected to each house of the General Assembly, or of the city council, as the case may be.

## Election.

All measures initiated by the people whether for the State, county, city or town, shall be submitted only at the regular elections, either State, congressional or municipal, but referendum petitions may be referred to the people at special elections to be called by the proper official, and such special elections shall be called when fifteen per cent of the legal voters shall petition for such special election, and if the referendum is invoked as to any measure passed by a city or town council, such city or town council may order a special election.

## Majority.

Any measure submitted to the people as herein provided shall take effect and become a law when approved by a majority of the votes cast upon such measure, and not otherwise, and shall not be required to receive a majority of the electors voting at such election. Such measures shall be operative on and after the thirtieth day after the election at which it is approved, unless otherwise specified in the Act.

This section shall not be construed to deprive any member of the General Assembly of the right to introduce any measure, but no measure shall be submitted to the people by the General Assembly, except a proposed constitutional amendment or amendments as provided for in this Constitution.

### Canvass and Declaration of Results.

The result of the vote upon any State measure shall be canvassed and declared by the State Board of Election Commissioners (or legal substitute therefor); upon a municipal or county measure, by the county election commissioners (or legal substitute therefor).

### Conflicting Measures.

If conflicting measures initiated or referred to the people shall be approved by a majority of the votes severally cast for and against the same at the same election, the one receiving the highest number of affirmative votes shall become law.

### *The Petition*

### Title.

At the time of filing petitions the exact title to be used on the ballot shall by the petitioners be submitted with the petition, and on state-wide measures, shall be submitted to the State Board of Election Commissioners, who shall certify such title to the Secretary of State, to be placed upon the ballot; on county and municipal measures such title shall be submitted to the county election board and shall by said board be placed upon the ballot in such county or municipal election.

### Limitation.

No limitation shall be placed upon the number of constitutional amendments, laws, or other measures which may be proposed and submitted to the people by either initiative or referendum petition as provided in this section. No petition shall be held invalid if it shall contain a greater number of signatures than required herein.

### Verification.

Only legal votes shall be counted upon petitions. Petitions may be circulated and presented in parts, but each part of any petition shall have attached thereto the affidavit of the person circulating the same, that all signatures thereon were made in the presence of the affiant, and that to the best of the affiant's knowledge and belief each signature is genuine, and that the person signing is a legal voter and no other affidavit or verification shall be required to establish the genuineness of such signatures.

### Sufficiency.

The sufficiency of all state-wide petitions shall be decided in the first instance by the Secretary of State, subject to review by the Supreme Court of the State, which shall have original and exclusive jurisdiction over all such causes. The sufficiency of all local petitions shall be decided in the first instance by the county clerk or the city clerk as the case may be, subject to review by the chancery court.

### Court Decisions.

If the sufficiency of any petition is challenged such cause shall be a preference cause and shall be tried at once, but the failure of the courts to decide prior to the election as to the sufficiency of any such petition, shall not prevent the question from being placed upon the ballot at the election named in such petition, nor militate against the validity of such measure, if it shall have been approved by a vote of the people.

### Amendment of Petition.

If the Secretary of State, county clerk or city clerk, as the case may be, shall decide any petition to be insufficient, he shall without delay notify the sponsors of such petition, and permit at least thirty days from the date of such notification, in the instance of a state-wide petition, or ten days in the instance of a municipal or county petition, for correction or amendment. In the event of legal proceedings to prevent giving legal effect to any petition upon any grounds, the burden of proof shall be upon the person or persons attacking the validity of the petition.

### Unwarranted Restrictions Prohibited.

No law shall be passed to prohibit any person or persons from giving or receiving compensation for circulating petitions, nor to prohibit the circulation of petitions, nor in any manner interfering with the freedom of the people in procuring petitions; but laws shall be enacted prohibiting and penalizing perjury, forgery, and all other felonies or other fraudulent practices, in the securing of signatures or filing of petitions.

### Publication.

All measures submitted to a vote of the people by petition under the provisions of this section shall be published as is now, or hereafter may be provided by law.

### Enacting Clause.

The style of all bills initiated and submitted under the provisions of this section shall be, "Be It Enacted by the People of the State of Arkansas, (municipality or county, as the case may be)." In submitting measures to the people, the Secretary of State and all other officials shall be guided by the general election laws or municipal laws as the case may be until additional legislation is provided therefor.

### Self-Executing.

This section shall be self-executing, and all its provisions shall be treated as mandatory, but laws may be enacted to facilitate its operation. No legislation shall be enacted to restrict, hamper or impair the exercise of the rights herein reserved to the people[409].

### § 2. House of Representatives.

The House of Representatives shall consist of members to be chosen every second year, by the qualified electors of the several counties.

### § 3. Senate.

The Senate shall consist of members to be chosen every four years, by the qualified electors of the several districts. At the first session of the Senate, the Senators shall divide themselves into two classes, by lot, and the first class shall hold their places for two years only, after which all shall be elected for four years.

### § 4. Qualifications of senators and representatives.

No person shall be a Senator or Representative who, at the time of his election, is not a citizen of the United States, nor any one who has not been for two years next preceding his election, a resident of this State, and for one year next preceding his election, a resident of the county or district whence he may be chosen. Senators shall be at least twenty-five years of age, and Representatives at least twenty-one years of age.

### § 5. Time of meeting.

The General Assembly shall meet at the seat of government every two years, on the first Tuesday after the second Monday in November, until said time be altered by law.

---

[409] This is the text as amended by Amendment Seven.

### § 9. Persons convicted ineligible.

No person hereafter convicted of embezzlement of public money, bribery, forgery or other infamous crime, shall be eligible to the General Assembly or capable of holding any office of trust or profit in this State.

### § 12. Powers and duties of each house.

Each house shall have power to determine the rules of its proceedings; and punish its members, or other persons, for contempt or disorderly behavior in its presence; enforce obedience to its process; to protect its members against violence or offers of bribes, or private solicitations; and, with the concurrence of two-thirds, expel a member; but not a second time for the same cause. A member expelled for corruption shall not, thereafter, be eligible to either house; and punishment for contempt, or disorderly behavior, shall not bar an indictment for the same offense. Each house shall keep a journal of its proceedings; and, from time to time, publish the same, except such parts as require secrecy; and the yeas and nays, on any question, shall, at the desire of any five members, be entered on the journals.

### § 15. Privileges of members.

The members of the General Assembly shall, in all cases except treason, felony, and breach or surety of the peace, be privileged from arrest during their attendance at the sessions of their respective houses; and, in going to and returning from the same; and, for any speech or debate in either house, they shall not be questioned in any other place.

### § 17. Duration of sessions.

The regular biennial sessions, shall not exceed sixty days in duration; unless by a vote of two-thirds of the members elected to each house of said General Assembly. Provided, that this section shall not apply to the first session of the General Assembly under this Constitution, or when impeachments are pending.

### § 19. Style of laws - Enacting clause.

The style of the laws of the State of Arkansas shall be: "Be it enacted by the General Assembly of the State of Arkansas."

### § 20. State not made defendant.

The State of Arkansas shall never be made defendant in any of her courts.

### § 21. Laws by bills - Amendment.

No law shall be passed except by bill, and no bill shall be so altered or amended on its passage through either house, as to change its original purpose.

### § 22. Passage of bills.

Every bill shall be read at length, on three different days, in each house; unless the rules be suspended by two-thirds of the house, when the same may be read a second or third time on the same day; and no bill shall become a law unless, on its final passage, the vote be taken by yeas and nays; the names of the persons voting for and against the same be entered on the journal; and a majority of each house be recorded thereon as voting in its favor.

### § 24. Local and special laws.

The General Assembly shall not pass any local or special law, changing the venue in criminal cases; changing the names of persons, or adopting or legitimating children; granting divorces; vacating roads, streets or alleys.

### § 25. Special laws - Suspension of general laws.

In all cases where a general law can be made applicable, no special law shall be enacted; nor shall the operation of any general law be suspended by the legislature for the benefit of any particular individual, corporation or association; nor where the courts have jurisdiction to grant the powers, or the privileges, or the relief asked for.

### § 34. Introduction of bills - Time limit.

No new bill shall be introduced into either house during the last three days of the session.

### § 35. Bribery of member of General Assembly or state officer.

Any person who shall, directly or indirectly, offer, give, or promise any money, or thing of value, testimonial, privilege or personal advantage to any executive or judicial officer, or member of the General Assembly; and any such executive or judicial officer, or member of the General Assembly, who shall receive or consent to receive any such consideration, either directly or indirectly, to influence his action in the performance or non performance of his public or official duty, shall be guilty of a felony, and be punished accordingly.

### § 36. Expulsion of member no bar to indictment.

Proceedings to expel a member for a criminal offense, whether successful or not, shall not bar an indictment and punishment, under the criminal laws, for the same offense.

### § 37. Laws - Enactment - Majority required.

Not less than a majority of the members of each House of the General Assembly may enact a law.

## Article 6. Executive Department.

### § 1. Executive officers.

The executive department of this State shall consist of a Governor, Lieutenant Governor, Secretary of State, Treasurer of State, Auditor of State and Attorney General, all of whom shall keep their offices in person at the seat of government and hold their offices for the term of two years and until their successors are elected and qualified, and the General Assembly may provide by law for the establishment of the office of Commissioner of State Lands.

### § 2. Governor - Supreme executive power.

The supreme executive power of this State shall be vested in a chief magistrate, who shall be styled "the Governor of the State of Arkansas."

### § 6. Governor, commander-in-chief of armed services.

The Governor shall be commander-in-chief of the military and naval forces of this State, except when they shall be called into the actual service of the United States.

### § 15. Approval of bills - Vetoes.

Every bill which shall have passed both houses of the General Assembly, shall be presented to the Governor; if he approve it, he shall sign it; but if he shall not approve it, he shall return it, with his objections, to the house in which it originated; which house shall enter the objections at large upon their journal and proceed to reconsider it. If, after such reconsideration, a majority of the whole number elected to that house, shall agree to pass the bill, it shall be sent, with the objections, to the other house; by which, likewise, it shall be reconsidered; and, if approved by a majority of the whole number elected to that house, it shall be a law; but in such cases the vote of both houses shall be determined by "yeas and nays;" and the names of the members voting for or against the bill, shall be entered on the journals. If any bill shall not be returned by the Governor within five days, Sundays excepted, after it shall have been presented to him, the same shall be a law in like manner as if he had signed it; unless the General Assembly, by their adjournment, prevent its return; in which case it shall become a law, unless he shall file the same, with his objections, in the office of the Secretary of State, and give notice thereof, by public proclamation, within twenty days after such adjournment.

## § 18. Pardoning power.

In all criminal and penal cases, except in those of treason and impeachment, the Governor shall have power to grant reprieves, commutations of sentence, and pardons, after conviction; and to remit fines and forfeitures, under such rules and regulations as shall be prescribed by law. In cases of treason, he shall have power, by and with the advice and consent of the Senate, to grant reprieves and pardons; and he may, in the recess of the Senate, respite the sentence until the adjournment of the next regular session of the General Assembly. He shall communicate to the General Assembly at every regular session each case of reprieve, commutation or pardon, with his reasons therefor; stating the name and crime of the convict, the sentence, its date, and the date of the commutation, pardon or reprieve.

### *Article 7. Judicial Department.*

## § 19. Circuit clerks - Election - Term of office - Ex-officio duties - County clerks elected in certain counties.

The clerks of the circuit courts shall be elected by the qualified electors of the several counties for the term of two years, and shall be ex-officio clerks of the county and probate courts and recorder; provided, that in any county having a population exceeding fifteen thousand inhabitants, as shown by the last Federal census, there shall be elected a county clerk, in like manner as the clerk of the circuit court, and in such case the county clerk shall be ex-officio clerk of the probate court of such county until otherwise provided by the General Assembly.

## § 23. Charge to juries.

Judges shall not charge juries with regard to matters of fact, but shall declare the law; and, in jury trials, shall reduce their charge or instructions to writing, on the request of either party.

## § 26. Punishment of indirect contempt provided for by law.

The General Assembly shall have power to regulate, by law, the punishment of contempts; not committed in the presence or hearing of the courts, or in disobedience of process.

## § 38. Justices of the peace - Election - Term - Oath.

The qualified electors of each township shall elect the Justices of the Peace for the term of two years; who shall be commissioned by the Governor, and their official oath shall be indorsed on the commission.

## § 46. County executive officers - Compensation of county assessor.

The qualified electors of each county shall elect one Sheriff, who shall be ex-officio collector of taxes, unless otherwise provided by law; one Assessor, one Coroner, one Treasurer, who shall be ex-officio treasurer of the common school fund of the county, and one County Surveyor; for the term of two years, with such duties as are now or may be prescribed by law: Provided, that no per centum shall ever be paid to assessors upon the valuation or assessment of property by them.

## § 47. Constables - Term of office - Certificate of election.

The qualified electors of each township shall elect the Constable for the term of two years, who shall be furnished, by the presiding Judge of the County Court, with a certificate of election, on which his official oath shall be indorsed.

### § 49. Style of process and of indictments.

All writs and other judicial process, shall run in the name of the State of Arkansas, bear test and be signed by the clerks of the respective courts from which they issue. Indictments shall conclude: "Against the peace and dignity of the State of Arkansas."

### § 51. Appeals from county or municipal allowances - Bond.

That in all cases of allowances made for or against counties, cities or towns, an appeal shall lie to the Circuit Court of the county, at the instance of the party aggrieved, or on the intervention of any citizen or resident and tax payer of such county, city or town, on the same terms and conditions on which appeals may be granted to the Circuit Court in other cases; and the matter pertaining to any such allowance shall be tried in the Circuit Court de novo. In case an appeal be taken by any citizen, he shall give a bond, payable to the proper county, conditioned to prosecute the appeal, and save the county from costs on account of the same being taken.

# Glossary

**accessory**   Someone who aids in the commission of a crime, but does not actually participate in the commission of it.

**accomplice**   Someone who actively participates in the commission of a crime.

**Act 300**   Another name for the *Arkansas Motor Vehicle and Traffic Laws*.

**actus reus**   A Latin legal phrase meaning the "guilty act;" a necessary element of all crimes.

**affirmative defense**   A type of defense where the defendant offers evidence that, if found credible, will negate criminal liability, even if the prosecution can prove all elements of the crime beyond a reasonable doubt.

**antishoplifting device**   "[A] mechanism or other device designed and operated for the purpose of detecting the removal from a mercantile establishment or similar enclosure or from a protected area within a mercantile establishment or similar enclosure."[410]

**appellant**   Someone who has lost a case in a lower court and is asking a higher court to rule on the cause.

**appellee**   The respondent in an appeal case; the person who won in the lower court and is now being sued in a higher court. In most criminal procedure cases, this will be the state or a branch of state government.

**Arkansas Rules of Criminal Procedure**   Rules set forth by the Arkansas Supreme Court for the regulation of criminal case processing by all criminal justice system components.

**arrest**   The deprivation of a person's liberty by lawful authority.

**assault**   Creating apprehension or fear of bodily harm.

**attempt**   "conduct [that] constitutes a substantial step intended to result in the commission of an offense."[411]

**attendant circumstance**   Facts relating to an event. For example, the age of a minor in a status offense is an important attendant circumstance.

**battery**   Generally, an unwanted contact or touching of another person. Most criminal statutes require intent to cause bodily harm.

---

[410] § 5-36-116
[411] *Mitchell v. State,* 290 Ark. 87, 717 S.W.2d 195 (1986)

**bestiality**    Performing or submitting "to any act of sexual gratification with an animal involving the sex organs of the one and the mouth, anus, penis, or vagina of the other."[412]

**beyond a reasonable doubt**    The standard of proof for a conviction in a criminal trial; a firm belief that the allegations made by the state at a criminal trial are true.

**burden of production**    (a.k.a. *the burden of going forward*) the obligation of one party in a case to present evidence.

**burden of proof**    The duty of proving a disputed point in court.

**capital offense**    An offense for which the death penalty is an authorized punishment.

**causation**    The law recognizes two major types of cause: *cause-in-fact* and *proximate* (a.k.a. legal) cause.

**cause-in-fact**    "But-for" causation; setting in motion a chain of events that lead to the harmful result.

**child**    A person under 16 years of age[413].

**civil law**    The body of law dealing with relationships between private citizens.

**civil rights**    Rights that belong to a person simply because they are a citizen.

**clear and present danger**    Threats that are both obvious and immediate.

**commercial occupiable structure**    "[A] vehicle, building, or other structure in which any person carries on a business or other calling. or in which people assemble for a purpose of business, government, education, religion, entertainment, or public transportation.[414]"

**complicity**    Aiding or abetting (encouraging) another in the planning or commission of a crime.

**computer crime**    Criminal activity where a computer or computer network is either the target of a crime or a tool used in the commission of a crime.

**concurrence**    The legal idea that the criminal act (actus reus) must be brought on by the criminal intent (mens rea).

**conspiracy**    An agreement to commit a crime.

**constructive intent**    Intent inferred when the harmful outcome should have been readily foreseen.

**criminal code**    Title 5 of the *Arkansas Code*. Most of the substantive criminal law of Arkansas, arranged by subject matter.

**criminal law**    A broad category of law concerned with regulating acts that harm society as a whole.

---

[412] § 5-14-122
[413] §5-4-701
[414] § 5-39-101

**cruel and unusual punishment**     A type of punishment prohibited by the Eighth Amendment of the US Constitution.

**culpability**     Blameworthiness; an individuals degree of liability in a criminal offense.

**damages**     Money awarded in civil suits.

**deadly force**     A degree of physical force that is likely to cause serious physical injury or death.

**defense**     Situational factors that reduce or eliminate culpability for an act that would otherwise be criminal.

**deliberation**     *See* **premeditation**.

**deviant sexual activity**     "Means any act of sexual gratification involving: The penetration, however slight, of the anus or mouth of a person by the penis of another person; or the penetration, however slight, of the labia majora or anus of a person by any body member or foreign instrument manipulated by another person."[415]

**double jeopardy**     Being tried twice for the same offense; also known as *former prosecution*.

**duress**     A defense based on the fact that the perpetrator was forced into action by the threats of another.

**element of a crime**     The component parts of a crime, each of which must be proven beyond a reasonable doubt to gain a conviction in a criminal case.

**enter or remain unlawfully**     "to enter or remain in or upon premises when not licensed or privileged to enter or remain in or upon the premises."[416]

**entrapment**     A defense based on the idea that the accused was convinced to do something that he or she would not ordinarily do by law enforcement.

**equal protection**     The Fourteenth Amendment guarantee that the laws of a state must treat an individual in the same manner as others in similar conditions and circumstances.

**evidence**     Broadly, anything that is used in court to established the truth of an alleged fact.

**evidence, direct**   Evidence that can stand on its own to prove the truth of an alleged fact.

**evidence, circumstantial**     Evidence that when taken together allows for an inference about an alleged fact.

**ex post facto law**     A law that criminalizes an act after the act is done.

**excuse defense**     A defense in which the actor admits committing the crime, but claims that some circumstance, such as insanity, should mitigate or eliminate criminal liability.

**felony**     A category of serious offenses usually punishable by one year or more in prison.

**fiduciary**     A legal relationship between parties that involves a high degree of confidence and trust.

---

[415] § 5-14-101
[416] § 5-39-101

**general intent**    Intent to perform a criminal act, but no intent to cause a particular harm or result.

**guilty plea**    An admission of guilt that amounts to a waiver of the right to a trial.

**harm** (resulting)    As an element of crimes, the resulting negative effect of the criminal act, such as the death of a person in murder.

**hindering**    The Arkansas statute equivalent to an *accessory after the fact* at common law.

**homicide**    The killing of a human being.

**hunch**    A level of proof that allows an officer no extraordinary search authority, but may result in further unobtrusive investigation.

**imprisonment**    Home confinement or incarceration in a detention facility operated by the state or any political subdivision, or a private correctional facility under contract with the state[417].

**in loco parentis**    Literally, *in place of the parent*; refers to the authority of the state to step in when such intervention is in the best interest of the child.

**incest**    A person commits incest if he or she marries, "has sexual intercourse with, or engages in deviate sexual activity with another person sixteen (16) years of age or older whom the actor knows to be: (1) An ancestor or a descendant; (2) A stepchild or adopted child; (3) A brother or sister of the whole or half blood; (4) An uncle, aunt, nephew, or niece; or (5) A stepgrandchild or adopted grandchild.[418]"

**inchoate offense**    Crimes that involve preparing for or seeking to commit another crime, such as solicitation.

intoxication    "A disturbance of a mental or physical capacity resulting from the introduction of alcohol, a drug, or another substance into the body."[419]

**judicial review**    The power of appellate courts to determine the constitutionality of laws and actions by agents of the state.

**justification defense**    A defense that attempts to show that what would otherwise be a crime is actually not because of the circumstances surrounding a particular event, such as killing in self defense.

**knowingly**    One of four levels of culpability under Arkansas law; The person "is aware that it is practically certain that his or her conduct will cause the result."[420]

**larceny**    The taking of the property of another with the intent to deprive the owner of it; This was one of the many property offenses brought together under the Arkansas theft statute, § 5-36-102.

**lesser included offense**    When a less serious crime has all of its elements in common with a more serious crime and both crimes are of the same generic class, then the less serious crime is a lesser included offense of the more serious crime.

---

[417] § 5-4-101
[418] § 5-26-202
[419] § 5-2-207
[420] § 5-2-202

**libel**    A false and malicious statement defaming a person's character in print form.

**liberty**    In criminal statues, the freedom of movement, such as that infringed upon by arrest or kidnapping.

**manslaughter**    A killing that would be murder but for some mitigating "severe emotional disturbance."[421]

**mens rea**    The mental element of crimes; the criminal intent.

**mental defect**    Mental retardation, brain damage or other biological dysfunction that cause dysfunction.

**mental disease**    "Substantial disorder of thought, mood, perception, orientation, or memory that grossly impairs judgment, behavior, capacity to recognize reality, or ability to meet the ordinary demands of life."[422]

**mental incapacitation**    A person is temporarily incapable of appreciating or controlling his or her conduct as a result of the influence of a controlled or intoxicating substance[423].

**minor**    "Any person under eighteen (18) years of age."[424]

**misdemeanor**    A relatively minor offense, punishable by no more than 1 year in jail.

**mistake of fact**    A criminal defense in some circumstances.

**mistake of law**    Almost never a criminal defense.

**motor vehicle**    "any self-propelled vehicle not operated exclusively upon railroad tracks, except snowmobiles and other devices designed and used primarily for the transportation of persons over natural terrain, snow, or ice and propelled by wheels, skis, tracks, runners, or whatever other means."[425]

**murder**    A general category of unlawful, intentional killings.

**negligently**    "A person acts negligently with respect to attendant circumstances or a result of his or her conduct when the person should be aware of a substantial and unjustifiable risk that the attendant circumstances exist or the result will occur."[426]

**no contact order**    A judicial order "prohibiting the defendant from approaching or communicating with particular persons or classes of persons, except that no such order shall be deemed to prohibit any lawful and ethical activity of defendant's counsel" and "prohibiting the defendant from going to certain described geographical areas or premises."[427]

**nolo contendere**    A plea that has the same effect as a guilty plea, but is not an admission of guilt.

**nondeadly force**    A degree of physical force that is not likely to result in serious bodily injury or death.

---

[421] § 5-10-104
[422] § 5-2-301
[423] § 5-14-101
[424] § 5-2-601
[425] § 4-90-202
[426] § 5-2-202
[427] *Ark. R. Crim. P.* Rule 9.3

**obscenity**    The Supreme Court has established that, to be obscene, material must meet a three-pronged test: (1) An average person, applying contemporary community standards, must find that the material, as a whole, appeals to the prurient interest; (2) The material must depict or describe, in a patently offensive way, sexual conduct specifically defined by applicable law; and (3) The material, taken as a whole, must lack serious literary, artistic, political, or scientific value.

**occupiable structure**    "A vehicle, building, or other structure: (i) Where any person lives or carries on a business or other calling; (ii) Where people assemble for a purpose of business, government, education, religion, entertainment, or public transportation; or (iii) That is customarily used for overnight accommodation of a person whether or not a person is actually present."[428]

**penal law**    See **Criminal Law**.

**pendency**    A state of being undecided.

**physical evidence**    Evidence in the form of physical objects.

**physical injury**    The impairment of physical condition, infliction of substantial pain, or infliction of bruising, swelling, or a visible mark associated with physical trauma[429].

**possession, actual**    Direct physical control of something.

**premeditation**    The process of planning or deliberating a course of action.

**possession, constructive**    Knowledge of the location and control over something without it being physically present.

**premises**    An occupiable structure or any real property[430].

**preponderance of the evidence**    The greater weight of evidence required to prevail in civil cases.

**prima facie evidence**    Evidence sufficient to raise a rebuttable presumption of fact.

**privacy, right to**    A constitutional right that is the basis for most search and seizure law.

**probable cause**    "Probable cause is where known facts and circumstances, of a reasonably trustworthy nature, are sufficient to justify a man of reasonable caution or prudence in the belief that a crime has been or is being committed."[431]

**procedural law**    The body of law that regulates how elements of the criminal justice system  treat those accused of crimes.

**profanity**    Irreverent speech or action.

**proximate cause**    Literally, the next or closest cause.

---

[428] § 5-2-601
[429] § 5-1-102
[430] § 5-2-601
[431] *Draper v. US* (1959)

**purposely** "A person acts purposely with respect to his or her conduct or a result of his or her conduct when it is the person's conscious object to engage in conduct of that nature or to cause the result."[432]

**real property** "All lands, including improvements and fixtures on them and property of any nature appurtenant to them or used in connection with them…"[433]

**reasonable suspicion** A standard of proof, less than probable cause, that requires a reasonable and articulable suspicion of criminal activity.

**receiving** A mode of theft involving receiving, retaining, or disposing of the stolen property of another person.

**recklessly** "A person acts recklessly with respect to attendant circumstances or a result of his or her conduct when the person consciously disregards a substantial and unjustifiable risk that the attendant circumstances exist or the result will occur."[434]

**residential occupiable structure** "a vehicle, building, or other structure: (i) In which any person lives; or (ii) That is customarily used for overnight accommodation of a person whether or not a person is actually present."[435]

**rule of law** The idea that everyone is bound by the law, even those who make the law and enforce it.

**serious physical injury** "means physical injury that creates a substantial risk of death or that causes protracted disfigurement, protracted impairment of health, or loss or protracted impairment of the function of any bodily member or organ."[436]

**sexual conduct** Actual or simulated sexual intercourse, deviate sexual activity, sexual bestiality, masturbation, sadomasochistic abuse, or lewd exhibition of the genitals or pubic area of any person or a breast of a female.[437]

**sexual contact** "any act of sexual gratification involving the touching, directly or through clothing, of the sex organs, buttocks, or anus of a person or the breast of a female."[438]

**specific intent** The intent to do something beyond the *actus reus* of a particular crime.

**strict liability** Crimes for which the usually necessary mental element has been removed; most violations are strict liability offenses.

**substantive criminal law** The part of the criminal law that specifies prohibited acts and omissions and specifies punishments for violations.

**theft consolidation statutes** Modern statutes that bring together many different species of property crime under one heading.

**tort** A civil wrong for which money damages are sought.

---

[432] § 5-2-202
[433] § 14-168-301
[434] § 5-2-202
[435] § 5-39-101
[436] § 5-1-102
[437] § 5-27-401
[438] § 5-14-101

**transferred intent**    The intent to harm one victim, but another is harmed instead; also known as "bad aim" intent.

**vehicle**    *See* **motor vehicle**.

**violation**    "an offense is a violation for purposes of the Arkansas Criminal Code if the statute defining the offense provides that no sentence other than a fine, fine or forfeiture, or civil penalty is authorized upon conviction."[439]

**void-for-overbreadth doctrine**    The idea that a statute will be unconstitutional if it is so broad that it can be interpreted to encroach on constitutionally protected rights.

**void-for-vagueness doctrine**    The idea that laws must be written in clear, unambiguous language so that a normal person can understand what is prohibited.

**weapon**    "any firearm, bomb, explosive, metal knuckles, sword, spear, or other device employed as an instrument of crime by subjecting another to physical harm or fear of physical harm."[440]

**weapon, deadly**    A firearm or anything manifestly designed, made, or adapted for the purpose of inflicting death or serious physical injury, or anything that in the manner of its use or intended use is capable of causing death or serious physical injury[441].

---

[439] § 5-1-108
[440] § 5-5-401
[441] § 5-1-102

CPSIA information can be obtained
at www.ICGtesting.com
Printed in the USA
FFHW012141130119
50161173-55077FF